The Story of Philosophy

James Garvey has a PhD from University College London and is secretary of the Royal Institute of Philosophy, editor of *The Philosophers' Magazine* and the author and editor of several books, including *The Ethics of Climate Change* and *The Twenty Greatest Philosophy Books*.

Jeremy Stangroom has a PhD from the London School of Economics. He co-founded *The Philosophers' Magazine* with Julian Baggini in 1997. He is the author and editor of numerous books, most recently *Why Truth Matters* and *Does God Hate Women?*

The Story of Philosophy

A History of Western Thought

James Garvey &
Jeremy Stangroom

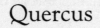

Quercus

First published as an illustrated edition in Great Britain in 2012 by
Quercus Editions Ltd

This paperback edition published in 2013 by Quercus Editions Ltd

55 Baker Street
7th Floor, South Block
W1U 8EW

A CIP catalogue record for this book is available
from the British Library

PB ISBN 978 1 78087 753 2
EBOOK ISBN 978 0 85738 582 6

10 9 8 7 6 5 4 3 2 1

Text designed and typeset by Ellipsis

Printed and bound in Great Britain by Clays Ltd. St Ives plc

Contents

The Story of Philosophy

Introduction

Wonder is the feeling of the philosopher,
and philosophy begins in wonder.

PLATO

Philosophy can't be pinned down. There are histories that attempt to stitch the whole convoluted thing up into a single long, coherent sequence of events. Other books are organized thematically. Here we have metaphysics. This is ethics. Here's what we know about the nature of knowledge. Similar books plough through the big questions. What exists? What can we know? How should we live? What does it all mean?

Some of these books are excellent, but they're all attempts to civilize something wild, something that mostly mistrusts authority, something that's really only human, something messy that moves around in several different directions at once. Maybe the best way to pass along a feel for this kind of thing is to do what people have always done when they've got a great deal of complicated information to convey, and that's tell a story. Stories are never the last word on the subject, they don't pretend to tell the whole truth, but there's often truth in them, truth you'd never see just by lining up all the facts. Humanity does not have a history of giving lectures round the campfire, and there's a good reason for this.

To get a handle on the story of philosophy, you need at least a little character development, a few plot twists, a murder, philosophers fleeing for their lives, others dying in obscurity, great projects doomed to failure, unlikely triumphs, accidental discoveries, disastrous love affairs, geniuses, idiots, monks, vagabonds and a demented German or two. But what matters most in all of this is our focus: the things that philosophers say, and the reasons they give for what they think is true. You'll hear a little about lives and events, but what holds the story together is ideas.

The result is a riot of philosophy, because that's what the thing itself is. Our table of contents bounces all over the place. Some chapters focus on giants like Plato and Aristotle, others take up movements and schools, and the rest consider concepts, themes, methods, phrases, events, problems and more. Much of it is historical, but we've abandoned all hope of seamless coherence. We've imposed a little narrative structure, tried to make connections where it might help, left out a lot that just didn't fit with the rest, but mostly we've let philosophy do its own thing and tried to keep up.

What you'll discover as you read on is that philosophy isn't really a slow build or burn, a calm, steady march out of the darkness and into the light of reason. There's something of that going on here and there, particularly at the start, but each generation struggles to find its own way. We get hold of something for a while and then lose it. We're sometimes distracted and spend centuries down blind alleys. Some problems are simply forgotten, but many are still with us, and have been for hundreds, even thousands of years. We climb out of obscurity and then fall back into it, maybe into a new, more complicated kind of obscurity. But we do keep climbing out. Philosophy is on to something. The story isn't easy, the plot isn't straightforward, but what good story goes in a straight line?

To find your way in, it will help to know something about the subject matter and methods of philosophy. Bear in mind, though, that philosophy is too large to be captured by any summary like this. Still, it's a good idea to get a few central terms and concepts on the table at the start. After that we'll cast an eye over the chapters of this book, and then you can get on with it.

Objects, knowledge, values and logic

Philosophy is usefully divided into various fields. There's a little room for disagreement about what counts as a major subdivision, but it doesn't really matter for our purposes how you slice things up. It's safe to say, anyway, that the subject falls into three or four main categories: metaphysics, epistemology, value theory and maybe logic.

Before we press this into better focus, the first thing to notice about the subject matter of philosophy is its abstract character. That's not to say that it's entirely divorced from everyday life. In fact, philosophical questions lurk one or two levels of abstraction away from ordinary, everyday concrete questions. You can stumble into them easily. 'What's your favourite sort of music?' I suppose I like jazz. 'Why do you like jazz?' It's beautiful. 'What do you mean by "beautiful"?' The third question is unlike the other two, and it lands us in the part of philosophy called aesthetics.

There's a jolt, a gear change from everyday questions to the abstractions of philosophy, and that's because philosophical questions aren't pursued for the same reasons as ordinary, practical ones. Philosophy, it gets said a lot, is born in curiosity, a plain desire to understand something, rather than the need to secure knowledge as a means to some other end. Someone might study genetics in the hope of producing more robust wheat crops. People read philosophy largely because they can't help it – they do philosophy for its own sake, not in an effort to get something else out of it.

Granted that philosophy's interests are abstract, just what are its subdivisions? We've already noticed aesthetics, which examines beauty, the value of art, the justification of aesthetic judgements and so on. Aesthetics itself is a part of value theory. While a painting might be good, there are other senses of good, and aesthetics' big brother is moral theory or ethics, which concerns itself with questions about how one ought to live. Ethics is broken down into normative ethics and meta-ethics. Normative ethics is an attempt to find a decision

4

procedure, a moral algorithm, rules or principles that might help us make decisions in particular cases and come to reasoned moral judgements. Meta-ethics is about the presuppositions behind our ethical concerns. Is morality relative? Are there moral facts? What do words like 'justice' and 'courage' really mean? Value theory is one of philosophy's main subdivisions, the one closest to practical life.

Another is metaphysics, the study of what exists in the broadest sense. Some standard questions in this neighbourhood will give you a feel for it. What is a substance? What does it mean for a substance to undergo change? How can many things share a single property, like being blue? What is a cause? What is an effect? What is a person? What is space? What is time? Does God exist? What is a mind? What is a body? Does the world exist independently of the mind? Is the world as it appears to us somehow illusory, and is there a deeper reality out there, hidden behind the limited information we have from our senses? Serious metaphysics is difficult stuff, and we'll find our way into some of these tangles in this book.

Another subdivision, called epistemology, concerns the nature of knowledge. Again, some questions will help you get a grip on it. What conditions have to be in place before we can say that we know something? Can reason discover truths independently of experience? Are some ideas innate? What role do the senses play in our efforts to know? Can we really, certainly and finally justify our beliefs beyond any doubt, and if so, how? Are there good reasons to remain sceptical? What are the limits of our efforts to know? Do the revealed truths of religion have a special status? Are there principles that govern the flow of ideas, just as there are laws of motion? These and other epistemological questions will occupy us almost from the start.

Value theory, metaphysics and epistemology are probably the three main parts of philosophical enquiry, but they certainly do not exhaust it. Philosophy bubbles over the sides of any container you try to put it in. Some people insist that logic should have its own category alongside the big three. Philosophers have almost always been concerned with the rules of right inference, and we should probably say that logic forms its own major subdivision, but we'll take this topic up in the next section.

Some argue that political theory should be lumped in with value theory, but many will say that political philosophy should stand on its own. Questions about political obligation and political organization are ancient ones that will also get some attention in this book. Others insist that the philosophy of language should have at least an honourable mention, so too the philosophy of science, the philosophy of mind, the philosophy of religion, the philosophy of mathematics, the philosophy of social science, the philosophy of psychology, the philosophy of physics, the philosophy of education – and at this point you've probably begun to suspect that one might philosophize about anything. You're right, which is the main problem with trying to think of philosophy narrowly as the study of metaphysics, value and knowledge. Part of the trouble is that philosophy's methods define it as well, or as badly, as its subject matter. There's considerable coherence when it comes to philosophical methodology, but historically it really is something of a zoo. Still, most philosophers pay attention to method, and it won't hurt to say something about arguments right at the start.

Tools of the trade

Probably what separates the first philosophers from the people who came before them was a concern with giving compelling reasons for their conclusions. This concern stuck. Views are not just presented, they're defended with argumentation.

An ordinary argument might be nothing more than two people making different claims: assertions launched from one side, and opposing assertions from the other. A philosophical argument, in contrast, involves people making different claims and backing those claims up with supporting reasons. Reasons can support a conclusion only if the whole argument itself – the premises and conclusion – hangs together logically. If everything lines up perfectly, if the premises are true and the argument has a valid form, then the conclusion follows necessarily.

But these sorts of knock-down arguments are rare in philosophy. Often the truth of the premises is in question, so you have to turn premises into mini-conclusions, and find a fresh set of premises to support them. Sometimes you can't really see the point of the conclusion, so you have to prowl around in the other things a philosopher says to narrow it down. A large part of reading philosophy is trying to understand arguments, and most of this work happens not on the page, but in the reader's head. A good rule of thumb is that if an argument seems obviously wrong, if a conclusion seems unbelievable, you've probably missed something somewhere. Just about all of the philosophers we'll consider in this book have stood the test of time for hundreds and hundreds of years. Probably that's because they've got the goods. If you don't see their point immediately, keep looking.

Philosophers not only make use of arguments, they've tried to find ways to formalize them, to study inferences in detail and see what works and what doesn't. This study, with all its symbolic trimmings, is philosophical logic. It's pursued formally in its own right, but philosophers have almost always had a commitment to constructing arguments that obey the rules of right reasoning.

Philosophers also generally have an interest in expressing themselves with clarity. So while a lot of the interpretive work is up to you, you'll find that some helpfully define their central terms, a few number their propositions, and many spell out axioms, draw distinctions and otherwise tell you exactly what they do or do not mean.

But there is a great deal of variation. Plato is as likely to hand you a serious argument as a metaphor or myth to advance his conclusions. Scholastic philosophers bury themselves, and you, in one hair-splitting distinction after another. Baruch Spinoza marches out premises like the steps of a geometrical proof. René Descartes is not above the odd literary device or two to persuade you covertly of the truth of his conclusions. Friedrich Nietzsche puts his claims in the mouth of a madman. Parmenides sings about the goddess Night, and passes on her metaphysical revelations in verse. Sometimes philosophers argue, and sometimes they pray. Reflection on methods, as is the case with subject matter, can only give us a partial grip on the story of philosophy.

This book

Now that you have a feel for the subject matter and methods of philosophy, a short overview of this book might help you find your way around it.

The philosophical tradition considered in this book is called 'Western' to distinguish it from the Eastern philosophies of Asia and the Far East, as well as the many other outlooks that originated in the cultures of other peoples. Western philosophy started in a Greek city around two and a half thousand years ago. The borders of its influence wobble back and forth as we move forward in time, taking in Europe, and sometimes parts of the Middle East and northern Africa, and eventually including the United States, Australia and other outposts in the present day.

The chapters are mostly self-contained, so you can hop about if you like. If you find Socrates boring, there's something wrong with you, but you should feel free to jump ahead to Aristotle and see if he grabs you. You'll get a feel for the flow of philosophy if you begin at the beginning and persevere all the way through, but there's nothing wrong with moving around as you see fit.

The first half of the book is organized mostly historically. We start with philosophy's prehistory – the *Odyssey*, the *Iliad* and the ancient Greek myths at the start of Western culture. The aim is to say what it was about that world that made philosophy possible. The following chapter, on the very first philosophers, takes up their metaphysical speculations, and we try to make sense of what seem to be very odd propositions. We then devote two chapters to philosophy's first heavy hitters: Socrates, Plato and Aristotle. The hope is to convey something of a feel for philosophy's deepest roots, and the sense in which, somehow, just three people largely set philosophy's agenda. The next two chapters cover the many schools of philosophy that surfaced in the years right up to the start of the Roman Empire. The Cynics, Stoics, Sceptics and Epicureans pursued wisdom at a time when philosophy was primarily a path to peace of mind, and their views resonate today. You'll meet some of philosophy's most memorable characters here.

Bravely, we devote two chapters to the philosophy of the medieval world, following philosophical interests as they shift in line with the rise of Christianity in the West. We take the opportunity to consider Islamic philosophers here too, as well as the Scholastics of the High Middle Ages. It's a neglected part of philosophy, but there's actually a lot of interest going on within it. What's more, modern philosophy is partly a reaction to medieval philosophy, and without a sense of what the medievals were up to, it's hard to appreciate the achievements of the moderns.

A chapter on the Renaissance and Enlightenment tracks the profound changes in our thinking about humanity, science and politics that are characteristic of the rise of modern philosophy. You'll read about humanism, have a look at Niccolò Machiavelli's infamous advice to rulers, and get a feel for the philosophical underpinnings of modern science. It's around here that things become messy.

Some of the following chapters consider particular movements or approaches to philosophy, while others focus on the thoughts of several philosophers coming at a single philosophical problem from different directions. It's partly chronological, but themes largely determine how thoughts are grouped from here on in. Fortified by a close look at philosophy's history, you'll be ready to consider the problems of modern philosophy, right up to some of the questions that philosophers are trying to answer in the present day.

We'll take up two views about knowledge that dominate the modern period – rationalism and empiricism. You'll see how each, inspired by advances in the budding sciences, tries to come to terms with the nature of human knowledge. It's a time of great philosophical ambition, with thinkers like René Descartes, Baruch Spinoza, Gottfried Leibniz, John Locke, George Berkeley and David Hume advancing arguments that are still pored over today. A bit later, we'll consider idealism, and in particular Kant's deep thoughts about the problems of metaphysics, and his alternative to both rationalism and empiricism. His recalibration of philosophy set the tone in many places up until the last century.

Next, the focus is politics, and the attempt to ground and understand political obligation in reason, rather than God or tradition. We'll take up the thoughts of Thomas Hobbes, John Locke and Jean-Jacques Rousseau, and move all the way on to Karl Marx and the philosophical underpinnings of the Communist revolution. All of their ideas established a foothold in Europe, but they had effects across the globe, and it's not going too far to say that they continue to shape the political landscape. We'll consider moral philosophy too, and find our way through the thoughts of Kant and the consequentialists, returning, once again, to Greek reflections on virtue.

Finally, we'll think through the main philosophical movements of the last century or so: existentialism and nihilism, and continental and analytic philosophy. We'll pause to consider the philosophy of mind as well, and the possibility that we're not at all sure how consciousness could exist in the physical world. We'll take up Søren Kierkegaard's Knight of Faith, Jean-Paul Sartre's notion of authentic existence, and

Nietzsche's dark thoughts on the crisis of value. We'll chart the rise of the philosophy of language and get to grips with Russell's method of logical analysis, as well as Wittgenstein's solution to the problems of philosophy. We conclude with an ill-advised glance forward, towards philosophy's future. In the end, you'll be right up to date, with a feel for the story of philosophy, through its history, all the way on to some of the problems of contemporary philosophy, and even a goodish guess as to where it is headed.

Have we left something out? Yes, of course we have, but we managed to get a lot in too. So take up and read the story of philosophy. By the time you finish it, you might be glad, as we are, that there is no happy ending. In fact there is no ending at all. It can sometimes feel as though philosophy, whatever it is, is only just getting started.

1
The Beginning of
Philosophy

The Greek Miracle

If you want to ensure a safe journey in your car, you might check the brakes, secure your seat belt and maybe poke the tyres to see that they're properly inflated. You probably would not set fire to a black bull to appease the gods. This distinguishes you from the Bronze Age Greeks, the men and women who began to think about the world in a new way around 3,000 years ago. To them, burning bulls to get what you wanted was an entirely sensible course of action. Consider these lines:

> Here on the shore the people were sacrificing black bulls to the dark-tressed Earth-Shaker, Poseidon. Nine companies of five hundred men sat there, each with nine bulls prepared for the sacrifice. They were tasting the innards, and burning the thigh-pieces to the god . . .

That's from the *Odyssey*, an epic poem about the adventures of the hero Odysseus as he travels home from the Trojan War. It's always been attributed to Homer, and we'll follow this tradition, but it's not clear that the poem has a single author. The stories were probably passed down orally through many generations, told many times, perfected by many artists. It's thought that someone, perhaps Homer, put a certain moral spin on the ancient stories he inherited from others, brought a kind of order to them, added certain poetic flourishes and finally his version became the standard one. However it came into being, the poem as we now know it is historically the second piece of literature in the Western world. It's the sequel to the first, Homer's *Iliad*, about the siege of Troy and the gods and human beings squabbling at the heart of it. In a sense these are our first real documents, the written beginning of all Western culture. And of course, you can find the roots of Western philosophy here too.

The Odyssey

Homer's Odyssey tells the story of Odysseus' adventures as he makes his way home after the Trojan War. He's been away fighting for ten years, and was captured and made prisoner for seven more by the nymph Calypso, who's fallen in love with him. Meanwhile, more than 100 'suitors' of his wife, Penelope, have spent the entire time enthusiastically trashing his house, eating his food and generally attempting to win over Penelope, who, unimpressed, stays faithful. Odysseus has the goddess Athena on his side, however, and she has him released and back at sea, heading for home, only for Poseidon to wreck his boat – Poseidon was on the side of the Trojans in the war, and now apparently has it in for Odysseus. Odysseus does not endear himself to Poseidon by later blinding Poseidon's son, the cyclops Polyphemus. Odysseus continues on his way, and some of his men manage to dodge cannibals, only to be turned into pigs by a witch. The rest avoid the song of the Sirens by plugging their ears with wax, and narrowly escape a sea monster and a whirlpool.

Finally Odysseus arrives home, in disguise, to have a clandestine and therefore honest look at what's been happening. He's not amused by the suitors. Athena persuades Penelope to arrange a test: whoever can string Odysseus' bow and blast an arrow through 12 axe heads wins her hand. Only Odysseus can do it, of course, and he celebrates by killing very nearly everyone. All the suitors die, the household maids who seemed to be on their side are hanged and a herdsman who provided them with goats has his nose, ears, hands, feet . . . and worse chopped off.

Homer's work contains many odd glimpses into the Greek mind, but those lines about animal sacrifice are particularly telling. Whether or not so many bulls met a sooty end on a Mediterranean shore is beside the point. What's weird is that those who sang the poems, and those who hung on every word, thought that burning a number of bulls for Poseidon was a good idea. But it's not something that anyone would seriously consider now. Why not? What has changed in the millennia that separate us from Homer?

The interesting thing from a philosophical point of view is the change in our rational expectations. There's no need to narrow it down too much at the start, but it's clear that, compared to the ancients, we look to different things when we want to go about the business of living or understand what's going on around us. It gets put in these sorts of ways: we have a scientific take on things, we search for causal explanations instead of supernatural ones, the forces that figure in our predictions and explanations of natural phenomena are devoid of personality, we demand a certain sort of logic in our arguments, we insist on a particular kind of evidence, and on and on.

We think in the way that we do because of a monumental intellectual shift that happened shortly after Homer's poem took shape. Some people who were part of a fairly quiet farming and trading community started asking questions that no one had ever asked before. Those people were the first philosophers, the Milesians, named after their city, Miletus, in a region that was then called Ionia but is now part of Turkey. You'll hear all about them in the next chapter. What they and a few others did has been called 'the Greek Miracle'. It didn't happen anywhere else, and it changed the course of human history. It's why we don't burn bulls. Within a generation, a handful of people in a few Greek settlements were no longer satisfied by talk of myths and gods. Suddenly, almost inexplicably, they invented rationality.

It's worth wondering about the world as it was before they changed it, and in thinking through some of this we'll get a grip on philosophy's primordial soup – the mindset that made philosophy possible. We'll start with the world view that Homer and another poet, Hesiod, partly created, and then try to set the stage for the first philosophers. Maybe you'll come to the conclusion that what happened in Miletus was wonderful, but not entirely miraculous. The world the first philosophers inherited was in a way primed for rational reflection, as we'll see.

Homer's world

It's hard to know what the Greeks might have thought about the world when the Homeric poems were coalescing. Scholars have tried to piece together what Homer takes for granted, reading between his lines, and there's at least some agreement about what one finds there.

The ancients seem to have thought that the world was more or less as it appears to be. The sky is what it looks like, a solid hemisphere enclosing a round, flat Earth. There's a kind of mist nearer the ground, filled with swirling clouds and vapours, called the Aither. Further up, near the Sun, the sky becomes fiery and hot, and perhaps beyond that point, in the starry heavens, you find the seat of the gods. There's a kind of symmetry here with what the Greeks thought was found in the levels beneath the Earth. First are the misty, cavernous, underground spaces called Tartaros. Beneath that is the realm of Hades, a kind of dark underworld of the dead.

Wrapped around the whole of the Earth is Okeanos, a flowing river that's the source of all the water we eventually see in streams, lakes and seas. There's speculation about the origin of this idea that everything rests on or emerges from water, and some argue that it derives from ancient civilizations that grew up around rivers and saw regular flooding, with the Earth 'emerging' from the waters each year. It's not a huge leap to think that the whole world might have arisen out of water in the same way.

It's worth noticing that even in this vision of the Earth, about as far back as we can go in Greek thinking about the way the world is, we find human beings telling stories that are, in a way, explanatory, that have a kind of logic to them that matches everyday appearances. Other cosmologies are not necessarily tied to sense experience in this way. One finds, for example, talk of 'earth parents' in some cultures, joining to create the world. Some early stories have it that the Earth is a severed part of a god. Others say that everything hatched from a cosmic egg. The Greeks never went in for that sort of thing. Maybe this is going too far, but there is the beginning of something like empiricism here, the view that knowledge is tied to sensory experience. Even in the earliest Greek view that we can tease out of the first bit of Greek writing we've got, there's the start of a commitment to the idea that our thoughts about the way the world is, and where it comes from, must fit in a certain way with what our senses tell us. This ancient Greek conception of the basic framework of the world might be naive, but it's not nonsense.

Homer's world is populated by human beings, of course – the Trojans, the Achaeans who lay siege to Troy, the various people Odysseus meets on his journey home – but it is also crowded with all sorts of non-human personalities. There are gods, titans, nymphs and mighty heroes with divine blood in their veins. There are also entirely bizarre mythical creatures like the Chimera, a fire-breathing combination of snake, goat and lion, and the six-headed sea monster Scylla. Much of this is just part of good story-telling, but the gods are more complicated and interesting than might at first be thought. Most noticeably, they are guilty of extraordinarily appalling conduct. They're not the sort of gods you'd like to be anywhere near.

We've come to expect the divine to be just, righteous and good, perhaps sitting in judgement in well-laundered white robes, but Homer's gods get up to all sorts of awful things. They become angry when slighted and inflict spiteful, childish, sometimes horrific punishments. They meddle in almost everyone's affairs. Some spend far too much time chasing young women or men – to take just one example, the father of the gods, Zeus, uses his godly powers to disguise himself as a familiar lover to trick a reluctant conquest into bed. The gods form allegiances, have family rows, then change their minds and swap sides. They intervene on behalf of those mortals they favour – sometimes through lies, the tacky manipulation of dreams, or perhaps doing some special pleading or granting favours in exchange for a service. If they've taken a dislike to you, you're seriously doomed. They'll wreck your life and your plans, sometimes behind the scenes but also directly and very thoroughly and entirely terrifyingly in person. Cowering in the middle of all this, ducking thunderbolts and hoping that the burnt bulls do the trick, are human beings. As Shakespeare has Gloucester put it in *King Lear*, 'As flies to wanton boys are we to the gods; they kill us for their sport.'

There is a lot of speculation about the meaning of the gods for the Greeks. One thing we can say with some certainty is that although thinking of events in terms of godly interventions might appear unsophisticated, there's something almost logical about it. When Homer tells us what the gods are doing and why they're doing it, he is in a way making sense of the chaos of events around him, offering a kind of explanation for everything from shipwrecks to the rise and fall of armies. He's positing an underlying order to the floods, wars and plagues, as well as the good fortune that might help a hero escape his prison. There's an explanation for the way things are – the world isn't just inexplicable and random – and if your side wins the fight against all the odds, maybe that's because Ares likes your style and has chosen to reward your bravery.

Without making too much of it, just as the Greek view of the dome of the heavens and the river round the Earth lines up with the way things look to the naked eye, there's a sense in which the world can appear governed by emotional impulse too. After all, the kind of events we're most familiar with, human actions are best explained in terms of emotion, impulse, desire and so on. We do what we do because of jealousy or love or hatred. Maybe the Earth shakes because Poseidon is annoyed by something you did. Again, this isn't too far away from rationality, is it?

The real Trojan War

Homer's writing might not be too far away from reality either. His poem, the *Iliad*, tells the story of the Greek siege of the city of Troy. The title comes from the Latin name for Troy, Ilium. The cause of the war, and at least a few complications that arise during it, has much to do with various parties abducting women. Paris, the son of Priam, king of Troy, steals Helen, who is the wife of Menelaus, the king of Sparta. She's the Helen of Troy you've heard about, and in Marlowe's *Doctor Faustus*, it's her face that launches a thousand ships. The thousand ships in question were actually launched by Menelaus' allies, the Achaeans, Homer's name for warriors from several Greek kingdoms.

The *Iliad* follows the various squabbles between kings and heroes, often fighting on the same side, as well as a number of interventions on the part of the gods. Armies meet on the field of battle, champions are chosen to fight for each side, truces are called and broken, and fierce fighting pushes the Greeks all the way back to their ships, then the Trojans are forced back to the walls of their city. Finally, the best Trojan fighter, Hector, meets the best Greek warrior, Achilles, and with a bit of help from Athena, Achilles kills him. In a spectacularly unsporting display, he immediately calls for a celebratory feast and drags Hector's body around behind his chariot for several days, until Hector's father buys the body back and gives him a proper funeral.

All thrilling and exciting, of course, but what's also interesting is that there might actually have been a battle of Troy, and a lot of this – no doubt minus the stuff about sea monsters and gods – could have a basis in fact. Scholars analysing the language of the poem have found evidence of its origin in oral tradition. Certain characteristic kinds of errors, mistakes that happen when a story is repeated over and over again, have been found in the poem. There are also examples of particular turns of phrase that serve as natural recall cues in Homer's lines. Such evidence could indicate that people had been passing the stories down for a long time before Homer's version took shape. Maybe people who saw the battle firsthand are the poem's original authors.

If that's too much of a stretch for you, a number of archaeologists maintain that a site that fits the narrative of the battle of Troy has been found in modern Turkey. Work is ongoing, and debate continues, but the place is the right age, in the right sort of spot, possibly the right size, and there's even evidence that is at least consistent with serious devastation at about the right time for the fall of Troy. A 'destruction layer' has been excavated, with signs of burning, caved-in walls, traumatized human bodies, arrow heads and, possibly, stock-piles of projectiles for slings – just the thing to have around if you are under siege.

Hesiod's order

As with Homer, we don't really know if Hesiod was one person or a name tagged on to the work of several poets. We're not sure if he came before or after Homer, but alongside Homer he contributed to what became the Greek world view. He's famous for two poems: *Works and Days*, a compendium of advice, largely about honest work; and *Theogony*, which explains the origins of the gods and how they acquired their various spheres of influence. Unlike those living in nearby states governed by powerful priestly classes, Hesiod and Homer, like the rest of the Greeks, were largely free to say what they liked about the gods, and add their own poetic gifts and intellectual inclinations to the mix. The result is remarkable.

Consider these lines from *Theogony*:

Verily first of all did Chaos come into being, and then broad-bosomed Gaia [Earth], a firm seat of all things forever, and misty Tartaros in a recess of broad-wayed earth, and Eros, who is fairest among immortal gods, looser of limbs, and subdues in their breasts the mind and thoughtful counsel of all gods and men. Out of Chaos, Erebos and black Night came into being; and from Night, again, came Aither and Day, whom she conceived and bore after mingling in love with Erebos. And Earth first of all brought forth starry Sky, equal to herself, to cover her completely round about, to be a firm seat for the blessed gods forever. Then she brought forth tall Mountains, lovely haunts of the divine Nymphs who dwell in the woody mountains. She also gave birth to the unharvested sea, seething with its swell, Pontos, without delightful love; and then having lain with Ouranos [Sky] she bore deep-eddying Okeanos [Ocean] . . .

What is fascinating is that even this mythological story has embedded within it what looks suspiciously like the roots of rational explanation, or anyway a kind of order. First there's Chaos, then Earth or Gaia appears, and the sorts of things you might expect to come from the Earth, like the mountains and the sea, really are 'brought forth' from it. Day follows or emerges from Night, and that somehow makes slightly better sense than Night coming from Day. The dawn does rise up out of the darkness, doesn't it? There is throughout a definite logic to what comes from what – it's not as though Day comes from mountains, which wouldn't sound right at all. The connections between various forces and the personalities of the gods make a kind of sense too.

The idea that Chaos appears first is itself worth lingering over for a moment. There's debate about how to interpret what's translated as Chaos here, and some suspect that the original Greek word is closer to the meaning of the English word 'gap'. Saying that Chaos exists first might be understood as positing an emptiness or nothingness at the start of everything. However, many understand Chaos not as a mere gap, but as a separation, a division, a space between what is earthly and what is skyward or heavenly.

The notion that the world took shape following an initial separation of some sort appears in a surprisingly large number of creation stories – Maori, Babylonian and Egyptian among them. It's also to be found in Genesis, along with familiar talk of night and day, sky and water:

> And God said, 'Let there be light', and there was light.
> God saw that the light was good, and he separated the
> light from the darkness. God called the light 'day', and
> the darkness he called 'night'. And there was evening,
> and there was morning – the first day. And God said,
> 'Let there be a vault between the waters to separate water
> from water.' So God made the vault and separated the
> water under the vault from the water above it. And it
> was so. God called the vault 'sky'. And there was evening,
> and there was morning – the second day.

Compare that to the Greek story. Having God do it all is explanatory in a way, but it's a less complicated, less interesting, maybe less informative way of explaining the origins of the world. There's nothing in Genesis of the logic of this thing following that thing, and how could there be? With God taking up all the space, there's just no room.

There is a little room, though, for speculation about why it is that talk of separation happens so frequently in the creation stories of such far-flung people. Perhaps this is all an echo of something near the very origins of human culture as such – something shared by the authors of many creation stories, not just Genesis. Talk of an initial separation runs deep, but it's hard to say anything reasonable that might explain its pervasiveness.

What we can say is that Hesiod brought a new rigour, a new order to the partly systematized world view we find in Homer. It's the fact of the order itself that is interesting. The world for Hesiod is an interconnected place that you can understand. There is a lot of begetting in his poem, and what you end up with is a kind of family tree of all the titans and the gods, as well as a story of how the gods came to power and what sort of power they have. Together his genealogy gives you a grip on which gods, and what spheres, are dominant over which others. It can provide you with a way to think about the world, as well as ideas about how to try to get what you want while you make your way through it. Hesiod's creation story, and the mythological family tree in it, is not told to legitimize a state or a king, as with many ancient myths. He's systematizing, explaining, ordering, and the result is on the way to a rational take on the way things are.

Beyond practicalities

So the world view inherited by the first philosophers was not exactly irrational. The structure of the world – the dome of the heavens, the underworld, the flat Earth and encircling ocean – all of this had a connection to what they saw with their own eyes. But the ancient Greeks weren't just interested in appearances – their talk of godly interference indicates that they suspected that there was something beyond appearance at work too. We've found in Greek thinking an attempt to rationalize the chaos of everyday events by looking for an underlying explanatory order in the actions of the gods. What's more, thanks to Hesiod, the human world and the gods who meddle in it are all part of a structured, ordered picture of reality, a place ready to be understood.

The world the Milesians found themselves in was approaching rationality, but it was nearly rational in another sense too – there was something like proto-science in it. But what the Greeks did when they encountered it was extraordinary, and it's the heart of the Greek Miracle.

By the time the first philosophers got down to business, the Greeks had already learned a lot from their industrious neighbours. Some of the philosophers and historians who came after Plato readily admitted that the Greeks learned geometry from the Egyptians. They also borrowed basic mathematics from the Babylonians – following them in dividing the day into an equal number of hours and using mathematics to pinpoint the turn of the seasons. The Babylonians taught the Greeks something about predicting the movements of heavily bodies too, but again this had more to do with arithmetic than observation.

The Egyptians and the Babylonians had a kind of mastery of these budding sciences for resolutely practical reasons. There are a number of different ways of looking at the achievements of both cultures at the time, but think just a little about these points, both made by more than one scholar. The Egyptians were very good at geometry largely because they had to be if they wanted to save money. Their system of taxation was based on usable land area, and you could claim a reduction in tax based on the surface area that dipped underwater when the Nile flooded. So you had to know some geometry, even if you just wanted to be a farmer. A good bit of Babylonian life was governed by religious considerations, and the religion at the time had to do with the gods of the heavens. So knowing what the planets and stars were up to, and when they would be up to it, turned out to have a bearing on everyday life. It was the practical application of both geometry and mathematics that was the great gift of the Egyptians and Babylonians.

The first philosophers probably had a large interest in the practical applications of geometry and mathematics, but while it satisfied the Egyptians and Babylonians, it wasn't enough for the Greeks. They moved on from practicalities and towards systematic and ordered answers to questions of great generality – into philosophy, in other words.

It is said that the first philosopher, Thales of Miletus, knew a lot about mathematics – in fact, we're not entirely sure what Thales knew. But legend has it that he used geometry to calculate the height of the pyramids and the distance of ships from the shore. While others stopped there, he went on to wonder what it is that pyramids, ships and everything else have in common that makes them all things. He wasn't content with spotting the fact that magnets could move certain bits of metal. He asked *why* magnets are the sorts of things that can move metal. For that matter, he wondered, why do some things move; what distinguishes animate from inanimate things? Plato and Aristotle agree on one thing, that philosophy begins in wonder, as opposed to trying to solve practical problems. It's not enough for philosophers to understand how things work. They need to know *why* things are as they are. That's true of Thales, and it's true of every other philosopher we'll consider in this book.

If wondering why in this way was beyond the Egyptians and Babylonians – and people everywhere else – how much further out of the ordinary run of things were the answers the Greek philosophers gave to their new questions. Their answers were rational answers. The Greeks, in a sense, invented rationality, because the answers they gave to their questions were new sorts of things in the world: reasoned conclusions. We'll focus on this a bit more in the next chapter, but from where we are now, it looks as though a few people in a Greek city came up with the novel idea of giving good reasons to support what they believed.

It's not entirely right to say that the Greeks departed from religion or mythology. Religious concepts figured in their thinking, and you can still be a philosopher and concern yourself with such things. What they did do was reject mere assertion. It was no longer enough to recite a few lines of Homer or say that something was simply so. Thales and the rest insisted on using reasons to back up what they took to be true. That was something new in the world.

There are all sorts of explanations for the Greek 'discovery of reason', if that's what it is. We've already glanced at some of them. As we've seen, Greek thinking about how the world is and how it works is already some way towards rationality. The creation story we find in Homeric thinking already makes a kind of sense, and coupled with Hesiod's divine family tree, we have a systematic, ordered world ripe for philosophical speculation. It's also true that in Miletus there was nothing like the Egyptian or Babylonian priestly class to get in the way of asking philosophical questions and rejecting dogmatic answers. And the first philosophers found themselves in a bustling trading port, with plenty of stimulating scientific input from abroad, the opportunity to travel, as well as leisure time for abstract reflection.

Does all of this explain the Greek Miracle? Irritatingly, it probably doesn't. All of these things make it seem just about possible that the first philosophers did what they did. But the world might have carried on forever without anyone insisting on reasoned conclusions, without anyone wondering why as they did. We might still burn bulls, but we don't. The inexplicable centre of the Greek Miracle is really the mysterious flash of genius owed to a handful of thinkers. They asked philosophy's first questions, and while their answers might strike you as stumbling, their questions are still very much with us.

The First Philosophers

It's the evening of 28 May 585 BCE. Thales, a prominent citizen of Miletus, is enjoying a moment of triumph. He has just witnessed a total solar eclipse that some years previously he had predicted would occur. He is well aware of the significance of his accomplishment. There is now no longer any need to invoke the gods to explain the workings of the world. It is clear that everything is under the governance of regular and predictable laws rather than supernatural caprice. What Thales doesn't know yet is that his achievement will bring him renown throughout the Greek world; and, more importantly, that it marks the birth of natural philosophy and of humanity's long stumble out of darkness into the light of reason.

This is a pleasing story about the origins of rational enquiry, but unfortunately it is probably mostly false. It is true that there was an eclipse on this date and that it was a significant event in the lives of the people of Ionia. The ancient historian Herodotus tells us that it occurred during the battle of Halys, fought between the Lydians and the Medes, neighbours of the Milesians, and that taking it to be an omen, the soldiers of both sides laid down their arms. However, it is unlikely that Thales knew the eclipse was going to happen, or that he understood even the most rudimentary aspects of the phenomenon. Not knowing is not the same as not predicting, of course, so it's possible he guessed and got lucky. But we have no good reason for supposing that this is the case. There are textual references to his apparent foreknowledge, but whether these are accurate or merely reflect the tendency to ascribe great deeds to celebrated figures, we don't know.

This story illustrates the difficulty of saying anything definitive about the lives of the earliest Greek philosophers – they're called 'the Presocratics', because they appeared before the large figure of Socrates, who we'll meet in the next chapter. The evidence we have about their lives comes from second-hand accounts, written long after they were dead, which reflect the prejudices and foibles of their authors. This is a shame, since it means we have to discard many tales that ought to be true simply because of their entertainment value. It would be wonderful to believe the ancient reporter Diogenes Laertius when he tells us in his *Lives and Opinions of Eminent Philosophers* that Heraclitus met his end after covering himself in cow dung and being inadvertently devoured by a pack of dogs, but probably it didn't happen. Similarly, the idea that

Empedocles ate a hearty lunch and then leaped into the flames of Mount Etna is satisfyingly poetic, but most likely not true.

We shouldn't be too discouraged, though, since things get a bit better when it comes to the *ideas* of the earliest Greek philosophers. Most of the Presocratics were thoughtful enough to write things down. Some of them, Democritus in particular, wrote an awful lot down. It's unfortunate, if not surprising, that none of their works survive intact, but we have been left with what scholars call 'fragments': words, sentences and occasionally whole paragraphs that were produced by the Presocratics themselves. We also have discussions of Presocratic ideas that crop up in later works, such as those by Plato, Aristotle, Plutarch, Clement, Diogenes Laertius and Simplicius. Put these together and we're on our way to getting a grasp of the issues that engaged the first philosophers.

Since we're telling the story of philosophy here, it would be nice if there were a clear narrative structure that governed the unfolding of Presocratic thought. It is certainly tempting to suppose that the Presocratic philosophers were talking and responding to each other, that their ideas were being tested in the court of reason, and that there was progress in the sense that earlier, weaker ideas came to be replaced by later, more robust ones. However, the reality is probably more haphazard than this. Not least, we don't know for certain just how familiar the major figures – Thales, Anaximander, Anaximenes, Heraclitus, Parmenides, Zeno, Empedocles, Anaxagoras, and Democritus – were with each other's work. Moreover, we're not even quite sure when they were working, either relative to each other or in absolute terms.

Nevertheless, it would be wrong to think there are no common threads running through Presocratic thought. The first is one we've already encountered: the earliest philosophers pioneered a novel and distinct way of looking at the world. They saw it as being ordered, amenable to reason and subject to its own internal logic, rather than chaotic and arbitrary. If Thales had been hit by lightning on his way home from the local *agora*, then (hopefully) he would have interpreted it as a natural event, not as a sign that the gods were displeased with him for his soothsaying about eclipses.

This shift in perspective might not seem like a big deal now but it was actually hugely significant. It opened up a space for the emergence of not just philosophy but science too. If the world is rule-governed, rather than arbitrary, then it is potentially intelligible, which means there is a reason for enquiring into its nature and looking for explanations of its various aspects. This is perhaps the second defining mark of Presocratic philosophy: it was concerned with what things are in a deep sense – with understanding the fundamental nature of things.

A little care is needed here. The idea that something has a 'fundamental nature' seems straightforward enough but it actually contains layers of complexity. So, for instance, it is possible that what is really important about a thing is its constituent elements, or how it came into existence, or its purpose, or some combination of these things. The significant point is that not everybody is going to agree about what matters most, and moreover what is thought to be important will vary over time. Therefore, while it is true that the Presocratics were united in their desire to understand the fundamental nature of things, it doesn't follow that they agreed about what counts even as an appropriate answer to that question. So, for example, a number of scholars have pointed out that the earliest Presocratic philosophers did not really have a concept of 'matter'. The question of what things were made of hadn't properly occurred to them. They were more interested in origins and motive power.

As we saw in the last chapter, though, there is one further thing about which they *were* all agreed – namely that claims about the nature of the world have to be supported by argument. This again was a dramatic break from the past. Pronouncements about the will of the gods would no longer do it; what counted was what could be *reasonably* asserted. According to philosopher and historian Jonathan Barnes, this emphasis on rationality and argument is the most remarkable and praiseworthy of the achievements of the Presocratics. It remains one of the defining characteristics of philosophy to this day.

This all sounds most encouraging. The Presocratic philosophers recognized the world as rule-governed and intelligible; they were interested in uncovering what things are in a deep sense; and they were committed to reason and argument as fundamental principles of enquiry. This is undeniably a good starting point. So what did they come up with?

Thales: a watery idea

Let's begin at the beginning, with Thales, the first philosopher. As far as we can tell, he believed that water is the origin of everything, that the Earth rests on a bed of the stuff, and that 'all things are full of gods'. He also thought magnets have souls. After the big build-up, these insights might seem a little underwhelming. Indeed, if, as the fanfare has it, it is true that Thales was 'the wisest man in Greece', it does rather leave us wondering what the other men were like. It perhaps also explains Diogenes Laertius' story that Thales was once led out of his house by an old woman to stargaze, whereupon he promptly fell into a ditch. She wondered, audibly, how someone who couldn't see what was under his own feet presumed to understand the heavens.

However, one should not feel too superior about the fledgling efforts of the first philosophers. It is extremely difficult for us to imagine ourselves not knowing what we always-already know – to borrow some terminology from linguistic theory. We are the products of the modern world, with all that that entails. If you're reading this book, then it's likely you're living in a society that has the methods and discoveries of the natural sciences as part of its background assumptions. It is nearly impossible for us to think ourselves out of this situation, and into the head of somebody who perhaps for the first time in history is looking at the world with something approaching a scientific spirit, and who has absolutely no prior knowledge or experience – his own or other people's – to draw upon.

If we attempt this imaginative leap, then Thales' speculations suddenly seem less absurd. Take the idea that water is the origin of everything. This is not such a strange notion when one remembers that life is dependent upon water, and that Thales lived in the Mediterranean, where this would have been an obvious fact of everyday life. Aristotle suggests that Thales hit upon his watery idea 'from seeing that the nutrient of all things is moist'. But maybe that wasn't it at all. Perhaps he was taken by the fact that water is able to change its form, turning to ice in cold weather and evaporating when it gets hot. Or maybe he was impressed by the way the Sun seems to draw energy up from the sea. In the end, it doesn't really matter. What matters is that he had *some* reason for thinking that water is the origin of all things. It wasn't simply an arbitrary leap of faith.

Thales' watery idea also has the merit of explanatory economy. His desire to reduce the complexity of the observable world to a single unifying principle was sound. It is a common thought to this day that the power and elegance of a theory lies in its ability to explain a lot of things in terms of very few things. This impulse to simplify was characteristic of Presocratic philosophy as a whole, and marked another departure from the past. However, parsimony in explanation doesn't equate with being right, and of course Thales wasn't right. He was completely wrong.

There is a general caveat here, which is that all this talk about Thales and what he might have thought is highly speculative. The truth is, we don't know what he thought. Aristotle, drawing upon an oral tradition, discusses his ideas, briefly and tentatively, on a couple of occasions, but that's pretty much it. The Thales one finds discussed in modern philosophical texts is largely an imaginative construct. He isn't quite conjured *ex nihilo*, but it's a pretty close-run thing. Probably he is best understood as the personification of philosophy's origin rather than as a fully formed historical figure. Any claim that it is possible to discover the real Thales in the pages of ancient texts should be treated with appropriate suspicion.

Anaximander: stuff that isn't stuff

Happily, Thales' contemporary, Anaximander, also a Milesian, is not quite so insubstantial. It is true we don't know a lot about him, but he at least managed to put pen to papyrus. In fact, he wrote a whole book, called *On Nature*, and also created a star chart and a map of the world. Unfortunately, aside from a single sentence from his book, none of these things survive, but then we can't have everything.

Anaximander, unlike Thales, did not regard water as the basic stuff of the universe. His big idea is altogether more esoteric. He thought that the basic stuff is limitless, indeterminate, eternal and invisible. He called it the Unbounded, or *apeiron*. It isn't an element exactly, certainly not in the traditional sense, but rather some other unspecified stuff from which everything else comes into being, and to which it returns after it is destroyed. So why believe in this mysterious stuff rather than something more tangible? We can't be sure, but one commentator suggests it is because Anaximander had observed the four traditional elements – earth, air, fire and water – changing into one another, and then resolved not to make any one of them the underlying stuff, positing something else instead.

Despite the weirdness of this, there is the germ of what will become an increasingly important idea here: namely that there is a difference between appearance and reality. The observable world – or in terms that would have been familiar to Anaximander, the *kosmos* – is changeable and finite. But the reality that underpins it, the Unbounded, out of which the *kosmos* is created, and which provides its sustenance and motive power, is limitless, eternal and perhaps even divine. The *kosmos* is not an illusion for Anaximander in the same way it seems to have been for Parmenides, as we'll see, but nevertheless he did understand its reality as being subordinate to the more fundamental reality of the Unbounded.

This does lead one to wonder how exactly these two domains interact with each other. Unfortunately, this is where things get both complicated and rather vague. Anaximander seems to have held that the *kosmos* is constituted by a set of opposing forces, the opposites, which stand in a relation of perpetual conflict with one another. This is the topic of the only surviving fragment of his work: '[The opposites] pay penalty and retribution to each other for their injustice according to the assessment of Time.'

Exactly what this means, or even inexactly, is not at all clear. It is possible that what he's getting at is that forces such as hot, cold, wet and dry are engaged in a constant battle for supremacy, with no one particular force being able to gain a decisive victory. So, for example, one can imagine the desert sun drying up an oasis only for it to be replenished again during a monsoon, or water extinguishing a fire only for it to be reignited at a later date. In this sense, the 'injustice' that occurs is the encroachment of one opposite upon the terrain of another, and the 'penalty' is the readjustment, and more, that occurs in the opposite direction.

This leaves Anaximander's curious statement that this process occurs 'according to the assessment of Time'. Some scholars explain this by invoking the Unbounded as a sort of cosmic referee. The idea is that the conflict between opposites is governed and regulated externally by the Unbounded, for which 'Time' stands as a synonym. Thus, for example, one might think of the orderly progression of days and nights, or perhaps of the unfolding of the seasons. However, this is all highly speculative, and though it fits with the idea that the Unbounded is the governing principle of the *kosmos*, we can't be sure if it's what Anaximander had in mind.

Moreover, it leaves untouched the question of how the

opposites, and indeed the more traditional elements of the *kosmos*, emerged out of the Unbounded in the first place. Here things are even more vague. Anaximander gestures in the direction of a 'separating out', driven by hot and cold forces. There is talk of 'whirls', a vortex, mist and maybe even some bark, but none of it makes much sense. Here is a later philosopher, Aristotle's student Theophrastus, doing his best to get a grip on it:

> He says at the generation of this world something generative of hot and cold separated off from the eternal, and from it a ball of flame grew round the air about the earth, like bark on a tree. When the ball burst and was enclosed in various circles, the sun and the moon and the stars came into being.

Probably the less said about this the better. If there is any philosophical interest here at all, it is that Anaximander's speculations are consistent with the idea that the *kosmos* has its own logic of development and was not brought into being by an act of God. This idea is common to all the Milesian philosophers, but it finds its most mature expression in the work of Anaximenes, pupil of Anaximander, and the third and final of the great philosophers of Miletus.

Anaximenes: air is everywhere

Anaximenes was not one for the sort of metaphysical flights of fancy favoured by his teacher. He eschewed talk of indeterminate, unbounded stuff in favour of something much more prosaic: he thought that air explained pretty much everything. The Earth and all the heavenly bodies stay where they are because they are supported by air. Living creatures are alive because they have been animated by air. And the fundamental stuff of reality – its *archê* – is air. This sounds like a replay of Thales, only substituting air for water, but actually there is enough that is novel in Anaximenes' account to make it interesting. In particular, he attempted to explain how it is that just one substance can account for all the variability found in the *kosmos*.

His idea is that air turns into other elements by a process of condensation and rarefaction. Hippolytus, a third-century Christian theologian who provides us with the fullest account of Anaximenes' views, explains it like this:

> As air is condensed and rarefied it appears different: when it is diffused into a more rarefied condition it becomes fire; wind, again, is air moderately condensed; cloud is produced from air by compression; when it is yet more condensed it is water, and then earth; and when it is as dense as possible it is stones.

In terms of this schema, then, fire is the most diffuse, rarefied form of air; next is normal air; then wind, which is normal air condensed; and then clouds, water, earth and stones, each one more dense than the rest. This process of condensation and rarefaction is driven by the continual motion of air, which, according to Anaximenes, is a prerequisite for any sort of change. He also hints that hot and cold have a role to play here, with heat being associated with diffuseness and frigidity with contraction.

As a description of reality, Anaximenes' speculations are about as hopeless as those of his predecessors – air is no more the foundation of reality than water or the *apeiron*. But again there is philosophical interest here that goes beyond the issue of the truth of any specific substantive claim. In particular, unlike in the cases of Thales and Anaximander, we can be pretty certain that Anaximenes believed not only that everything in the observable world *originated* from his basic stuff, but also that everything is *made out of it*. Moreover, he offered a broadly naturalistic explanation of how the variability and complexity of the observable world emerges out of the uniformity of a single substance. In these senses, he is a decidedly more modern figure than either of his Milesian predecessors.

Anaximenes, 25 years the junior of Anaximander, probably flourished in the middle of the sixth century BCE, a period that marked the beginning of the end of Ionia as a distinct centre of economic power and cultural excellence. The

Persians under Cyrus the Great conquered the region in 546 BCE, and although Miletus managed to avoid much of the upheaval at first, the city was eventually captured and enslaved by the Persians in 494 BCE. Ionia soon lost its place near the centre of the Greek world, but there is one more Ionian philosopher of note from this period: Heraclitus of Ephesus.

Heraclitus: flux and chaos

Heraclitus is perhaps the most diverting of the Presocratic philosophers. Not, it must be said, for his philosophical output, which is frustratingly unclear, but rather for his curmudgeonly nature. He was described in antiquity as being 'haughty' and 'overweening', but really this is putting it mildly. He is ancient philosophy's bad-tempered Rottweiler. He said of Homer, and the warrior poet, Archilochus, that they should both be beaten with sticks. Pythagoras fared little better, being dismissed as 'the prince of lies'. And as for his compatriots, the Ephesians, he thought they would do well to kill themselves.

The cause of all this fuss seems to have been the inability of people to see the world as Heraclitus saw it. Thus, for example, he complained that 'Most men do *not* have thoughts corresponding to what they encounter, they do not know what they are taught, but imagine that they do.' He said that people tended to sleepwalk through their lives: 'Other men are unaware of what they are doing when awake, just as they are of what they forget about in sleep.'

However, there is an irony here, in that it isn't at all clear how Heraclitus himself saw the world. Even in antiquity, he was considered notoriously obscure. Diogenes Laertius reports that when Socrates was asked what he thought of Heraclitus' writing, he replied: 'What I have understood is good; and so, I think, what I have not understood is; only the book requires a Delian diver to get to the bottom of it.' Socrates was perhaps being a little overoptimistic, since probably a Delian diver would also struggle. But there is merit in effort, so let's see if we can make some sense out of Heraclitus' musings.

Perhaps the best jumping-off point is his most well-known epigram, one of more than a hundred surviving fragments, which states that 'You cannot step twice into the same rivers; for fresh waters are flowing in upon you.' This is typical of Heraclitus' style – short, enigmatic (or annoying, depending on your perspective) and subject to multiple interpretations. In one sense, it is obvious what he is getting at. A river flows continuously, which means each time somebody steps into it, they're going to be surrounded by different water, thereby making it a different river. The issue, though, is how we interpret this claim: what does Heraclitus intend us to take from it?

It is here that things get tricky. One reading suggests that Heraclitus believed rivers are characterized *only* by flux and lack any sort of solid identity; and, by extension, assuming the river to be a metaphor for the whole of reality, that flux is constitutive of the entire world. Nothing is permanent. This seems to have been what many of the philosophers and commentators of antiquity took him to have meant. So, for example, Plato attributed to him the belief that 'all things flow and nothing remains still'. Aristotle tells us that:

> . . . the view is actually held by some [i.e., Heraclitus] that not merely some things but all things in the world are in motion and always in motion, though we cannot apprehend the fact by sense perception.

It would be nice if we could just leave it at this and move on to other, less gnomic Greeks, but unfortunately there is more to be said. Of particular significance is the fact that other fragments suggest Heraclitus did not intend such a radical conclusion. Consider, for example, fragment 49a: 'We step and do not step into the same rivers; we are and are not.'

It is tempting to suppose that Heraclitus is simply asserting a contradiction here: we both do and do not step into the same rivers. However, a more charitable reading has it that he is wrestling with the problem of identity through change. Specifically, in this case, he's trying to work out whether something can still be the same thing even if its constituent elements have changed completely. If it turns out it can be, then there is sense in saying that we both step and do not step into the same rivers. A river can be continuously changing in terms of its make-up, yet remain the same river.

The idea that an apparent contradiction might express an

underlying unity is characteristic of Heraclitus' work. Consider these epigrams:

> The way up and the way down are one and the same.

> The sea is the purest and the impurest water. Fish can drink it, and it is good for them; to men it is undrinkable and destructive.

> Hesiod is most men's teacher. Men think he knew very many things, a man who did not know day or night! They are one.

All of these involve contradictions that dissolve on further examination. Something is up or down depending on one's perspective. At the top of a hill, all ways point downwards; at the bottom, the way is up. Similarly, salt water is pure or impure depending on whether an organism is set up to tolerate it. Fish are, humans aren't. And day and night both form part of the same 24-hour cycle.

These sorts of thoughts have led many scholars to propose that Heraclitus was advocating what is called the 'identity of opposites': phenomena such as day and night, up and down, might appear to be contradictory, but they are in fact identical. If this is right, then, in Heraclitus' terms at least, the existence of flux and conflict is compatible with the proposition that the world manifests a fundamental harmony, that all things are 'the same'.

But really we can't make too much of this. For a start, Heraclitus hasn't done anything like demonstrate the 'identity of opposites'. On some readings, his efforts are an object lesson in confusion and overgeneralization. We should not judge him too harshly, of course, since he lived long before people had worked through the various nuances of meaning attached to notions such as 'identity' and 'difference'; nevertheless, his ideas on these matters do not stand up to scrutiny. So, for example, while we understand what he's getting at when he says that night and day are the same, we also know that two different things don't become one thing just because they share something in common.

The other reason for caution is the standard one when it comes to the Presocratic philosophers: we just can't be sure about his intended meaning. The usual problems are compounded in the case of Heraclitus by his deliberately oracular style, which is reflected in wildly differing translations of his fragments and divergent views among commentators as to how they should be interpreted. Jonathan Barnes, commenting on this free-for-all aspect of Heraclitean scholarship, notes that:

When . . . Hegel came to Heraclitus, he was moved to an extravagant effusion: 'Here we see land! There is no proposition of Heraclitus which I have not adopted in my logic.' A prominent opponent of Hegelianism is no less effusive: Heraclitus' fragments, far from adumbrat-

53

ing teutonic dialectics, reveal 'a thinker of unsurpassed power and originality', a Greek Wittgenstein. The truth is that Heraclitus attracts exegetes as an empty jampot wasps; and each new wasp discerns traces of his own favourite flavour.

There is a temptation, perhaps justified, to be pretty cynical about this sort of thing. There are, of course, dangers in making sweeping statements about the merits of a philosopher taken seriously by a lot of people who know an awful lot about the field. Nevertheless, reading the standard treatments of Heraclitus' work, one is struck by a sense that it's an exercise in futility to try to determine exactly what he intended. Perhaps the moral of the story is that if you want to be understood by posterity, then probably you're better off avoiding aphoristic paradox and punning as your modus operandi.

Parmenides: all is one

It will probably be a relief to hear that Parmenides, the greatest of the philosophers of Elea, a city in southern Italy, did not indulge in aphorism or oracular pronouncement. On the contrary, he is notable for being the first of the Presocratic philosophers to employ a systematic argumentative style, where it seems his intention was to lead the reader inexorably from premises to a particular conclusion. It is somewhat ironic, then, that he chose to work in hexameter verse. It is even more ironic that he wasn't much good at it.

We don't know a lot about Parmenides' life, but it seems he was born into a prominent Ionian family sometime around 515 BCE, and that he spent most of his life in Elea, which is a little to the south of Naples. There are rumours that he was taught by the poet Xenophanes, and that he met Socrates, but it is likely that neither of these things is true. However, we do know a fair bit about what he thought, since, largely courtesy of the Neoplatonist scholar Simplicius, we still possess some 120 continuous lines of his writing. From these we find out that Parmenides learned all he knew about philosophy not from Xenophanes, nor from any other mortal, but rather from a goddess:

> The goddess graciously received me and took my right hand in hers; and she spoke and addressed me: 'Young man, companion to the immortal charioteers, who come to my house with the mares who carry you, welcome . . . You must learn all things, both the unwavering heart of persuasive truth and the opinions of mortals in which there is no true warranty.

The surviving lines form part of his epic poem *On Nature*, which is split into three sections: a prologue, which deals with his encounter with the goddess; the 'Way of Truth', in which the goddess expounds an entirely novel theory of being; and the 'Way of Opinion', in which, for reasons best known to herself, she outlines a broadly naturalistic account of the world that she readily admits is false.

Parmenides' idea, explicated in the 'Way of Truth', is that it is only possible to think or say anything about being, or *what is*. Once one grants this premise – and it should be said from the outset that there is no good reason to do so – then all sorts of radical consequences follow. For a start, it does away with the idea that things can come into existence from nothing, a notion that Parmenides claims is unintelligible: 'That it came from what is not I shall not allow you to say or think – for it is not sayable or thinkable that it is not.'

It also rules out the possibility of change, since if something has changed it implies that it is not now what it once was, which again is disallowed on the grounds that it is necessary to abandon all talk of what is not. And for the same reason, we cannot think or talk of anything ceasing to exist, since this implies the negation of being, which has the consequence that what exists must be eternal.

It is not unreasonable at this point to think that maybe Parmenides' goddess has quaffed a little bit too much of the good stuff before endeavouring to enlighten him, since it certainly seems that things are perfectly able to come into existence, change and go out of existence. Parmenides, of course, would have accepted that this is how things seem, but he would have denied that the way things *seem* is the way things are. It might appear that creation, change and extinction are possible, but this is an illusion, a consequence of the unreliability of sense experience, which belongs properly to the realm of opinion or appearance.

Parmenides doesn't stop with the claim that all change is

ruled out. He pushes his idea that it's only possible to think of *what is* until it elicits further radical conclusions. Motion, change and diversity are impossible. What exists is uniform, indivisible, perfect, divine, everlasting, complete and . . . round. All this adds up to an account of reality that is completely at odds with that provided by Heraclitus. Where Heraclitus sees turbulence and flux, Parmenides sees uniformity, stability and permanence. The Parmenidean universe is a singular, unchanging, undivided, perfect unity.

So what should we make of all this? Perhaps the first thing to say is there is no doubt that Parmenides' ideas were original and significant. According to many scholars, he is *the* pivotal figure in Presocratic philosophy. Certainly it is true that his metaphysical speculations on the nature of being, or *what is*, were a different sort of thing than anything that had gone before. It is also true that his ideas would come to have a major effect on the thinking of Plato, and thereby on the course of Western philosophy as a whole.

Moreover, there is much to admire in the pioneering aspects of his philosophical work. As already mentioned, he was the first of the Presocratic philosophers to make use of systematic argument with the aim of demonstrating that particular conclusions had to be true given the truth of certain premises. It is also perhaps not too much of a stretch to see Parmenides as being the earliest exponent of a philosophical approach known as 'rationalism', which holds that it is possible to derive truths about the world from purely intellectual reflection. He might be the first idealist too.

However, all this comes with a large caveat: it is clear that the specific arguments advanced by Parmenides are erroneous, since the conclusions he drew from them are obviously absurd. In fact, it is pretty easy to identify where he went wrong: right at the beginning, when he claimed that it is not possible to think or say anything about *what is not*.

Such a thing certainly seems possible. It makes sense, for example, to say that unicorns do not exist, or that Sherlock Holmes is only fictional, or that the writing of this book has not yet been completed. But are we referring to anything when we talk about Sherlock Holmes? If not, how can our words mean anything?

It is easy to get into philosophical trouble when talking about things that do not exist. As we'll see in a chapter on logical analysis, it took 2,000 years and some advancements in logic to sort through the metaphysical tangles first encountered by Parmenides. Even so, we're still not sure why Parmenides thought that we cannot legitimately talk about what does not exist. He is frustratingly unclear on this issue, which means it is only possible to gesture at an explanation. The heart of it *seems* to be that he conceptualized thought and being as if they were the opposite sides of the same coin, thereby supposing that thought implied being. In one sense, this impulse is understandable – it is not a particularly contentious idea to think that thought must be *of* something. But the mistake comes in thinking that this something must necessarily exist (and, therefore, that it is not possible to think of *what is not*). If you're in any doubt that this is a mistake, consider, for example, that if it were true, it would be possible to confirm the existence of any hypothetical entity simply by thinking of it. And also, arguably at least, that anything that could exist must exist.

Not surprisingly, Parmenides' ideas did not gain widespread acceptance beyond the immediate circle of his fellow Eleatic philosophers. Achilles and the Tortoise is one of Zeno's classic paradoxes of motion, which seem to show that if space (and/or time) is infinitely divisible, then motion is not possible at all. Constructed in defence of Parmenides' idea that all is one, it has the following form: Imagine that Achilles is taking on a tortoise in a race, and he gives the tortoise a head start. Although Achilles is much quicker than the tortoise, it is possible that he'll never be able to catch his dawdling opponent. This possibility rests on the fact that whenever Achilles reaches a point where the tortoise has been, the tortoise will have moved on a little further, even if only by a small amount.

At the beginning of the race, the tortoise has a headstart over Achilles. Very rapidly, Achilles gets to the point where the tortoise started the race, but the tortoise has moved forward. Achilles then gets to the position the tortoise had reached at the point at which Achilles got to the tortoise's original starting position, but again the reptilian menace has gone a bit further. And the race carries on in this fashion, with Achilles getting ever closer to the tortoise, but never actually catching her.

Another version of this paradox emerges if one considers what it takes to walk across a room. To do so, necessarily you must cover half the distance before you complete the journey. However, you can't cover half the distance until you cover half of half the distance, and you can't cover half of half the distance until you cover half of that distance, and so on, ad infinitum. It seems then that you will never get started.

We know, of course, that people do cross rooms, and that Achilles would have caught the tortoise in a race, which means that something must be wrong with Zeno's argument. However, it is not clear exactly what. The most popular approach is probably to argue that the paradox is dissolved by the fact that mathematics shows that an infinite series ($\frac{1}{2}$ + $\frac{1}{4}$ + $\frac{1}{8}$ + $\frac{1}{16}$ . . .) has a finite sum, which means that there is some finite amount of time it will take to traverse the series.

But even if we don't quite know what to do with Zeno's paradoxes, the one thing no one does is accept them as proof of Parmenides' views. In fact, in one of his dialogues, Plato suggested that Parmenides became something of a figure of fun because of the ideas he espoused. But it is also true that the philosophers who came after him were in various ways responding to the challenges laid down by his philosophy. This was particularly true in the case of Plato, whose theory of forms can be understood as an attempt to hold on to the

Parmenidean idea that what is ultimately real is unchanging and eternal, without it being necessary to jettison the realm of sense experience altogether. But, as we'll now see, Plato saw something in Heraclitus too.

The Love of Wisdom

The Presocratics are called 'Presocratics' for a very good reason. The appearance of Socrates on the philosophical scene really does mark a clear transition from one set of concerns to another. As the Roman philosopher and statesman Cicero puts it, 'Socrates called philosophy down from the heavens.' Even if you give the Presocratics their due for taking the first steps towards rationality, you never really know what to say when they tell you that all is water or that everything is really one. But you can have a conversation with Socrates. He didn't go in for obscure speculation about the fundamental nature of reality. He didn't say anything unsettling about magnets. What matters to him are much more human questions. What does it mean to be just? What is courage? How should one live? At least we think that's what concerned him.

By almost all accounts, Socrates' preoccupation with moral questions annoyed just about everyone in Athens. He called himself a gadfly or horsefly, buzzing around, nipping away, and jolting people out of complacency and into more careful thinking. If you were on the business end of his constant questions and endless arguments, it was probably incredibly irritating. And he continues to annoy us, more than 2,000 years later, because although he's almost certainly the most influential philosopher in Western history, we know almost nothing about what he really believed. This is largely his own fault, because he claimed that he didn't actually know much about anything. His wisdom, he said, consists in the fact that he knows that he knows nothing, while everyone else persists in the mistaken belief that they know quite a bit. Perhaps most annoyingly of all, he never wrote down even a sentence of philosophy. There is no Socratic corpus. We've got nothing on him.

But in an excellent accident of history, standing right next to Socrates while he bothered his fellow Athenians was Plato, his student and, thankfully, not just a philosophical genius but a literary one too. Plato wrote dialogues, kind of philosophical transcripts, with Socrates usually asking questions, getting answers, ripping the answers to shreds and then insisting on better answers. The dialogues have good philosophical arguments in them – reasons being offered in support of conclusions – but even if they didn't, we would still read them for their beauty, charm and style. They're works of art in their own right. Plato paints portraits, sets scenes, tells jokes and seems to be the master of a huge range of literary devices.

The result is entirely three-dimensional characters arguing about things that end up mattering to you. Here's the best news of all: probably every one of Plato's dialogues has survived.

Based on those, and a few other sources, we can piece together something of Socrates. He wasn't much to look at – short, pudgy, bald, snub-nosed – and what he lacked in looks he failed to make up for in personal hygiene. Nevertheless, he had a much younger wife, Xanthippe, as well as an eye for handsome young men. He sometimes heard a voice in his head, and he fell into a kind of stupor or 'fit of abstraction', which would leave him staring into space, maybe puzzling something out, for long hours. What he had in abundance was debating prowess. According to a contemporary, Xenophon, he 'could do what he liked with any disputant', and he did, regularly cutting some jumped-up Athenian down to size in front of an audience of young men who followed him around and listened to his every word. He saw war in his youth and fought heroically by all accounts. He might have worked as a stone cutter, but by the time of most of the dialogues he's an old man nearing 70, with no visible means of support and an obsession with virtue.

What did he actually think? Although we probably have all of the dialogues, it's not as simple as reading Plato as though he were a court reporter. Over time, as Plato's own philosophical outlook dawned on him, it's thought that the Socrates in the dialogues becomes more and more a mouthpiece for

Plato's own take on things. So to varying degrees of certainty, the dialogues are grouped into early, middle and late works, with the earliest probably giving us the best clues about the thoughts of the historical Socrates, and the later dialogues expressing Plato's own remarkable views. So we'll start with the Socrates of the early dialogues, move on to Plato's philosophy, and finally say something about the enormous influence that Socrates and Plato have had on philosophy.

Knowing what's good for you

Socrates is the hero of almost all of Plato's dialogues, and in the early ones a regular pattern emerges. Socrates encounters someone who thinks he knows about some aspect of morality or another, for example, courage. Sometimes his interlocutor is a friend, or someone who just wants to join Socrates in the pursuit of wisdom, but often it's a pompous Athenian who wrongly thinks he knows his stuff. Socrates asks for a definition of a general term. What is courage? He gets an answer, and then with further questions teases out trouble. Maybe he finds some sort of contradiction. Perhaps what gets said eventually shows that the original definition was too narrow or too broad – some act that should count as courageous is ruled out or something that isn't courageous is ruled in. Perhaps in the course of deeper reflection the person finds that what they said at the start leads on to something that just isn't right. They try again, make a new and hopefully more considered attempt at a definition, and Socrates goes on with more questions.

As example of Socratres in action might make this more clear. Plato describes a young man called Euthyphro who is on his way to court, where he plans to sue his own father for allowing a slave to die of exposure. In a fine display of Socratic irony, Socrates says that Euthyphro must be an expert in both religion and morality, and must have 'made great strides in wisdom' to be confident enough to bring his own father to justice. 'Rare friend,' Socrates exclaims, 'I think that I cannot do better than be your disciple!' Would Euthyphro perhaps take a moment to enlighten Socrates concerning the true nature of piety? Euthyphro bites, and Socrates takes him apart very quickly.

Euthyphro says that piety is exactly what he is exhibiting in prosecuting his father, but Socrates objects that at best he's merely given an example of piety, not a definition. He tries again: piety is what pleases the gods. Socrates points out that different gods are pleased by different things – some gods are pleased by actions that displease others. Are we to say that some things are both pious and impious? Euthyphro tries a final time: 'What all the gods love is pious and holy, and the opposite which they all hate, impious.' Socrates presents him with this dilemma: is the pious or holy loved by the gods because it is holy, or is it holy because it is beloved of the gods?

Socrates uses those two options to show that Euthyphro has given only an attribute of piety (it's loved by the gods), and not a proper definition. It's an ingenious bit of reasoning, but perhaps more interesting is the fact that the dilemma is the inspiration for what is still regarded as a serious objection to religious morality. Divine command theory, as it's called, holds that morality is grounded entirely in what God commands. But does God command what's good because it is good, or is it good because it is commanded by God?

If God commands what's good because it's good, then He is just following some standard of goodness that isn't Him – so divine command theory is false if it says that morality is determined by God alone. If what's good is good just because God commands it, then morality looks arbitrary and much less meaningful than most of us take it to be. Morality is nothing deeper than the whim of the divine. Awful actions might have been morally acceptable had God commanded them. Debate, as you might imagine, rages on.

Socrates' procedure of seeming to tease out knowledge by asking questions is the inspiration for the appropriately named 'Socratic method' of enquiry and learning. In the early dialogues at least, he never really presents his own positive view, never settles on a definition of anything. Instead he guides his interlocutors to deeper insights through meticulous interrogation. He's helping others gain self-knowledge, enabling them to come to grips with who they really are and what they actually believe. The injunction 'Know thyself' appears several times in Plato's dialogues. In a characteristic line, Socrates says to Phaedrus that he has no time to think about mythology, because he does not yet know himself, and if he hasn't even managed that, he's not going to waste time investigating anything else.

Socrates says in several places that what matters most is the soul, the inner self, and coming to understand oneself and live accordingly is probably fundamental to the Socratic mission. Socrates thinks he's up to something akin to midwifery – bringing forth knowledge that's already within us if only we take the time to engage in philosophy and think things through. Once we have that knowledge, we must be true to it, and that means we have to live in accord with it. This is probably part of the reason why, despite never really settling on a definition at the end of the early dialogues, Socrates thinks his time is well spent. Even if he and his fellows haven't discovered the nature of courage, they know better what they think and who they are.

Given the endless questions, it's hard to find a positive doctrine, but it's clear that Socrates thinks that there's a connection between possessing virtue and being able to give a definition of virtue. If you can't say what courage is, he seems to believe, you don't know what you're talking about when you talk about courage. You therefore can't really be courageous. Perhaps that's too strong, and it would be more careful to put it like this: unless you can say exactly what virtue is, you've got little chance of actually attaining it, because you don't know what you're aiming for. However we unpack this view, it's pretty clear that Socrates holds that there is a strong connection between virtue and knowledge. How he really understood that connection, though, is open to question.

What we can say with confidence is that the 'Socratic paradoxes' are attributed to the historical Socrates by many early sources. He's credited with thinking that virtue is knowledge, that weakness of will is impossible, that no one does wrong willingly, that all wrong-doing is owed to ignorance. These notions are paradoxical because it's not difficult to think of plenty of examples of people doing wrong while knowing exactly what they're doing. Weakness of will is just about everywhere. So what was he thinking?

It's controversial, but he might have believed that if a person really has a comprehensive grip on virtue, then he or she would never choose vice. If we knew what we were doing, what we were willing, when we chose evil – if we could see the harm we cause not just to others but to our own inner lives – we'd never do it. So we only ever choose to do something morally wrong because we don't fully know what virtue is. For Socrates, perhaps, all wrong-doing is an expression of ignorance, a lack of knowledge of the good.

Beyond this blurry picture, it's hard to pin down Socrates' philosophical views. With Plato, though, it's a different story. He had a lot to say.

Plato's worlds

While Socrates' concerns were probably almost exclusively ethical, Plato branched out. His dialogues say a great deal about metaphysics, epistemology, politics, the philosophy of mind, religion, language, aesthetics and, of course, ethics. From where we are in time, it looks like Plato raised most of the central questions that set the philosophical agenda in the West. Aside from a blip in the Middle Ages, we've been worrying about largely what he worried about. And his answers still occupy us. It's hard to imagine what it would take for Plato to go out of style.

But we should be cautious when wondering about what Plato himself believes. The dialogues present different philosophical claims from the points of view of different people. Positions change, perhaps indicating that Plato changed his mind over time. Quite often, the dialogues raise questions that are never clearly resolved. It's tempting to think that Plato expresses his views entirely through Socrates, but even Socrates is sometimes at a loss or even heavily outgunned – a young Socrates has his philosophical outlook kicked in by an older, wiser Parmenides in a dialogue of the same name. Plato leaves a number of questions open.

Nevertheless, there is a real temptation to think that Plato is carrying on in his mentor's footsteps. By the time he's writing the middle dialogues, in particular the *Republic*, it looks very much like he's trying to fill in some of the blanks left by Socrates. We can do no more than glance at a part of this here, but according to this line of thinking, the major problem Plato grapples with is the problem of universals. His theory of forms is proposed to solve it.

In asking for definitions of courage, piety, justice and so on, Socrates quite regularly rejects responses that are nothing more than lists of examples. He knows there are just people, just decisions and just societies, but he's not after individual instances of justice, he says. He wants to know what it is that all just things have in common that makes them all just.

Philosophers see a distinction here between particulars and universals. The world is full of particular objects. In this room there's a pile of old books, and many of them are hardbacks in the same series, uniformly rectangular with covers coloured the same dismal shade of maroon. These books have at least two properties or attributes in common: they're all maroon, and they're all rectangular. In philosophical jargon, the books are particulars – unique space-time occupants, which might undergo change over time, with properties like being maroon and rectangular. But what is maroon itself? What is rectangularity?

The properties of things are a species of universal. The property maroon appears quite a lot in this room – it shows up four times in the books and again in three chairs and one scarf. Maroon is, in a sense, not at all like the many particular objects in the room. For one thing, maroon is not unique in the way a particular book is. In fact it's the repeatability of universals, in this case maroon's capacity to be in more than one book at once, that makes them 'universal' in the first place. It also makes them seriously weird. How can different objects share the same property? How can properties be in more than one place at a time? How should we understand the relationship between universals and particulars?

As we saw in the last chapter, Heraclitus and Parmenides, both in their own ways, seem overwhelmed by the very idea of change. Heraclitus' more gnomic pronouncements – 'we step and do not step into the same rivers; we are and are not' – seem to show him struggling with the idea that something can somehow still be the same thing even though its parts have changed. Parmenides is moved to even more radical claims. For him, the notion of change is incoherent, so he denies its reality. How could something be 'not now what it once was'? It just makes no sense at all.

Change is metaphysically confusing, but for Plato it takes on an epistemological dimension too. Everything around us changes – the pages of these old books were once crisp and white, but now they're brittle, dusty and yellowing. So how can we really say that we know anything about them? You might think you know that the book you are holding is rectangular, but what if you drop it or bend it or get frustrated and set it alight? How can you know anything at all about this book, when everything about it is subject to change?

Knowledge, Plato seems to have thought, is immutable. His inspiration might well have been mathematics. If two coplanar lines are perpendicular to the same line, then they are parallel to each other. That proposition is known – it's known once you look it up, anyway – and it's going to stay knowable no matter what gets dropped, bent or burnt. If you know something, really know it, your knowledge can never become false. But what could possibly secure permanent knowledge in a world of ever-changing, particular things?

Plato's rather alarming solution to this tangle of problems is to say that universals really exist in another, unchanging world. He calls universals 'forms', and if there's a maroon book and a maroon chair, there's also Maroon or the form of Maroon, which is, in itself, perfectly maroon. A maroon book, as Plato puts it, imperfectly copies Maroon itself: it 'participates in' or 'has a share in' the universal, the form Maroon. You'll see quickly that if there's an unchanging world of forms, there's a solution to the question of what makes the permanence of knowledge possible too. When I know something, my knowledge really is immutable, because the true objects of knowledge are unchanging forms.

So Plato posits two worlds: the world of becoming and the world of being. The world we're in is a realm of particular objects, the world of becoming. Here, various temporary, individual things have an ever-changing set of properties – they become what they are, change, and perhaps cease to be. The changes to their properties depend on something that stays reassuringly the same, the forms.

The forms exist in a perfect, unchanging world of being, and they underwrite the properties we see merely reflected in the maroon books of our changing world. Plato's theory of forms, in effect, synthesises the insights of both Heraclitus and Parmenides. It must have looked at the time like a stunning way to cope with two competing philosophical world views. Heraclitus is right, and everything we see around us, including the rivers, is constantly changing. Parmenides is right too, because all the changing things we see are in a way illusory, less than real, merely imperfect copies of what truly exists, which is unchanging and perfect. Plato has the best of both worlds.

Cave men

Slightly interesting, clever, but a bit crazy, you might think. Why should anyone believe in an unchanging realm of forms that no one can see? What's real is the world all around us. Plato has anticipated your response, and he has a kind of answer for you in the famous cave allegory, which Socrates relates in the *Republic*.

Socrates asks Glaucon to imagine a group of people who have spent their lives tied to a wall in a darkened cave. There's a fire behind them, and between the fire and their backs others carry aloft stone and wooden carvings of animals and people. This casts shadows over the heads of the prisoners and on to the wall in front of them. Being stuck all their lives and knowing no better, they mistake the shadows for real objects and the echoes of those behind them for the sounds of the shadows. They give each other prizes for who can recognize the shapes the best.

But suppose, Socrates says, that one of them is freed. If he turns around he'd be blinded by the fire, confused by the shapes, and maybe he'd want very much to return to his shadows. Suppose further that we drag him, no doubt protesting loudly, out of the cave and into the light. He'd be even more confused, blind, lost and desperate for his cave, but eventually maybe his eyes would start to adjust. He sees not shadows or puppets, but real objects for the very first time. Finally he looks upon the Sun and comes to see how it illuminates the real objects of the world. He wouldn't really want to return to the cave, but imagine that he does, perhaps to help free his friends.

He's at a serious loss when he's back in the dark – unable to feel his way around, unable to make out what for him are dim shadows on the wall. The prisoners mock him, think that he's crazy, and he has some trouble making himself clear. He's no good at spotting the shadows any more and looks a bit stupid from their point of view – no prizes for him. Socrates asks Glaucon, 'Wouldn't it be said of him that he went up and came back with his eyes corrupted, and that it's not even worth trying to go up? And if they were somehow able to get their hands on and kill the man who attempts to release and lead them up, wouldn't they kill him?'

We're the ones stuck in the cave, of course, and the world that we see is the world of becoming, nothing but darkness and illusion, filled with mere shadows, imperfect copies of the perfect forms in the world of being. Out there, under the Sun, is a world of real objects, which awaits our discovery through philosophical investigation. You might be right to say we can't see the forms, but we can intellectually grasp them. The Sun, many think, represents the form of the Good, which might be a kind of super form or ultimate reality. If only we could know the Good, it would shed light on all the other forms.

Even from this short account of the cave, it's clear that Plato's conception of education – dragging someone kicking and screaming out of the darkness – is a little unnerving. His portrait of the philosopher as blinded, ridiculed, hoping to help but failing to get others to see the light, can be a little affecting too, particularly when you think of Socrates' eventual fate.

The theory of forms, whether or not you buy into it, is an ingenious, bold solution to the problem of universals. It also makes knowledge possible, even for those of us stuck in this shifting world of becoming. It makes sense of Socrates' quest for definitions, because there really are forms of Justice and Courage and Piety out there to know. It also bolsters the meaning of Socrates' constant questioning, and gives a solid grounding to the Socratic method itself. Plato argues that before we are born, our souls visit the world of being and contemplate the forms. The truth is inside us if only we try hard to think things through and remember. Socrates was right to ask his questions. It's the best way to help others recall what they already know.

The third man

Perhaps the most lethal objection to Plato's theory of forms is one he raises himself in *Parmenides*, a dialogue in which a young Socrates meets the older philosopher Parmenides and his student Zeno. The objection is now called 'the third man argument', and this is probably owing to Aristotle's version of it.

Plato holds that whenever there's one property common to many things, there's a form for that property. Suppose two grains of rice are white. Then according to the theory of forms, there's a form White, and the rice 'participates' in White. But Plato also says that the form of White is itself white – indeed, it's perfectly white. We've now got three things with a property in common, so we're going to need another form – call it White2 – in virtue of which all three things share a property. Similarly, Plato is a man, so there must be a form Man, in which Plato, like all other men, has a share. The form Man is himself a man – the most perfectly manly man, too – so it looks like we need a third man to explain what is common to Plato and the form Man. You can see where this is headed. Plato's theory of forms leads on to a regress and, according to most scholars, the regress is both infinite and vicious.

Why did Plato bring it up? Did he change his mind about the theory of forms? The theory shows up again in *Timaeus*, and if that work comes after *Parmenides*, as many believe, it suggests that Plato didn't believe the objection was decisive. Then again, in the *Laws*, thought to be Plato's last work, it merits no mention at all.

The death of Socrates

At least three Athenians, probably representing many more, brought Socrates up on charges of impiety and corrupting the youth. It's thought that the 'corrupting the youth' business had something to do with his many followers, who no doubt emulated him and interrogated (and therefore annoyed) their fellow citizens. Perhaps the charge was political and someone was actually worried that Socrates' occasionally anti-democratic views might rub off on the young men of Athens. The impiety charge – they said he didn't believe in the gods of the city and introduced new deities – might have been rooted in the voice he heard in his head, his 'personal spirit'. Some think Socrates was critical of the traditional view of the gods as concerned with the lives of human beings. Others wonder whether at least some of his lines of questioning could have been interpreted as flirting with atheism.

There's also a lot of speculation about what was really behind the charges. Some say he had a connection to the Thirty Tyrants – puppets of the old enemy of Athens, the Spartans – who briefly ruled just a few years before. He was often in the company of aristocrats, who had little time for people power. When democratic feelings ran high, he must have been the focus of some anger. He was a friend, possibly a lover, of Alcibiades, who earned every Athenian's hatred by swapping sides to Sparta. Maybe everyone had just had enough of the questions. Perhaps he finally humiliated the wrong person or made too many influential enemies.

If we don't know exactly why it happened, we have Plato's word for what might actually have happened. The charges are read and Socrates responds. His defence is, of course, masterful. At one point he cross-examines an accuser, drawing out a contradiction in the claim that Socrates doesn't believe in the gods, yet believes in a spirit – but how could that be if spirits are children of the gods? He's found guilty by a close vote, and is given the chance to propose his own punishment. He suggests a tiny fine, as well as free room and board for life from the state as reward for his efforts to improve the virtue of the citizens of Athens. His 500 judges are not amused, and they vote in favour of the prosecution's proposal: death by drinking a poison potion of hemlock.

It's pretty clear that Socrates has the chance to escape, but he doesn't. He might have expressed a smidgen of remorse and avoided the death penalty in the first place. He could have promised to stop philosophizing and he might have got away with his life. Some say he'd just had enough of living, others that he convinced himself that he'd have the chance to continue his investigations with the honoured dead in the afterlife. The legend that stuck has it that he thought that 'the unexamined life is not worth living'. He drank the poison, walked around until his legs went numb, lay down and died in the company of those with whom he'd talked philosophy. He was the first true philosopher in the original sense of that word, the first 'lover of wisdom'. If he couldn't philosophize – if he couldn't pursue the wisdom he loved – he'd rather be dead.

Socrates' legend fanned out from his Athenian cell. Various Greek and Roman schools of thought took their inspiration from different aspects of the Socratic legend – as we'll see, the Stoics, Sceptics and Cynics were the first and most influential. Socrates was certainly the largest influence on Plato. Together, they shaped the thoughts of Plato's student Aristotle. It's hard to think of a philosopher since who hasn't been affected in some way by Plato, Aristotle or both. As the philosopher Alfred North Whitehead famously said, 'The safest general characterization of the European philosophical tradition is that it consists of a series of footnotes to Plato.' That's almost not an exaggeration. You can trace the beginning of just about every serious philosophical dispute or position back, somehow, to questions first raised by Socrates in Plato's dialogues.

If Plato provides us with the subject matter of philosophy, Socrates is the exemplar of its style and practice. We still do philosophy largely as he did it, through the give and take of conversation, by asking questions and giving answers – in university seminars, conferences, tutorials, viva examinations, cafés and blogs. It's every philosophy student's secret hope to emulate Socrates at least a little: the tenacity and integrity, following every argument wherever it leads, going on no matter what, and being able to reduce anyone to a gibbering wreck with a few incisive questions. More than two millennia later, Socrates is still corrupting the youth. There's something very satisfying about that.

Purpose

In 1511 Raphael daubed the finishing touches to a master-piece on a Vatican wall. His painting *The School of Athens* depicts in the grand style of the high Renaissance about 20 ancient Greek philosophers, artists, politicians, mathematicians and other luminaries. Some figures are deep in contemplation, others hold forth to attentive little groups of acolytes, a few peer over the shoulder of some great thinker who fiercely scribbles wise words on a tablet. But the eye is drawn quickly to the two bold characters in the centre of the scene. A venerable Plato – bald head, greying beard, flowing robes – strides manfully beside a handsome, youthful Aristotle, whose short brown beard and hair make him look a little like a rugged lumberjack. What's most striking, though, is how Raphael depicts their right hands.

Plato points a graceful finger to the heavens, away from this illusory world of shadow towards an ideal realm of perfect forms. Aristotle is having none of it. With a steady hand held out flat, he indicates where our attention ought to be, down in the messy diversity of this world, where answers to our questions can be found if only we pay careful attention to the ordinary things all around us. Was Aristotle really anything like the marginally dashing figure in Raphael's painting? Our best lead comes once again from the endlessly disconcerting reports of Diogenes Laertius: 'He had a lisping voice . . . He had also very thin legs, they say, and small eyes; but he used to indulge in very conspicuous dress, and rings, and used to dress his hair carefully.' One hopes it was just a phase.

We know Aristotle was born in 384 BCE, in Stagira, a coastal city in what is now the Chalcidice peninsula in Greece. His father was a physician and friend of King Amyntas of Macedon, and his mother was from a moneyed family in Chalcis. Both were dead by the time Aristotle was about ten – it's not clear how and why, but there's nothing suspicious about it – and he was adopted by Proxenus, then the court physician to King Amyntas. Aristotle almost certainly grew up in the middle of great wealth, power and privilege.

When he was 18 he arrived at the centre of the intellectual world, Plato's school in Athens, the Academy, where he remained for 20 years, in the company of other high-flying philosophers who were also drawn to Plato. When Plato died around 347 BCE, his nephew inherited the Academy, and Aristotle left Athens. He spent some time travelling, pausing in Asia Minor, and on the island of Lesbos to study marine life. Soon after he returned to his native Stagira, Philip, the new

King of Macedon, summoned him to court as tutor to his son. As Alexander the Great, Philip's son eventually defeated the Persians and commanded a vast empire stretching down from Greece through modern Turkey and Syria into Egypt and eastwards through Iraq, Iran, Pakistan and India.

Historians have been drawn to this historical conjunction: a philosopher with a mind as powerful as Aristotle's having influence on someone as historically significant as Alexander the Great at an impressionable age. What did Aristotle teach him? Plato's conception of a philosopher-king must have been well known to Aristotle. As Plato puts it in the *Republic*, 'Until philosophers are kings, or the kings and princes of this world have the spirit and power of philosophy, and political greatness and wisdom meet in one, and those commoner natures who pursue either to the exclusion of the other are compelled to stand aside, cities will never have rest from their evils.' Did Aristotle try to turn the young heir into a philosopher-king? We actually have no idea what he might have tried to convey to Alexander, and we don't know whether any of the cities he ruled were better for it.

We also don't know exactly what happened at the end of Aristotle's life. When Alexander the Great died, the pro-Macedonian government in Athens fell, and given his courtly connections Aristotle might have been in some danger. The Athenians, who were nothing if not consistent, charged him with impiety. The legend has it that he would not let them 'sin twice against philosophy', and he fled. He died within a

THE STORY OF PHILOSOPHY

year, possibly owing to long-standing trouble with his stomach.

Legends to one side, we know that Aristotle spent a lifetime with the means to study whatever took his interest, and quite a lot took his interest. The scope of his work is staggering. As a young man in the Academy, he mastered the dialogue form and, according to Cicero, 'if Plato's prose was silver, Aristotle's was a flowing river of gold'. When he finally founded his own school in Athens, the Lyceum, he produced still more. Diogenes Laertius attributes a huge number of books to Aristotle, 'the whole consisting of four hundred and forty-five thousand two hundred and seventy lines'. According to one scholar, this is the equivalent of about 6,000 modern pages.

Among other things, he wrote about ethics, logic, politics, metaphysics, physics, mathematics, poetry, aesthetics, mind and theology, and composed several treatments of the works of his philosophical predecessors (sometimes running to several volumes). Given the enormous impact his work has had on every branch of philosophy, it's amazing to think that most of his vast output has nothing to do with what we'd recognize as philosophical enquiry. Much of what he engaged in is clearly biology. He had great descriptive power and produced books of detailed observation and careful classification. As Darwin put it, 'Linnaeus and Cuvier have been my two gods, though in very different ways, but they were mere schoolboys to old Aristotle.'

Aristotle makes great strides in a huge number of different academic disciplines, but what is even more remarkable is that he's inventing many of those disciplines along the way. He does something even more fundamental than this, too. In the course of his many writings, he regularly spells out what others have had to say on a given topic, identifies the presuppositions and aims distinctive of that particular domain, works out what counts as evidence in it, defines its relevant terms, and gets on with solving its particular problems. It's not clear that anyone before Aristotle thought to break areas of enquiry down like this and say what is distinctive of each one. So not only did he contribute to a huge number of disciplines, he seems to have invented the very idea of a discipline in the first place.

What has come down to us, though, is not a flowing river of gold. We have less than a third of his enormous output, and the eloquent work just didn't get through. Ancient commentators distinguish between his exoteric writings, polished pieces of admirable style that he wrote for public consumption, and his esoteric writings, technical notes for use within the school by himself and other philosophers.

To give you a feel for the breadth of his interests, here is a list of the topics of some of the books mentioned by Diogenes: justice, poets, the erotic, riches, the soul, prayer, nobility of birth, pleasure, colonists, sovereignty, education, the Good, Plato's dialogues, economy, friendship, suffering, sophistry, species and genera, property, virtue, 'one book on things which are spoken of in various ways', anger, ethics, seventeen books about 'divisions and divisible things', motion, four books on 'contentious propositions', syllogisms, method, thirteen books of definitions, passions, mathematics, the voluntary, honour, just actions, the arts, rhetoric, poetry, style, advice, nature, many books about the doctrines of a large number of philosophers and philosophical schools, nine books on animals, eight books on anatomy, anatomical questions, compound animals, mythological animals, impotence, plants, physiognomy, medicine, units, signs of storms, astronomy, optics, motion, music, memory, the work of Homer, the first elements, mechanics, stone, fourteen books of 'things explained according to their genus', rights, victors at the Olympic and other games, tragedies, plays, laws, interpretation, examinations of various constitutions, proverbs, books about different sorts of political organization, collections of letters and several books of poems.

Most of this is now lost, and no one is entirely sure how the books that we've got survived. There's a story that Aristotle's writings were inherited by his successor at the Lyceum, Theophrastus. Aristotle's influence dissipates for a short time after his death, and some explain this by maintaining that his work somehow simply vanished. They say that the work passed from Theophrastus when he died to a nephew, who didn't know what to do with it, so he hid it all in a cave, where it remained undisturbed for 200 years. The works were supposedly rediscovered and passed to Andronicus, then the 11th head of Aristotle's school, around 60 BCE. The story goes that he pieced it all back together and made it available in a collection for the first time. The last bit of the story, minus the cave, might well be true. Many scholars believe that the Aristotelian corpus as we have it – its division into various books, its order – is owed to Andronicus' efforts. We still read what is essentially his edition of Aristotle's work.

The surviving corpus consists mostly of technical works in progress. Some of it is polished, but the majority is something like modern lecture notes and summaries, definitions, lists of problems, and worked and reworked drafts that don't necessarily hang together. Reading Aristotle can be a slog – you don't get the shimmering prose of Plato. But there's something much more intimate about Aristotle's writing. You can sometimes think you've caught an honest glimpse of his astonishing intellect, unadorned by distracting literary devices.

Even less than a glimpse is all we'll manage here, but we'll start with his work on logic, consider his understanding of explanation, move on to his accounts of matter, form and cause, and conclude by touching briefly on his understanding of the good life.

The blueprint for rationality

As the empiricist philosopher John Locke puts it, 'God has not been so sparing to men to make them barely two-legged creatures, and left it to Aristotle to make them rational.' Locke almost isn't going too far here. Aristotle invented logic, or at least he invented its philosophical study. Careful argumentation has been the focus of philosophy ever since, and it's been done almost entirely on Aristotle's terms.

Aristotle's logic depends on the notion of a syllogism or deduction. As he puts it, a syllogism is 'speech in which, certain things having been supposed, something different from those supposed results of necessity because of their being so'. The 'things having been supposed' are the premises of an argument. The conclusion is the different proposition that 'results of necessity'. Premises are built up out of subjects and predicates – this thing (subject) has that property (predicate), all these things (subject) do not have this property (predicate), and so on. Premises can either affirm or deny that the subject has a predicate. When it all lines up, and the conclusion follows, you've got a syllogism.

Perhaps the most famous example of an argument will make all this much more clear:

Socrates is a man.
All men are mortal.
Therefore, Socrates is mortal.

The expression 'Socrates is a man' is a premise that affirms of the particular subject Socrates that he has the predicate or property of being a man. The expression 'All men are mortal' affirms of the general term 'man' that all such things have the predicate of being mortal. The conclusion follows of necessity, that is to say, if the premises are true, the conclusion has to be true too. They are, and it is: therefore, Socrates is mortal.

Aristotle calls a syllogism like this one 'perfect', because no further premises need to be added to make the conclusion follow. To give you a feel for the basic forms of syllogism identified by Aristotle, consider these perfect ones:

All As are B. All Bs are C. All As are C.

All As are B. No Bs are C. No A is C.

Some As are B. All Bs are C. Some As are C.

Some As are B. No Bs are C. Not all As are C.

By making explicit the formal relationships of terms in an argument, Aristotle produced a logical system of extraordinary power. It formed the basis of his conception of scientific enquiry too. For Aristotle, a 'demonstration' is an explanatory syllogism. It's an argument that shows why the conclusion is true. This notion of demonstration, and his accompanying analysis of logical inference, dominated philosophical accounts of logic until the work of Gottlob Frege a little more than 100 years ago. Many, including Kant, thought there was simply no more to say. Aristotle had said it all.

It is Aristotle's notion of demonstration that makes scientific enquiry largely what it is too. Scientists study the world the way they do, seek explanations of a certain sort, largely because of his account of what it means to demonstrate a truth. For perhaps 2,000 years, Aristotle has provided humanity with its blueprint for rationality in not just philosophy, but science as well.

The four causes

The story goes that philosophers call the abstract study of being 'metaphysics' because of an editorial decision and a title that accidentally stuck. The book in which Aristotle takes up metaphysical matters comes after his book on natural things, '*ta phusika*' or 'physics'. '*Meta*' is Latin for 'after' or 'adjacent', and the thought is that originally 'metaphysics' just meant 'the book that comes after the book on natural things'. Aristotle's *Metaphysics*, anyway, is rough going. Avicenna – probably the greatest mind of the Islamic Golden Age – said he read it 40 times and still didn't understand it.

But it begins simply enough, with the famous line, 'All men by nature desire to know.' The ultimate sort of knowing, Aristotle says, is wisdom, an understanding of 'the why of things'. He breaks this kind of knowing down into the 'four causes' or four sorts of explanation, four fundamental answers one might give to questions asked about a thing. The four causes are the material cause, the formal cause, the efficient cause and the final cause. These are not Aristotle's terms, but they're useful for keeping things straight.

The material cause is 'that from which' a thing comes into being. Bronze is the material cause of a bronze statue, because the statue comes from a lump of bronze. If we ask what the statue is, we might be satisfied to learn what it's made of, namely bronze. The material cause preoccupied the Presocratics, focused as many were on identifying the fundamental stuff that makes up everything. But for Aristotle, identifying the material cause of a thing conveys only a partial understanding of it. There's more to the statue than just the bronze.

The second cause, the formal cause, is considerably more complicated than just working out what material makes up a thing. Aristotle calls it 'the form or pattern' of a thing, which suggests that the shape of the statue is its formal cause. But he also says the formal cause is 'the definition of the essence' of a thing, which makes it sound like more than just the shape. He explains this with the following spectacularly unhelpful example: 'the ratio 2:1 and number in general are causes of the octave'. What could he possibly mean?

'Form' here refers not merely to shape and pattern, but also to *how matter is arranged*. This suggests a principle behind the organization. For Aristotle, sometimes a thing is arranged one way rather than another because of what the thing is. There's a connection here, in other words, between how the thing is shaped and the definition or essence of that thing – it's shaped that way because of what it is. You might ask, 'Why is this thing a table?' and I could answer, 'It's a table because it has a flat top supported by four legs. That's how it was built, why the parts were arranged like that, because that's what kind of thing a table is.' That sort of answer specifies the table's shape, but it also says something about the 'definition of its essence'. If you remind yourself that an octave is a musical chord consisting of two notes, where one is twice as high in pitch as the other, the 'form or pattern' of an octave is the ratio 2:1. An octave is what it is because of the organizing principle behind the arrangement of those notes.

The third cause, the efficient cause, is 'that from which the change or the resting from change first begins'. The word 'efficient' is from the Latin '*facere*', meaning to make or to do, and the efficient cause is what creates, makes or originates something. Aristotle tells us that an adviser is the efficient cause of an action that's eventually undertaken, the father is the efficient cause of a child, and in general the maker is the efficient cause of the thing made. Why is that statue here? The sculptor, its efficient cause, created it.

The last cause Aristotle identifies is the most intriguing, influential and certainly infamous of the four: the final cause, 'the end, i.e. that for the sake of which a thing is'. Aristotle believes that everything in nature has a *telos*, a purpose, an aim or direction – uncovering the purposes behind and within absolutely everything is fundamental to the way he interprets and understands the world. He gives us the example of health as the final cause, the end, goal or purpose, of a fortifying walk. The idea is that something is what it is partly because of its purpose, because of the goal at which it aims.

The first two sorts of cause have to do with matter and form, two notions that are fundamental to Aristotle's metaphysics. It's worth considering them in a bit more detail. It will help us when we come to his conception of human happiness, and it will also give us a taste of his solutions to some of the problems that confused his predecessors.

Matter, form and change

For Aristotle, all the objects around us are combinations of matter and form, and it's this conception of objects that gets him around the difficulties that troubled Heraclitus and Parmenides, and led Plato to posit the theory of forms. Plato couldn't find a way to think about change that made knowledge of this changing world possible. He also had trouble with universals and the notion that different things could somehow share the same property – lots of books being the same shade of maroon, for example. As we saw in the last chapter, he posited the world of being, and filled it with unchanging forms that could serve as objects of knowledge. The things in our world that share a property are, you'll recall for Plato, participating in the same form.

For Aristotle, however, the forms are not off in another realm of being – in fact for him form can only exist with matter making it up. (He suggests that form without matter is God, but otherwise, form is in matter.) The form of the table is right there, in the structure of the table you can see with your eyes. It's this insistence on the importance of the reality all around us that Raphael is getting at in his painting, and it's behind almost every aspect of Aristotle's philosophy.

Aristotle formulates a number of objections to Plato's notion of forms – including the third-man argument – but what really seems to bother him is that Plato's forms are not explanatory. They're no help at all in trying to understand universals, change, permanence, knowledge or any of the philosophical tangles that interested philosophers almost from the start. Saying that all tables are tables because they 'participate in the form Table' doesn't help us understand anything, because the relationship of participation itself is obscure. And exactly how does the thought that the form of Table is permanent help us understand change, or work out what happens when a table falls apart or is put together?

Putting forms in the world, first of all, answers Plato's question about the possibility of knowledge. How can we have knowledge of tables in this ever-changing world? Aristotle has already told us: examine a large number of them and find the four causes. Contemplation alone won't do the job. You've got to roll up your sleeves, pick things apart and observe.

If you think of objects as combinations of matter and form, you are also on your way to thinking about change without needing Plato's extra world of being. When an object undergoes change, sometimes what's changing is its form. If I build a brick wall, the bricks are the matter and the wall shape is the form. If the wall collapses, we can understand this instance of change as a change in form. The matter persists through change.

There's also a sense in which things change not by falling apart, but by becoming something else. To understand this, Aristotle relies on a distinction between actuality and potentiality, which complements his distinction between matter and form. The potential to be a wall is in the matter, in the bricks, not the form. I couldn't have built a wall out of cream, but bricks have the right potential for becoming a wall. The actuality of the wall, though, depends on the form being realized, not the matter. In at least one sense of potentiality, as Aristotle uses the term, a thing with potential has the capacity or ability to be in another, more completed state. The idea that the wall is 'more complete' is interesting. Potentialities are expressions of 'natures' – things are what they are not only because of what they are, for Aristotle, but also because of what they nearly insist on becoming.

He tells us that potentiality is indefinable, but he tries to spell it out with these examples: 'Someone waking is to someone sleeping, as someone seeing is to a sighted person with his eyes closed, as that which has been shaped out of some matter is to the matter from which it has been shaped.' A sleeping person has the potential to wake. A person with her eyes closed has the potential to see. And some matter has the potential to be shaped into something like a wall. The potential is a kind of resting actuality, which emerges when we wake up, open our eyes or build a wall.

Notice, in all this, that it's not just bricks and other human artefacts that have their potential spelled out in terms of purpose. Aristotle thinks that natural objects have purposes too. Things have natures that aim at a goal. It's in the nature of rocks to seek their natural place on the ground (so they fall when you drop them), and it's in the nature of fire to seek its natural place in the heavens (so it rises). It's in the nature of an acorn to become an oak tree. For Aristotle, purpose is absolutely everywhere. Given that Aristotle sees human beings right alongside other living things in the natural world, it's unsurprising that he understands the good life for human beings in terms of purpose too. His account of morality is remarkable and powerful – it's still part of the way philosophers think about moral goodness and human happiness. And, like everything else in Aristotle's thinking, it's shot through with purpose.

Living well and being good

We have space only to speed past Aristotle's understanding of morality and living well, but even a short consideration of his work here is enough to convey a feel for its richness. Aristotle begins his account of ethics by saying, 'Every art and every investigation, and similarly every action and pursuit, is considered to aim at some good. Hence the Good has rightly been defined as "that at which all things aim".' If we're not to go around in circles, there has to be one overarching, supremely valuable good, and Aristotle argues that the supreme good for us is happiness. It's desired for itself, not as a means to some other higher good. But what is happiness? Aristotle's answer depends on two difficult concepts: virtue and the soul. Both are tied to purpose.

He argues that a craftsperson is good if she does what's distinctive of her craft well. In Aristotle's terminology, this is a matter of *arête*, which is translated variously as 'virtue' or 'excellence'. Being an excellent sculptor is exercising the virtues distinctive of the sculptor – precision, an eye for form and balance, and so on. Or to use the terminology we've already got on the table, a virtuous or excellent sculptor fully actualizes her potential as a sculptor. Examples can be multiplied: a virtuous horse gallops well, a virtuous knife cuts well, in short, a virtuous or excellent anything does what's distinctive of that thing well.

Why not think that there's something distinctive about human beings in this sense too? Living a human life well would therefore consist in doing what's distinctively human well. So what is distinctive about being human?

Aristotle's answer depends on a slightly treacherous conception of soul. One thing is clear: he is not talking about anything religious at all. For him, soul is an active principle characteristic of living things. It's tied to his understanding of form, and you can think of it in different, interconnected ways. Maybe one of these formulations will help: soul is the way a living structure is organized, it's the form of living matter, living matter's actuality, or the 'that in virtue of which' a living thing is the thing that it is.

The main thing to bear in mind is that all living things have a soul in Aristotle's sense, because all are organized so as to be alive. When the relevant organization goes, when the form is lost, the living thing dies. Plants have a vegetative soul and grow and reproduce as they do. Animals have this plus a locomotive soul that enables them to move, as well as a sensitive soul that enables them to perceive the world. Human beings have all this, as well as a rational soul. What is distinctive about us is our capacity to think as we do.

So Aristotle argues that 'the good for man is an activity of the soul in accord with virtue'. Happiness , the ultimate good, consists in doing what's distinctively human well. What's distinctively human is understood in terms of the rational part of the human soul. To be happy, then, we have to exercise rational excellence – we have to be the best thinkers we can be.

From here, Aristotle can go in two directions, because for him there are two sorts of rational activity. Reason might guide one's actions, or one might use reason to reflect, to engage in rational contemplation. It's the first of these sorts of rational excellences that receives the most attention, because Aristotle unpacks it, partly, in terms of the famous doctrine of the golden mean.

He claims that virtuous action, doing the morally right thing, is the mean between two extremes. Vices of excess and deficiency lie on either side of the middle path, which is itself the right course of action. So, for example, one might be properly courageous and avoid the two extremes of cowardice on the one hand and foolhardy bravado on the other. It's easy to misinterpret Aristotle here. He's not arguing for absolute moderation in all things, because he says that the mean is different for different people in different contexts. Sometimes the right amount of wine to consume is enough to get you drunk.

Morally right conduct, for Aristotle, is an expression of a virtuous character, and doing the right thing depends on the context you're in. Being virtuous is a matter of doing the right thing at the right time, with the right feelings, in the right way and for the right reason. There's no set of moral rules to follow. In this messy world, the morally right action changes with context, depends on all sorts of factors, so you can't say what is right without knowing the facts of the case. Even in his account of morality, Aristotle embraces the diversity in the world that Plato rejects. The result is a profound conception of right and wrong, even if, as some worry, there's not much practical advice in it.

Aristotle's thoughts about purpose stuck in the minds of just about everyone who came after him. His views shaped not only philosophy, but what eventually became our scientific attempts to understand the natural world itself. It took a genius like Newton to shake us free of Aristotle's thought that objects move towards their natural place. It took a mind like Darwin's to think us past the idea that animals and their parts fulfil inner purposes. For hundreds of years, throughout the Middle Ages, Aristotle was referred to as 'The Philosopher'. There simply was no one else who mattered as much.

2
Hellenes & Romans

Cynics, Stoics and Sceptics

Peering back through the centuries, it can seem as though a handful of Presocratics, Socrates, Plato and Aristotle were the only serious philosophers alive and at large in ancient Greece. But this is only a quirk of our distant temporal perspective, a trick of the historical light.

Those now cursed with the epithet 'minor Socratics' were probably much more than the name suggests. A few might have known Socrates well and must have been moved when he died. Perhaps they really did see themselves as minor Socratics in some sense, as carrying on the great man's mission, but others went off in different intellectual directions, building on insights of their own. Almost all were well known in their day, and for generations their work was studied carefully. We barely remember their names, and in most cases just fragments and whispers survive, but they attracted students, opened schools, wrote hundreds of books, and got on with pursuing wisdom as they understood it.

It might have gone on in that way for a while, but something dramatic happened to the Western world, and to philosophy, following the death of Alexander the Great in 323 BCE. As his vast empire collapsed into violent factions competing for land and wealth, new centres of trade and learning coalesced in Africa, Asia Minor and the Middle East.

Rome – once an independent city the size of Athens – gobbled up territory until, from the point of view of those within it, the whole world was the Roman Empire. While the Romans clearly had a handle on soldiering, admin and occupation, they were the muddy-booted children of uncouth farmers compared to the Greeks. As the Romans prospered and aspired to greater sophistication, they looked to Greek culture.

The Romans marched across Europe, North Africa and the Middle East, embedding outposts of Greek thinking in alien worlds. New philosophical outlooks appeared, no doubt owing in part to the novel mix of ideas stirred up by the times. Eastern superstitions mingled with Greek logic. Entirely new lines of thought opened up.

Philosophical ideas that got a start in and around Athens were, within a few hundred years, debated and discussed all over the Roman world. Beggars living on city streets, even former slaves, found consolation in Greek conceptions of fate and virtue. Roman emperors and senators made Greek philosophy their own. Greek thoughts were in the heads of people at every level of Roman society. And, of course, the Romans brought their own notions and agendas to the table. The result wasn't entirely Greek or Roman, but a new intermingling of ideas.

From the death of Alexander to the battle of Actium and the start of the Roman Empire in 31 BCE, Hellenistic philosophy takes centre stage. These points in time are just conventions – one sort of philosophy didn't stop and another start on a particular afternoon – and some of the philosophers we'll consider in this chapter fall outside those dates. But the philosophy of this era really is a departure from what came before it. The fear and uncertainty that resulted from the collapse of Alexander's world and the turmoil accompanying the Roman consolidation of power had everything to do with it. The world was no longer a pleasant backdrop for reflection on universals, particulars and the good life. As Bertrand Russell puts it in *A History of Western Philosophy*, 'Aristotle is the last Greek philosopher who faces the world cheerfully; after him, all have, in one form or another, a philosophy of retreat.' If philosophy was born in curiosity and wonder, it began its formative years as a means of escape from uncertainty and ill fortune. It became a path to peace of mind in an unsettled world.

The times changed very quickly at first. As A. A. Long and D. N. Sedley write in their treatment of the early days of Hellenistic philosophy, 'If Aristotle could have returned to

Athens in 272 BC, on the fiftieth anniversary of his death, he would hardly have recognized it as the intellectual milieu in which he had taught and researched for much of his life.'

The Academy that Plato founded and Aristotle's Lyceum were still around, of course, but both schools were transformed. The Academy was run by Arcesilaus, who ushered in its so-called 'Middle Age' by turning from Plato's intellectualism to a kind of ultra-Socratic Scepticism. Cicero tells us that Arcesilaus professed to 'know nothing, not even his own ignorance'. The slightly insipid Strato of Lampsacus was the uninspiring head of the Lyceum at the time, presiding over its slow decline by replacing philosophical enquiry with the study of the natural world. For a time Aristotle's philosophy passed entirely into obscurity. No one knows why.

What is remarkable is not just that those two famous schools had changed so much in so little time, but that the best-known philosophers in Athens were not even within them. The philosophical descendants of Plato and Aristotle had been brushed aside. Athens was under the sway of entirely new thinkers.

What were they talking about, and who were they? Hellenistic philosophy is dominated by the Stoics and the Epicureans. We'll take up the Epicureans and their main influence, the Atomists, in the next chapter, but we turn now to the Stoics. To understand them, however, we'll have to consider two other schools of philosophy. The best place to begin is with

Diogenes the Cynic. If you're well mannered and easily offended, you might want to look away now.

The dog philosophers

Ancient reporters have passed on an unusually large number of stories about Diogenes of Sinope. He was probably hard to forget. We know he wrote books, but only the anecdotes survive. It is in a way fitting that we have the stories and not the writing. His life might have been a better expression of his philosophy.

We don't know for certain but it seems Diogenes had a penchant for wordplay and seemed ready to wade into, and win, any verbal dispute. He wasn't above using his fists either. He rejected all aspects of tradition, the dictates of culture, and the rules of civilized life as artificial, unnatural encumbrances that only get in the way of freedom and genuine happiness. Virtue, for him, was to be found in living according to one's natural endowments, rather than seeking happiness in money, fame, the accumulation of objects or devotion to the dictates of society.

Diogenes rejected social conventions wholesale. He begged for food or foraged for what he could in the marketplace, slept in an old wine barrel, and wore little more than simple cloth. He dealt with his 'bodily requirements' as and when he had the need, and there's talk of him urinating publicly (occasionally on people who perhaps did not grasp the implications of his views with sufficient clarity), defecating in a theatre, advocating free love, eating whatever and whenever he chose (including a raw ox foot, which might have killed him) and engaging in open, shameless masturbation.

He shouted at people in the streets, making fun of their petty conformity, and they shouted back, calling him a dog for living as he did. 'Cynic' comes from the Greek word '*kynikos*', meaning 'canine' or 'dog-like'. The word as it is in English retains something of its ancient meaning – seeing the worst in people, particularly focusing on their selfish attachments. Diogenes the Dog, as he was called, was the exemplar of the Cynic sage. He was wretched and poor by the measures of society, but by his own lights happy, free and rich in virtue.

As you might expect, he didn't get on very well with Plato, who allegedly called him 'Socrates gone mad'. There's some truth in this. If he wasn't a gadfly, Diogenes certainly hounded his fellow citizens in a Socratic manner, all in the name of virtue. He made sport of what he took to be their vain and ridiculous attachment to things that don't really matter, and there are echoes of Socratic irony in his snarl. He also shared Socrates' disdain for money and social standing, as well as his insistence on simplicity, being true to one's principles, and self-mastery. But even Socrates slept in a bed.

It is said that Plato held a banquet for some visiting friends, and somehow Diogenes crashed the party, stomping around and ruining Plato's fine carpets. 'Thus I trample on the empty pride of Plato' was his way of pointing out that happiness cannot lie in trying to inflate one's standing with finery. He allegedly threw away one of his own few possessions, a cup, after seeing a boy drink from his cupped hands. 'That child has beaten me in simplicity,' he said. He jettisoned his spoon too, after noticing another boy scooping up lentils with a crust of bread.

The carpet incident might have been on Plato's mind in another story that has come down to us, by way of Diogenes Laertius. Diogenes the Dog appears to gatecrash one of Plato's lectures:

> When Plato was discoursing about his 'ideas', and using the nouns 'tableness' and 'cupness'; 'I, O Plato!' interrupted Diogenes, 'see a table and a cup, but I see no tableness or cupness.' Plato made answer, 'That is natural enough, for you have eyes, by which a cup and a table are contemplated; but you have not intellect, by which tableness and cupness are seen.'

He also took issue with Plato's insistence on definitions, objecting in particular to what he probably took to be Plato's shallow definition of man as a 'featherless biped'. Was there not more to a human being than this? Diogenes made the point by appearing with a plucked chicken, saying, 'This is Plato's man.' We don't have Plato's response, but you can easily picture him slapping himself in the forehead.

A number of notable Cynics followed Diogenes, including a husband-and-wife team, the hunchbacked Crates of Thebes and Hipparchia of Maronea. Crates, it is said, gave away a fortune to follow Diogenes, and lived on entirely equal terms with Hipparchia, who has a claim to be the first female philosopher. Crates started a tradition of Cynic literature – he left behind work with inspired titles such as *Knapsack* and *Praise of the Lentil* – largely parodies that aimed at unseating received opinion.

There's another tradition the Cynics might have had a hand in. Some have argued that there are just too many similarities between the teachings of Jesus and Cynic philosophy for it to be merely a coincidence. Was Jesus influenced by a Cynic? The Cynics were certainly operating at the right time and possibly the right place. Was he, some historians argue, actually a typical Cynic figure of the age?

Jesus certainly could have come into contact with Cynics. Gadara, just 30 kilometres from Nazareth, a day's walk from the Sea of Galilee, was home to a number of famous Cynics, including the satirical author Menippus. There is even some tantalizing biblical evidence for the possibility that Jesus encountered a Cynic. It was in 'the country of the Gadarenes' that he came across a lunatic, living in rags among the tombs, possessed by the demon Legion. Diogenes the Dog, of course, was called a madman too. Could this episode point to an encounter between Jesus and a Cynic?

Certain expressions and teachings of Jesus are even more suggestive. 'Blessed are the poor, for theirs is the Kingdom of God' and similar exhortations praising poverty and simplicity certainly are in line with Cynic teaching. Consider this famous passage from the Gospel of Matthew:

> And behold, one came up to him, saying, 'Teacher, what good deed must I do, to have eternal life?' And he said to him, 'Why do you ask me about what is good? One there is who is good. If you would enter life, keep the commandments.' He said to him, 'Which?' And Jesus said, 'You shall not kill, You shall not commit adultery, You shall not steal, You shall not bear false witness, Honour your father and mother, and, You shall love your neighbour as yourself.' The young man said to him, 'All these I have observed; what do I still lack?' Jesus said to him, 'If you would be perfect, go, sell what you possess and give to the poor, and you will have treasure in heaven; and come, follow me.' When the young man heard this he went away sorrowful; for he had great possessions.

When you read those lines, it is extremely hard not to think of Crates of Thebes giving away his fortune so that he could follow Diogenes.

But the Cynics went quiet, and seem to have all but vanished in the shadow of the Stoics and the Epicureans, until the first century, when they reappeared, of all things, as devastating political critics. They and other philosophical schools were deemed so threatening that philosophers were banished from the city of Rome more than once. Though many Cynics gave sermons on the simple life and handed out pamphlets decrying convention, the paradigmatic Cynic had nothing to do with politics or organized philosophical instruction. Groups of begging Cynics, or lone sages haranguing a crowd with talk of virtue, were common enough in parts of Rome.

Before they went quiet, though, the Cynics made one last contribution to philosophy. It's said that Zeno of Citium travelled in 313 BCE to Athens, where, inspired by the legend of Socrates, he decided to devote his life to philosophy. He asked around, searching for the sage of the day, the person most like Socrates, and was pointed to the Cynic Crates of Thebes, who happened to be passing by. Zeno became his disciple. He also studied at Plato's Academy for a time, but it was his contact with Cynicism that had the most profound effect on him. Eventually he gathered disciples of his own around him and taught at a well-known landmark along the Agora, a kind of covered space decorated with murals, half open to the air through a row of columns. It was called the Painted Porch, in Greek the '*stoa poikile*'. He and his followers, the people of the porch or *stoa* people, turned the Socratic madness of Diogenes the Dog into a world view synonymous with calm, imperturbability and steadfast indifference. It was the start of Stoicism, one of the most dominant and powerful schools of philosophy for perhaps the next 500 years.

The Stoics' indifference

None of the work of the early Stoics survives, but three names are attached to the very beginning of Stoicism. Zeno, its founder, divided the Stoic curriculum into the study of logic, physics and ethics. His successor Cleanthes was an impoverished ex-boxer who couldn't afford paper and scribbled the sayings of Zeno on what he took to be the next best thing: oyster shells and ox bones. It is said by some that he was a bit dim.

But Cleanthes' successor, Chrysippus, clearly had the philosophical goods and, along with Zeno, seems to have been the brains behind the rise of Stoicism. He was a master of argumentation and wrote several hundred books, including some highly technical analyses of logical inference. He also had an irritatingly high opinion of himself, as well as a mildly endearing flair for vulgarity – Diogenes Laertius tells us that one of his histories devotes 'six hundred lines to what no one could repeat without polluting his mouth'. But by most accounts he was instrumental in the rise of Stoicism. As an ancient line has it:

For if Chrysippus had not lived and taught,
The Stoic school would surely have been nought.

He was remarkably unkind to his master Cleanthes, saying at one point that he just wanted to learn the school's dogma from him – he'd work out the proofs for himself. It's likely that Chrysippus refined Zeno's set-up into what is almost certainly the first genuinely systematic school of philosophy. The Stoics claimed that their philosophical system was like an orchard – logic was the protective wall around it, physics was the soil and the trees, and ethics was the fruit.

Logic, for the Stoics, encompassed not just the rules governing right inferences but also what we would now call epistemology or theory of knowledge, as well as the philosophy of language. They founded their views on a certain sort of 'grasping of the impressions of the mind', a move that invited the attack of the Sceptics. Stoic logic was viewed by later thinkers as a competitor to Aristotle's work. Much of it was stimulated by Sceptical critiques – hence the thought that logic is like a protective wall.

Stoic physics has it that the world is in some sense a living, rational, divine creature. In a nod to Heraclitus, they held that the world began in a great cosmic conflagration, and so it shall return in an endless repeating cycle of fiery beginnings and endings. Throughout each identical phase, every event is predetermined, governed by fate and entirely for the good. The world itself is made up of material bodies, permeated by a divine rationality that underlies and directs all change according to a benevolent plan.

It was the Stoics' conception of ethical conduct, however, that is most responsible for the movement's spread and influence. If Stoic logic was beyond you, you could still manage a grip on its ethical outlook, and many did. Stoic ethics was a departure from the dark musings of the Presocratics and the complexity of the Academy and the Lyceum. For the first time, philosophers produced a philosophical framework that spoke directly to everyday people. Following in the footsteps of Diogenes the Cynic and Socrates, the Stoics argue that what matters most is virtue, and virtue consists entirely in living in accord with the whole of the divinely ordered universe. But how could anyone do otherwise, how could anyone fail to live in accord with nature, if everything is predestined and governed by fate?

The divine plan will work itself out no matter what, and there's nothing anyone can do about that, but what one can do is react to events in the right way, which is to say harmoniously, virtuously, in tune with the flow of things. A Stoic image that makes the point is of a dog tied to a wagon. When the wagon moves, the dog can tranquilly walk along beside it or be dragged, yelping and choking. Either way, it is going to follow the wagon. So too with a human life. We can be dragged kicking and screaming and protesting or – and you can spot Diogenes' DNA in this – we can recognize what really matters, and live according to nature.

But thanks to the Stoic notion of 'preferred indifferents', we don't have to seek virtue with Diogenes in the bottom of a barrel. Writing in the fifth century, the chronicler Joannes Stobaeus reports:

> Zeno says that . . . of those things which exist some are good, some bad, some indifferent. Good are . . . wisdom, moderation, justice, courage, and all that is virtue . . . Bad are . . . folly, intemperance, injustice, cowardice, and all that is vice . . . Indifferent are . . . life and death, reputation and ill-repute, pleasure and exertion, wealth and poverty, health and sickness, and things like these.

There are two notions at work in this sort of Stoic claim. First, the thought is that conventional goods – health, wealth, social standing, fame and the other large things most people pursue – could, depending on the circumstances, be to one's detriment or benefit. If you inherit a lot of money and then squander it in a brief yet memorable blast of debauched decadence, the money didn't really do you any good. It might even have made things worse. Strictly speaking, money and the rest aren't actually good in themselves. Only virtue is good no matter what.

Second, the acquisition of conventional goods is 'not up to us'. As the Stoic Epictetus puts it, 'Up to us are opinion, impulse, desire, aversion . . . Not up to us are body, property, reputation, office.' Whether or not you end up healthy, wealthy and famous depends on the luck of the draw. You can't do anything about it, and anyway, given the goodness of the divine plan, it's all for the best. So such things are classed as merely 'indifferent' by the Stoics. There is nothing gained in worrying about them, therefore it is irrational to do so. A Stoic might, however, regard the conventional goods as preferable – they are, in Stoic terminology, 'preferred indifferents' – but whether and when we acquire them is 'not up to us'. Health, reputation, even living and dying are therefore matters of indifference. Maybe ending up in a fine house is preferable to sleeping in a barrel, but the Stoic is indifferent either way. It's this indifference to one's fortunes that is still reflected in English when we say, if someone meets disaster with equanimity, that he or she is 'being philosophical about it'.

What matters, however, is virtue, and that is entirely up to us, because it is in us – it's our attitude to the world around us. There's a straight line from this thought through the Cynics and back to the Socratic idea that virtue is knowledge, and what matters most is the inner you, your soul. In the hands of the Stoics, these views became something more than philosophical doctrine: Stoicism was a way to find peace in a difficult world, largely by controlling one's impulses. As the Stoic emperor Marcus Aurelius puts it in his *Meditations*, 'A cucumber is bitter. Throw it away. There are briars in the road. Turn aside from them. This is enough. Do not add, "And why were such things made in the world?"'

But all of this should not suggest that the philosophy of this age is characterized entirely by the stilted reflection of imperturbable Stoics, with the occasional howl of a Cynic momentarily fracturing their composure. Other schools of thought jostled alongside them. A large part of Hellenistic philosophy can be understood as a protracted disagreement between the Stoics and Epicureans on the one hand, and the Sceptics on the other. At issue was the very possibility of securing knowledge.

The suspension of judgement

Depending on how you count them, two or three schools of Scepticism emerged in Greece and Rome. The oldest begins with Pyrrho, who was active around 300 BCE, the second with Arcesilaus and the Sceptics of Plato's Academy, and finally a Scepticism motivated by Pyrrho, owed to Aenesidemus in the first century BCE and carried on by Sextus Empiricus into the second century.

It is said that Pyrrho travelled with Alexander's army to India, where, intriguingly, he found inspiration among 'naked wise men'. Whatever he discovered in his travels, he then suspended judgement in all matters – neither affirming nor denying any proposition, holding on to no opinion – and so found a kind of peace. His friends, it's said, were constantly yanking him out of the way of traffic, steering him away from cliffs and other hazards, and generally stewarding him out of danger as he wandered around, unmoved and unconcerned by anything at all. According to Diogenes Laertius, 'He used to clean all the furniture of the house without expressing any annoyance. And it is said that he carried his indifference so far that he even washed a pig.'

Pyrrho wrote no books of philosophy, and reports of what

he actually believed, coming to us second- and third-hand, are difficult to decipher. His student, Timon, says that Pyrrho considered three questions. First, what are things like by nature? His three-part answer admits of various translations, but some take it that he said that things are indifferent, unstable and indeterminate. How should we be disposed towards things? We should have no opinions about them. What is the result of this attitude? Pyrrho tells us that our reward is freedom from anxiety.

The Academic Sceptics didn't write much either, preferring instead the flow of verbal argumentation. Inspired by Socrates' endless scrutinizing and questioning, as well as Plato's use of the dialogue form, they cranked out arguments for and against any proposition. Reason, it was thought, leaves us with equally compelling arguments all around, so we can't profess to know anything.

The Academics' skill was satisfyingly in evidence in 155 CE, when philosophical emissaries from the Academy, the Lyceum and the Stoic school were dispatched to Rome. The Academy's representative, Carneades, lectured breathtakingly and entirely convincingly in favour of justice, to the edification of the young men in attendance. The next day he delivered an equally persuasive lecture against justice, comprehensively overturning everything he had said before. His Roman hosts, fearing for the virtue of his audience, threw him out of the city.

There were more general sceptical arguments too, Agrippa, a philosopher active near the end of the first century, aimed to show that knowledge is impossible, because no knowledge claim can ever be justified. There is, in other words, no such thing as a real justification. The argument, sometimes called Agrippa's trilemma, goes like this.

Suppose you claim to know some proposition (p). One might ask if you know p or are just assuming it. If you claim to know it, it's fair to ask how you know it, to insist on your reasons for thinking it is true, your evidence for p, in other words. Suppose you then give reasons (r). Whatever your reasons, one can ask once again if you know r or are just making assumptions. You've got to claim to know r if r counts as justification for p. According to Agrippa, you now have just three choices, and none of them are justifications. You might continue to give reasons indefinitely ($r1$, $r2$, $r3$ . . .) and never reach a justification. You might make a dogmatic assumption (r, damn it!), and just assert what you believe without justification. Or you might repeat something you already said (p, $r1$, $r2$, $r3$, $r1$, whoops!), and reason in a circle, but circular reasoning is not justification.

Agrippa argues that none of these moves delivers a justification for p and, therefore, all belief is assumption, not knowledge.

Some philosophers quibble with the set-up and claim that the burden of proof isn't always on the person who claims to know. Others maintain that there are more kinds of justification not mentioned by Agrippa. Some attempt to wriggle free while playing by Agrippa's rules, by trying to find a way to say that one of his choices really does count as giving a justification. What's wrong with giving an indefinite supply of reasons? What's wrong with a foundational assumption? What's wrong with circularity if it's not vicious? It's not hard to think of Agrippa's replies. What is hard to think about, though, is the possibility that we don't exactly know what we're talking about when we talk about knowledge. Agrippa, almost by accident, seems to point to that possibility.

The Sceptics of the Academy were most exercised by the positive assertions of their adversaries, the Stoics and the Epicureans. The Stoics in particular argued for their conclusions based on foundations rooted in certain sorts of allegedly unmistakable sense perceptions. The Sceptics arrayed what they took to be equally compelling arguments against the possibility of any such justifications. The school descended, for a time, to concerning itself with little more than formulating counterarguments and objections to the positive claims of others.

It was too much for Aenesidemus, who departed the Academy to return to what he took to be the more profound teachings of Pyrrho, and so began a third wave of Scepticism. Aenesidemus formulated the Ten Modes, forms of argument that put reason and sensory reports into different sorts of conflict. The hope was that the modes might be levelled against any dogmatic assertion. Considering one will give you a feel for the rest:

> The third mode is that which has for its object the differ-
> ence of the organs of sense. Accordingly, an apple
> presents itself to the sight as yellow, to the taste as sweet,
> to the smell as fragrant; and the same form is seen, in
> very different lights, according to the differences of
> mirrors. It follows, therefore, that what is seen is just as
> likely to be something else as the reality.

The argument aims to undercut any claim to know about the
properties of an object based on sensory information. How
can we know what an apple really is, when our senses report
such different things compared to one another? Whatever the
reality is, it's as likely to be something else as what our senses
tell us.

Aenesidemus returned Scepticism to its roots. Pyrrho's
escape from anxiety in the suspension of judgement was now
the ultimate point of philosophical argumentation. In this
way, Pyrrhonian Scepticism is much more in keeping with
the spirit of the Hellenistic age than the Scepticism of the
Academics, more in tune with the aims of the Cynics and the
Stoics. On that harmonious note, we turn to the Epicureans,
the other large school of this time, who thought their way
through to tranquillity in an entirely different way. Philosophy, for Epicurus and his followers, takes the sting out of
death. It even enables you to duck the wrath of the gods.

Atomists and Epicureans

The inevitability of death casts a long shadow over our lives. The cultural anthropologist Ernest Becker, in his book *The Denial of Death*, claims that our fear of it haunts us like nothing else: 'It is the mainspring of human activity – activity designed largely to avoid the fatality of death, to overcome it by denying in some way that it is the final destiny for man.'

The example of Socrates, who went to his own death willingly and calmly, will likely seem to most of us almost beyond comprehension. The story below, on the other hand, which appeared in the *British Medical Journal* in 1958, is altogether more familiar:

'The old lady was put in the ambulance and, sinking fast, was driven to a famous teaching hospital. By the time she was wheeled into the casualty ward she had breathed her last. But the young and efficient casualty officer was far from being dismayed. All the resuscitation services that the hospital could provide were mobilized, and for eighteen hours the patient's heart was kept beating . . . Mercifully enough, this determined battle was fought in vain. When asked later what had been the point of it all, the casualty officer gave a very significant reply . . . He had one duty, and one duty only: to do all that lay within his powers to ward off death.'

The thought that death is something to be warded off at all costs is not peculiar to the modern age. Indeed, we have reason to think that as far as the ancient Greeks were concerned, Socrates' equanimity in the face of death was an exception rather than the rule. Christine Sourvinou-Inwood, a scholar of ancient Greece, for example, argues that attitudes towards mortality in the Greek world underwent a sea change around 700 BCE, after which time death became something to be feared in much the same way as it is in the present day.

Certainly, the fear of death was considered to be a significant impediment to human happiness by Epicurus, the founder of Epicureanism, which, alongside Stoicism, is the second great school of Hellenistic philosophy.

Epicurus

Epicurus was born in Samos, an Athenian colony – and also, incidentally, the birthplace of Pythagoras – in 341 BCE. The details of his formative years are sketchy, but Sextus Empiricus reports that he was drawn to philosophy in his early teens after his schoolteachers were unable to give satisfactory answers to his questions about Hesiod's cosmogony. He probably studied under the philosophers Pamphilus and Nausiphanes. He unkindly called Nausiphanes 'the Mollusc', but it was the Mollusc who seems to have introduced him to Democritus' atomistic ideas. These formed the bedrock of his philosophical world view.

Epicurus first started teaching in Mytilene, before being forced to move to Lampsacus, where he established his first school. However, it was in Athens, at a school he founded in 306 BCE (or thereabouts) named 'the Garden' – so called because it was located in a garden that was apparently situated halfway between the competing schools of the Stoics and the Academics – that Epicureanism really took off as a distinctive philosophical approach.

The Roman Stoic philosopher Seneca reports that the Garden had the following inscription on its gate:

Stranger, here you will do well to tarry; here our highest good is pleasure. The caretaker of that abode, a kindly host, will be ready for you; He will welcome you with bread, and serve you water also in abundance, with these words: 'Have you not been well entertained? This garden does not whet your appetite; but quenches it.'

Epicurus, it is said, was true to this sentiment, welcoming all into his school, including, scandalously at the time, women and slaves. However, though the school emphasized the importance of community and friendship, it was organized along clear hierarchical lines, with Epicurus very much its master. As Seneca put it, 'In that famous fellowship every word that was spoken was uttered under the guidance and auspices of a single individual.'

Epicureanism was very much a missionary philosophy. Its converts were required to swear an oath of allegiance to the principal doctrines of Epicureanism, and were expected to preach the Epicurean message. Epicurus enjoined his disciples 'to apply it in their own households, to take advantage of all other intimacies and under no circumstances to slacken in proclaiming the sayings of the true philosophy'. According to the Epicurean scholar Norman DeWitt, this proselytizing aspect of Epicureanism meant it was able to flourish independently of schools and tutors, allowing it to penetrate into small towns and villages where there were no places of learning, and to win converts from social groups that would normally be unmoved by the ideas of a philosophical system.

In many ways, Epicureanism was a quasi-religion. Epicurus himself was venerated almost as a Messiah figure. Cicero, for example, tells us that Epicureans would often have the image of their master on paintings, cups and rings. It is also significant that the Epicurean message was passed down virtually unaltered over the centuries, so much so that *The Nature of Things*, the philosophical poem of the Roman poet Lucretius, is considered to be an accurate representation of the ideas of Epicurus, even though it was written some two hundred years after his death.

Epicurus was something of an applied philosopher, in that his concerns were largely practical. In particular, he wanted to show how rational reflection could help to dispel the fears and superstitions that undermined people's happiness. In this sense, Epicureanism can be seen as part of the general Hellenistic reaction against the grand theorizing of Plato and Aristotle. It was in some ways a return to the philosophical style of Socrates, who, as we have seen, was similarly concerned with how we should live. However, in Epicurus' hands, this took on a much more personal aspect, since he believed that the main aim of philosophy was to lead people into a state of *ataraxia*, or tranquillity.

We saw a similar thing with the Cynics, Stoics and Sceptics in the last chapter, but on the face of it, this still seems a slightly odd way to think about the purpose of philosophy. Perhaps that's because we now see philosophy as a discipline that aims at uncovering the truth about things. Why think that such a practice will lead to peace of mind? Anybody who has struggled with formal logic, or sat through a lecture on Hegel's *Phenomenology*, will probably be sceptical of philosophy's tranquillity-inducing properties. But the ancient view of philosophy as a route to peace in life is not as odd as it might at first seem.

The issue of how we view our own mortality is instructive in this respect. Epicurus did not accept that fear of death is an inevitable part of the human condition. Rather, he saw it as being rooted in erroneous thinking, as a sort of cognitive mistake. If this is right, then philosophy holds out the promise of a kind of salvation: show people where they go wrong when they fear their own death, and there's a chance they'll fear it no longer, or at least feel a little better about it.

To this end, Epicurus deployed two arguments he hoped would show the irrationality of the fear of death. The first of these is known as the 'no subject of harm' argument. It holds that:

Death . . . is nothing to us, seeing that, when we are, death is not come, and, when death is come, we are not. It is nothing, then, either to the living or to the dead, for with the living it is not and the dead exist no longer.

The argument here is simple: we're not going to be around to experience the state of being dead, so there's no need to fear it. Death can't be bad *for us*, since once we're dead there will be no 'us' for whom it could be bad. Non-existence is entirely unproblematic, since it isn't something that happens to anybody.

The second argument is known as the 'symmetry' argument, and it is nicely encapsulated in Mark Twain's pithy dismissal of the terrors of non-existence: 'I do not fear death. I had been dead for billions and billions of years before I was born, and had not suffered the slightest inconvenience from it.' In other words, being dead is the same as being unborn, and since we have all been unborn without it being any sort of a problem, there is nothing to fear in the thought that we shall return to what is effectively the same state.

Neither of these arguments is decisive. In particular, there is a complicated debate to be had here about whether it is rational to fear losing what one values about life, including the fact of living itself, if one knows that one will have no awareness of having lost those things. However, there is also a more straightforward puzzle about Epicurus' argument: what grounds does he have for claiming that we won't experience the state of being dead? After all, plenty of people believe precisely that we will survive our physical death.

Perhaps the first thing to say here is that there was no consensus view among the ancient Greeks about what happens after death. Probably the most common belief was the one found in Homer's *Odyssey*. He portrays the souls of the dead as living shadowy half-lives in Hades (the underworld), deprived of memory and psychologically disconnected from their previous existence. This view that consciousness only survives death in a very weak sense is the nearest thing to an officially sanctioned Hellenic view of the afterlife.

But there were other ideas floating around. Plato probably believed that the soul is immortal. Certainly, in the *Phaedo* he has Socrates arguing strongly in favour of the proposition that the soul does not perish on bodily death. Moreover, in a number of dialogues he indicates a belief in the doctrine of metempsychosis – the view that at death, or after a suitable interval, the soul passes into another body. He ties this to his idea that all learning is in fact recollection:

> The soul, then, as being immortal, and having been born again many times, and having seen all things that exist, whether in this world or in the world below, has knowledge of them all; and it is no wonder that she should be able to call to remembrance all that she ever knew about virtue, and about everything . . . for all enquiry and all learning is but recollection.

In contrast to this esotericism, Epicurus' idea about what happens upon death is much more down to earth. He thought the soul is made up of tiny atoms, and that upon the demise of the body, it disperses into a giant void never to be seen again. He did not pluck this notion out of thin air, but rather built on the ideas of the two great atomist philosophers, Leucippus and Democritus.

The atomists

The atomists were notable among their contemporaries for the singular achievement of getting things basically right. No doubt this was more a matter of luck than judgement, and in the details they got things quite wrong, but nevertheless their ideas anticipate modern science in a quite striking way.

We know virtually nothing about Leucippus of Miletus, except that it's possible he was an admirer of Zeno, that he taught Democritus, and that he lived in the fifth century BCE. Unfortunately, it's also possible that he didn't exist at all. Epicurus, for example, seems to have doubted it, and it was a matter of some dispute among 19th-century scholars. Despite the possible setback of not actually existing, Leucippus is named by most historical commentators as one of the originators of the ideas that form the bedrock of atomist theory. Aristotle, for example, credits Leucippus and Democritus *jointly* as the source of the idea that the only things that exist are atoms and the void.

Fortunately, we know a little bit more about Democritus. He was born in Abdera, on the coast of Thrace, sometime around 460 BCE. Diogenes Laertius tells us that he travelled widely, visiting Egypt and Persia, and possibly even India and Ethiopia. We're not sure how impressed he was by his travels. He allegedly said that he'd rather discover a single causal law than be crowned the king of Persia. In between travelling, he managed to write some 80 works on a diverse range of topics such as ethics, music, mathematics and cosmology. None of these texts survive intact, but there remain a large collection of fragments, and from these it is possible to piece together the details of his philosophy.

Democritus' central claim is that the universe is populated by two kinds of things: atoms and void. The atoms are infinite in number, indivisible, solid, and vary in shape and size, some being scalene, some hooked, some concave and some convex. They are constantly on the move within the similarly infinite void. The objects of the everyday world come into existence as a result of the collisions that inevitably occur:

> . . . overtaking each other they collide, and some are shaken away in any chance direction, while others, becoming intertwined one with another according to the congruity of their shapes, sizes, positions and arrangements, stay together and so effect the coming into being of compound bodies.

This idea that the manifold objects of the everyday world are made up of varying aggregates of atoms allowed the atomists to reconcile the arguments of the Eleatics (Parmenides, Melissus and Zeno) against change and plurality with the data of sense perception. The basic stuff of reality is unchanging and eternal, but it combines together to form the objects of our experience. Nothing *fundamentally* new is created as a result of the collisions and combinations between atoms, but this is compatible with the *appearance* of change and multiplicity.

The similarity between this view and the modern scientific idea that the atom is the basic building block of matter is obvious. However, it would be wrong to take this as evidence that the atomists were engaged in something akin to science proper. In fact, their endeavours were every bit as much an instance of speculative metaphysics as were those of the Eleatics. Or, to put this another way, like Parmenides, they were in the business of deriving truths about the empirical world by reasoning from first principles. So, for example, Democritus argued that sweet and bitter flavours arise because of the different shapes of atoms: bitter flavours being caused by atoms that are angular and jagged, and sweet flavours originating in round, smooth atoms. This argument makes sense in terms of the principles of atomism, but clearly it has no empirical warrant.

However, there are a couple of senses in which atomist theory does enjoy a genuine affinity with modern science. First, it is committed to a thoroughgoing materialism – even thought is to be explained in terms of the actions of atoms. And second, it relies on an entirely mechanistic explanatory framework. The atomists were avowed determinists, believing that everything that happens does so because of strict causal laws. They had no use for the sort of forward-looking, teleological explanations so beloved of Aristotle. The universe does not exist in order to fulfil the purposes of a Creator; rather, it exists and takes the form it does because of the inexorable working-out of physical laws.

It might be thought that Democritus' commitment to materialism would rule out a notion such as the soul, but in fact it just meant he conceived of it in materialist terms. Aristotle reports that Democritus believed the soul to be composed of spherical atoms, which he compared to the motes that we see in shafts of light coming in through windows. The consensus among commentators is that Democritus did not think the soul is immortal. Rather, on the death of the body, the atoms that constitute the soul break apart and disperse into the void.

Epicurus redux

This idea brings us back to Epicurus, whose philosophy, in most respects, is straightforwardly Democritean. As we noted earlier, Epicurus, like Democritus, believed the soul was made up of atoms:

> . . . we must recognize generally that the soul is a corporeal thing, composed of fine particles, dispersed all over the frame, most nearly resembling wind with an admixture of heat, in some respects like wind, in others like heat.

He was also clear that the soul perishes on the death of the body:

> When the whole frame is broken up, the soul is scattered and has no longer the same powers as before, nor the same notions; hence it does not possess sentience either.

It is this idea that allowed him to argue that death means the end of us. The soul is the seat of sentience; on the dispersal of the soul, sentience is extinguished, and we cease to exist. We have no reason to fear non-existence. Therefore, we should not fear death.

Epicurus also offered a naturalistic account of the gods. Residing in the *intermundia*, the spaces between worlds, they too are composed of atoms, although godly atoms are of the finest sort. Epicurus' gods are immortal, unconcerned with human affairs, immune from pain and peril, and exist in a state of perfect tranquillity. We have no reason to fear the gods, but equally there is no reason to think we can affect them in any way. Epicurus was not averse to the occasional religious ritual, perhaps, for example, to celebrate the excellence of the gods, but we should not think that by such means we can win their favour.

The problem of evil

In order to bolster his claim that the gods are unconcerned with human affairs, Epicurus deployed what is considered to be the earliest statement of "the problem of evil", which, roughly speaking, refers to the difficulty of explaining how there can be evil in the world if it is also true that a perfectly good, all-powerful and all-knowing God exists.

His argument has the following form:

God . . . either wishes to take away evils, and is unable; or He is able, and is unwilling; or He is neither willing nor able, or He is both willing and able. If He is willing and is unable, He is feeble, which is not in accordance with the character of God; if He is able and unwilling, He is envious, which is equally at variance with God;

if He is neither willing nor able, He is both envious and feeble, and therefore not God; if He is both willing and able, which alone is suitable to God, from what source then are evils? or why does He not remove them?

The basic argument here is that any being worthy of being called God ought to be both willing and able to remove evil from the world. Therefore, given that there is evil in the world, it seems that God is either unwilling or unable (or both) to do so. If he's unable, then he's feeble; if he's unwilling, then he's morally flawed.

Epicurus deployed this argument presumably in order to support his contention that the gods are simply not interested in human affairs. However, the argument doesn't actually appear in any of his extant works, but rather is found in a treatise called 'On the Anger of God', written by the early Christian apologist Lactantius. Not surprisingly, Lactantius does not think that Epicurus' argument is decisive, arguing that without knowledge of evil there is no wisdom, and therefore evil is necessary and justified, since the good of wisdom outweighs the bad of evil.

This sort of response to the problem of evil is termed a theodicy. The idea of a theodicy is to show there is no contradiction in believing in an omnibenevolent, omniscient, omnipotent deity and also that there is evil in the world. Theodicies vary in form and complexity, but often come down to the idea that though we might not know it, we are actually living in the best of all possible worlds.

Pleasure as good

This view of the Gods as being disinterested in human affairs, which is sometimes called "polydeism", is an important part of the Epicurean philosophy of happiness. The gods are fundamentally absent from the world. So we have no reason to dread the possibility of divine capriciousness or retribution, and we might as well get on with enjoying our lives. However, this freedom from the gaze and judgement of the gods, when combined with the thoroughgoing materialism of Epicurus' philosophy, brings with it a problem. How do we know the right way to live if there is no ultimate source of value, if there is no transcendent realm to which we can refer to make sense of notions such as virtue, justice and piety?

The answer Epicurus gives to this question is that *pleasure* is the ultimate good:

> . . . we call pleasure the alpha and omega of a happy life. Pleasure is our first and kindred good. It is the starting-point of every choice and of every aversion, and to it we come back, inasmuch as we make feeling the rule by which to judge of every good thing.

This got him into a lot of trouble. The difficulty is that it seems potentially to justify pretty much any behaviour. Want to spend your life watching daytime television and stuffing down doughnuts? Perfectly reasonable, so long as it brings you pleasure. Enjoy napping? No problem, why spend your life awake if you're happier snuggled up under the bed covers?

Not surprisingly, Epicurus' opponents seized on his advocacy of what looks at first sight like a fairly crude hedonism as a stick with which to beat him. They portrayed him as ignorant, licentious and gluttonous, interested only in the pleasures of the flesh. The Stoic philosopher Epictetus, for example, said of Epicurus that his idea of the worthy life amounted to 'eating, drinking, copulation, evacuation and snoring'. Diogenes Laertius recounts numerous slanders against Epicurus, including that he routinely vomited twice a day as a result of his drinking, spent his time chasing women and young men, and wasn't much able to get up from his sofa – which leads one to wonder how he managed with the women and young men.

However, as far as we can tell, there wasn't a great deal of truth in these accusations. Diogenes Laertius dismisses them as slightly crazy. Epicurus was not an out-of-control hedonist, but rather an advocate of moderate pleasures. He did not think we should pursue wild parties and fleshy excitement, since to indulge in such things would result in a spiral of desire that would inevitably cause frustration and misery in the long run. Instead, we should seek merely the absence of pain:

> When, therefore, we say that pleasure is a chief good,
> we are not speaking of the pleasures of the debauched
> man, or those which lie in sensual enjoyment . . . but
> we mean the freedom of the body from pain, and the
> soul from confusion.

Although pleasure *in and of itself* is always a good thing, it does not follow that we should actively pursue every sort of pleasure. On the contrary, we should avoid those pleasures that are likely to set us up for unhappiness in the future, perhaps, for example, because they result in a craving that cannot be satisfied, or lead to ill health. Pleasures rooted in a compelling desire are necessarily double-edged, since desire is inextricably bound up with pain and frustration. Therefore, it is prudent to cultivate a state of bodily and psychological equilibrium, where desire is minimized, and the quiet pleasures can be enjoyed.

There are, of course, difficulties with this argument. Not least, it seems a little too convenient that the sorts of behaviours ruled out by the moral codes of ancient Greece are also those that Epicurus disavows on the grounds that the pleasures they involve are the wrong kinds of pleasures. Nevertheless, it remains true that the accusation levelled against Epicurus by his opponents that he was an apologist for Bacchanalian excess is unfounded.

However, though Epicurus was a long way from being an advocate of a sensualist hedonism, there are still problems in putting pleasure right at the heart of an ethical theory. In particular, it risks reducing all our relationships and dealings with other people to an instrumental calculation about costs and benefits. Thus, for example, although Epicurus stressed the importance of friendship, and was said personally to be a good and loyal friend, he argued that friendships should be pursued for the rewards they bring, not for their own sake. Similarly, he claimed that while there is no principled reason for behaving justly towards other people, such behaviour is desirable since it is the best way of avoiding the fear of retribution that goes with unjust behaviour. As he puts it: 'Injustice is not intrinsically bad; it has this character only because there is joined with it a fear of not escaping those who are appointed to punish actions marked with that character.'

It is quite easy to see why this sort of thing will have offended the proponents of more austere forms of morality. The Stoic Cicero, for example, complains that Epicurus' idea that thoughts about pleasure and pain motivate all our choices is 'a doctrine in the last degree unworthy of the dignity of man'. He points out that good men endure pain and danger for country and for friends, 'not only not seeking pleasure, but actually renouncing pleasures altogether, and preferring to undergo every sort of pain rather than be false to any portion of their duty'.

The notion that there might be duties that have nothing to do with pleasure simply doesn't feature in the Epicurean schema. This put Epicureanism on a collision course with Platonism, Stoicism, and then later, in the second and third centuries CE, with the early Christian apologists. Tertullian, for example, suggests that Epicurean and other Greek philosophical doctrines were demonic in origin. Although Epicureanism was popular and influential for around 500 years, with its reach eventually extending to the far edges of the Roman Empire and beyond, its decline when it occurred was rapid.

A number of factors conspired to precipitate its demise. The rise of Christianity, which we'll consider in the next chapter, closed down the space available for an alternative world view such as Epicureanism to flourish. Put simply, in the battle of ideas between the two belief systems, Christian monotheism proved to be the more enduring, no doubt helped by the fact that it became the official religion of Rome. While Epicureanism faded rapidly, Christianity developed the sorts of institutional structures that enabled it to survive the vagaries of history.

The decline of the Roman Empire, and the advent of the 'dark ages', is also part of this story. Christianity gradually became enmeshed in the social fabric of European society, which meant it was able to survive, and even flourish, in the chaotic years between the fall of Rome and the beginnings of the Renaissance. However, this was not true of Epicureanism, and almost inevitably Epicurean philosophy all but disappeared.

But this was not the end of Epicurus. His ideas were rediscovered in the 17th century by the philosopher Pierre Gassendi, who developed a neo-Epicurean challenge to the philosophical system of René Descartes. Although it is true to say that Epicureanism is no longer a living philosophical system, it is nevertheless the case that echoes of Epicurus' ideas can be found in much humanist and egalitarian thought.

3
Religion

Faith and Reason

Augustine of Hippo, the first great Christian philosopher, was peculiarly interested in sex. This is not unprecedented among philosophers, despite their reputation for other-worldliness. Jean-Paul Sartre, for example, was notorious for his lasciviousness. As we'll see in the next chapter, Peter Abelard, a Scholastic philosopher of the 12th century, managed to get himself forcibly castrated after an entanglement with a much younger lover. However, what makes the case of Augustine particularly interesting is the way in which the revulsion he felt as a result of the 'carnal corruptions' of his youth, when combined with certain Greek and Christian themes, led him to an ascetic world view that came to dominate Christian thinking for more than a millennium.

Unfortunately, this was not necessarily to the betterment of humankind. As Bertrand Russell notes, it is strange that at a time when the Roman Empire was crumbling, Augustine was more concerned with preaching the merits of sexual purity and the damnation of unbaptised infants than with the fate of civilization. Russell goes on to add that: 'Seeing that these were the preoccupations that the Church handed on to the converted barbarians, it is no wonder that the succeeding age surpassed almost all other fully historical periods in cruelty and superstition.'

However, whatever the fallout from his ascetic morality, there is no doubting Augustine's importance as a thinker. Not only was his work integral to the development of philosophy and theology in the Western tradition from the fourth century until at least the Renaissance, his treatment of particular issues – for example, his relativistic theory of time, and his critique of the Pelagian 'heresy' – remains of interest to this day.

Augustine was born Aurelius Augustinus in the North African town of Tagaste in 354 CE to Patricius, his pagan father, a town administrator, and Monica, a devout Christian, who was the formative influence in his life. Augustine received a classical education, and then under the patronage of Romanianus, a wealthy citizen of Tagaste, studied rhetoric at the university in Carthage, during which time he turned his back on Christianity, began to live a hedonistic lifestyle, and espoused a belief in the Manichean religion. At this time, he also started a 13-year affair with a young woman, whose name he never divulged, but who he clearly loved and with whom he fathered a son, Adeodatus.

In 383 CE, he travelled to Italy, where he stayed for five

years, during the latter part of the time working as a professor of rhetoric in Milan. It was while in Milan, under the influence of his mother and Bishop Ambrose, that he converted to Christianity, the story of which forms the backdrop to his best-known work, *Confessions*. Augustine was baptised in 387 CE, by which point he had already written a number of his most important early works, including *Against the Academicians* and *Soliloquies*.

In 388 CE, he travelled back to Carthage, never again leaving North Africa. He founded a monastery, gave money to the poor, became a noted polemicist against Manicheism, the religious belief he had espoused as a young man, and was ordained a priest in Hippo Regius in 391 CE. In 395 CE, he became Bishop of Hippo, a position he retained until his death in 430 CE. He spent the last 40 years of his life writing copiously and working tirelessly in an effort to spread the message of Christianity across North Africa.

Original sin and puddly concupiscence

We know about Augustine's youthful sexual adventures because he tells us about them in his autobiographical work, *Confessions*, which takes the form of a dialogue with God, charting the course of his life from childhood until his conversion to Christianity at the age of 33. The work is dominated by themes of regret and guilt.

I did not keep the moderate way of the love of mind to

mind – the bright path of friendship. Instead, the mists of passion steamed up out of the puddly concupiscence of the flesh, and the hot imagination of puberty, and they so obscured and overcast my heart that I was unable to distinguish pure affection from unholy desire. Both boiled confusedly within me, and dragged my unstable youth down over the cliffs of unchaste desires and plunged me into a gulf of infamy.

To love and to be loved was sweet to me, and all the more when I gained the enjoyment of the body of the person I loved. Thus I polluted the spring of friendship with the filth of concupiscence and I dimmed its lustre with the slime of lust.

Augustine believed that as a result of the fall of Adam, human beings are irremediably mired in sin, including the sin of sexual lust. God created Adam with free will, which meant Adam could have refrained from sin, but instead he chose to break the one rule ordained by God: he ate fruit from the Tree of Knowledge. As a result of this act of disobedience, Adam and Eve lost the gift of God's grace, and became enslaved by sin. Their corruption was passed down to all their progeny – the whole of humanity – and as a result human beings are fundamentally wicked and deserving of eternal damnation.

That Augustine meant all this to be taken quite literally is evident from his treatment of the theme of wickedness in

Confessions. For example, he insists that newborn babies manifest wickedness even in the cradle:

> I would fling my arms and legs about and cry, making the few and feeble gestures that I could, though indeed the signs were not much like what I inwardly desired and when I was not satisfied – either from not being understood or because what I got was not good for me – I grew indignant that my elders were not subject to me and that those on whom I actually had no claim did not wait on me as slaves – and I avenged myself on them by crying. That infants are like this, I have myself been able to learn by watching them . . .

He also makes a big play out of an incident in his youth that saw him stealing some pears from a tree. He notes that the fruit was not tempting in and of itself. The pleasure was in the violative nature of the act. There was no inducement to evil but the evil itself.

> I loved my own undoing. I loved my error – not that for which I erred but the error itself. A depraved soul, falling away from security in thee to destruction in itself, seeking nothing from the shameful deed but shame itself.

Augustine did not believe that human beings are able to rescue themselves from sin. There is no way we can attain grace through good behaviour or deeds, for example, since we are depraved to the core. Happily, though, God allows at least some of us to get to heaven – although Augustine seems to think not very many of us. By virtue of His grace, the elect from among us will have their sins washed away and enter the kingdom of heaven. The rest of us are destined to suffer hellfire and eternal damnation.

The City of God

This idea, that humanity is divided into two great camps, finds its most striking expression in *The City of God*, Augustine's magnum opus. In this work, he argues that since the time of Adam's fall, history has been characterized by the struggle between two great cities, each governed by a specific principle of conduct. On the one hand, there is the City of God, where love for God and His rules, by virtue of His grace, is dominant; on the other hand, there is the City of Babylon, which is predestined to join the devil in eternal torment, and which is governed by the love of self and the flesh.

In broad terms, this distinction corresponds to the division between the Christian Church and the secular, pagan state. Thus, for example, Augustine stresses the way that secular states such as Assyria and pagan Rome were founded and sustained through the use of violence and oppression. However, his idea was not precisely empirical – rather moral and spiritual, which means this correspondence is necessarily imperfect. Not least, the City of God existed long before the birth of Christ and the emergence of the Church. Also, mere membership of the Church does not guarantee moral rectitude. If the principle of a person's conduct is love of the self, then regardless of their relationship to the Church, they belong to the City of Babylon.

There is no doubt that Augustine considered the Christian Church to be superior and in some sense primary to the state. The clear implication of his position is that a state can only be fully just if it is informed by Christian principles of conduct. In this sense, he stands *against* the separation of Church and state, a view that became orthodox in the Middle Ages, particularly with the rise of the power of the papacy, and partly as a result of the theoretical support Augustine's writings provided.

Where's the philosophy?

To the modern mind, all this talk of sin, wickedness, damnation and grace probably seems a little odd, and certainly not particularly philosophical. It is hard to imagine, for example, a discussion of the fate of digested human flesh at the resurrection occurring in the pages of technical philosophical journals like *Mind* or *Analysis* as it does in *The City of God*.

There are a number of points to raise in this regard. The first is that while in the present day we make a clear distinction between philosophy and dogmatic theology, Augustine would not have recognized it. It's not so much that he would not have understood the difference between rational argument and revelation, but rather that his concern, certainly in the latter part of his life, was to understand the world and humanity's place in it in light of what he took to be the truths of Christianity. The Jesuit philosopher Frederick Copleston expresses the point like this:

> Augustine did not play two parts, the part of the theologian and the part of the philosopher who considers the 'natural man'; he thought rather of man as he is in the concrete, fallen and redeemed mankind, man who is able indeed to attain truth but who is constantly solicited by God's grace and who requires grace in order to appropriate the truth that saves.

The second point is that it is possible to identify aspects of Augustine's work that are properly philosophical. One example is the argument he makes in *Soliloquies* in favour of the immortality of the soul. It's not a particularly good argument, but it doesn't depend upon revelation or theological speculation for its conclusion. Augustine's starting point is the claim that although true things may cease to exist, Truth itself is eternal. And given that Truth exists, it must exist in something that is also eternal, 'For whatever is cannot survive in anything, if the thing in which it is does not survive.' He goes on to argue that reflection on the nature of necessary truths such as those of geometry and mathematics shows that the home of Truth must be the soul (or mind). It follows, therefore, that the soul is immortal.

Augustine makes a similar sort of argument as a proof of God's existence. It begins with the claim that the mind is aware of necessary and unchanging truth, 'which thou canst not call thine, or mine, or any man's, but which is present to all and gives itself to all alike'. Put simply, the idea here is that there are eternal truths that in some sense transcend and rule the mind. These truths cannot be changed by the mind, and they are not themselves changeable in the same way that the mind is changeable. However, equally, they are not free-floating – they have to be grounded in something. Not surprisingly, this something turns out to be God: 'Thee do I invoke, God, Truth, in whom and by whom and through whom are all things true which are true.'

The final point to make here is a little more involved. Augustine's work is both a dialogue with the great philosophers who came before him, and also heavily influenced by certain Platonic and Neoplatonic ideas. The dialogue aspect is straightforward enough. So, for example, *The City of God* treats us to a survey of philosophy from the time of Thales, in which Augustine considers how well the ideas of earlier philosophers stack up against what he takes to be the truths of Christianity. It is clear that he is most impressed by Plato and the Platonists who followed him. For example, he says that from among the disciples of Socrates, Plato was the one who 'shone with a glory which far excelled that of the others, and who not unjustly eclipsed them all'. He places Platonism above all the other philosophical schools: 'Let Thales depart with his water, Anaximenes with the air, the Stoics with their fire, Epicurus with his atoms.'

The Platonists didn't get everything right, though. In particular, they were wrong about polytheism, wrong about the transmigration of souls, and wrong in not recognizing the divinity of Christ. However, of all the earliest philosophers, they came closest to the message of Christianity, and Augustine suggested that if Plato and his followers had been born a little later, then they too would have been Christians. The common ground between Platonism and Christianity is seen most clearly in the rejection of materialism, the belief in the soul's immortality and the idea that there is a transcendent realm from which all material things ultimately derive their being.

Neoplatonism

Perhaps the most prominent of the Platonic themes found in Augustine's work is the idea that the earthly realm is markedly inferior or impoverished when compared to the divine realm. This is one of the signature claims of Neoplatonism, associated most clearly with Plotinus, the last great philosopher of antiquity. Unfortunately, however, here we run into choppy waters, because Plotinus' ideas are more than a little obscure. If you have a taste for florid language, and you've never come across a conceptual distinction that you haven't been tempted to subdivide further, then maybe you'll get along with Plotinus. For everybody else, though, it's a struggle. Still, Plotinus is incredibly important in the history of Christianity – in large part precisely because of his influence on Augustine – so it's worth saying something about his ideas.

Plotinus' central metaphysical claim is that all Being is caused by 'the One'. This sounds straightforward enough, even if a little implausible, but unfortunately it isn't at all clear what the One actually is, or even if it is anything at all. Russell says of it that it is indefinable, and in regards to it 'there is more truth in silence than in any words whatever', which hardly inspires confidence that enlightenment is immediately going to be forthcoming. It is said variously to be equivalent to God, the Good and Beauty; and it crops up in Plato's *Republic*, where it is termed 'the Idea of the Good', and also in his *Parmenides*.

To the extent that it is possible to say anything at all about the One, it is that it is absolutely simple, indivisible, without attributes and beyond all Being. There are echoes of Parmenides here, but with the added difficulty that Plotinus has to explain how it is possible to produce the universe in all its multiplicity from something that is absolutely simple – whereas Parmenides only has to explain the *appearance* of multiplicity. The explanation Plotinus offers, though far from convincing, is 'emanationist' in form. It holds that the universe issues from the One, moving away from the perfection of the One, as a matter of necessity. This process is characterized by a number of 'emanations' or principles, hierarchically organized, each less perfect than the preceding emanation, and all ultimately derived from the One. The most important of these are: *Nous* (Thought or Intellect), World-Soul, individual souls and the material world.

If the One is rather shadowy, then the whole business of how these emanations emerge from each other is black as night. We can say that Plotinus' thoughts about emanation are motivated by a commitment to the Presocratic idea that the complex must be explained in terms of the simple, and also by the view that contingent phenomena must ultimately be explained in terms of something that itself requires no explanation. Thus he ends up with a conception of the One as absolutely simple, self-caused and the cause of everything else in the universe.

Augustine as a Plotinian

So how does Augustine fit into this picture? This, of course, is a complicated issue, but the simple answer is that, especially in his earlier works, he largely accepts the Plotinian conception of reality. In particular, he regards God as the source and origin of the various stages of plurality and multiplicity that exist below God. He equates God with Being, Truth and Good-ness, and emphasizes the contrast between the intelligible world of spiritual truth and the sensible world of material objects.

This contrast between the intelligible and sensible realms allows Augustine to argue that if we turn our gaze towards the intelligible world, towards God, in other words, and cease to be seduced by the glitter of the material world, then we'll find eternal, abiding Truth and solace from the troubles of everyday life. This idea finds its most poetic expression in his famous description in *Confessions* of a quasi-mystical experience he shared with his mother at Ostia:

> . . . we gradually passed through all the levels of bodily objects, and even through the heaven itself, where the sun and moon and stars shine on the earth. Indeed, we soared higher yet by an inner musing, speaking and marvelling at thy works.
>
> And we came at last to our own minds and went beyond them, that we might climb as high as that region of unfailing plenty where thou feedest Israel forever with the food of truth, where life is that Wisdom by whom all things are made, both which have been and which are to be. Wisdom is not made, but is as she has been and forever shall be . . .

There are, of course, aspects of the Plotinian world view that Augustine does not accept. In particular, in contrast to the Neoplatonic denial of divine agency, he insists on the voluntary nature of God's activity, and argues, contrary to Plotinus, that there was a single moment of creation – although he also thought that God remains active in the development of the universe. Needless to say, it's no surprise that Augustine on occasion departs from the Neoplatonist line, since his aim is not to develop Neoplatonism, but rather to take its insights and combine them with what he believes to be the truths of Holy Scripture.

Islamic philosophy

Although the Middle Ages has a reputation for intellectual underperformance, it just isn't true that vast tracts of time went by during this era without anything much of interest happening. Therefore, it is with a certain amount of sheepishness that we must now fast-forward about 600 years to consider how some of these issues concerning faith and reason played out amongst the great philosophers of the Islamic golden age. If we were constructing a purely chronological account of the story of philosophy, there would be little justification for such a leap. However, when it comes to philosophical *importance*, thinkers such as Ibn Sina and Ibn Rushd just outrank their earlier Western counterparts such as Pseudo-Dionysus and John Scotus Eriugenia.

Part of the significance of early Islamic philosophy is that it was the main channel through which Aristotle was rediscovered in the Western world. However, the Muslim philosophers who worked around the turn of the first millennium did not espouse anything like a pure Aristotelianism, but rather made use of both Aristotelian and Neoplatonic concepts, while at the same time attempting not to depart too far from Islamic orthodoxy.

Ibn Sina

The greatest of the early Muslim philosophers was Ibn Sina, known as Avicenna in the West, who was born near Bukhara in Central Asia in 980 CE. He was absurdly precocious, studying medicine from the age of 13, and successfully treating the sultan of Bukhara before he was out of his teens, for which he was rewarded with access to the sultan's library.

It is easy enough to identify Neoplatonist themes in Ibn Sina's work. For example, in order to explain how the world comes into being, he relies on an emanationist account that is every bit as jaw-droppingly convoluted as Plotinus'. It involves God, one, simple and eternal; God's self-knowledge; a first awareness; an intellect; a soul; a celestial body; a second intellect; and a lot more of the same all the way down to the Active Intellect, which, much to everybody's relief, is responsible for the generation of our world. Ibn Sina argued that God, the supreme intellect, is the highest object of human understanding. The fundamental structure of reality, as it emanates from Him down through the various levels, is available to human thought through the faculty of reason.

This is the fairly standard Neoplatonist conception that we came across in both Plotinus and Augustine, and, of course, it suffers from the same plausibility deficit. However, Ibn Sina does move away from Neoplatonism in other aspects of his metaphysics. Take, for example, his proof of God's existence. This relies on Aristotle's distinction, set out in his *Categories*, between necessary and possible existence. If we examine the objects that make up the world, we won't find anything about their essences that explains why they exist. Their existence is merely *possible*, which is to say that they might not have existed. However, the fact that any object might not have existed leaves us without an explanation for its existence. It seems to follow, then, that its existence must have been necessitated by something else; or, to put this more precisely, its existence must have been the consequence of the essence of another existent object. This means we end up with a chain of essential causes, which must terminate somewhere in order to avoid an infinite regress. The termination point is an entity that exists *necessarily*, which does not derive its existence from outside itself. This, of course, is God, the Necessary Existent.

Al-Ghazali and the Hellenization of Islam

A question that immediately springs to mind here is to what extent Ibn Sina's views are properly considered Islamic. His conception of God, for example, is highly esoteric, and it is hard to imagine it was the sort of thing that average Muslim believers had in mind when they offered up their prayers to Allah. It is perhaps not surprising that Ibn Sina came under attack for views that were deemed un-Islamic. The most significant of his accusers was the Islamic theologian and mystic al-Ghazali (known as Algazel in the West), whose major work, *The Incoherence of the Philosophers*, was an attack on what he saw as the Hellenization of Islam in the work of philosophers such as al-Farabi and Ibn Sina.

Al-Ghazali's attack is multidimensional – commentators have identified at least 17 different points of contention – but perhaps the most interesting issues have to do with God as a freely acting agent able to intervene in the world in any way that he chooses. Consider, for example, the question of whether the heavens are created. The Islamic philosophers who were the focus of al-Ghazali's ire tend to argue that they were not. Ibn Sina's view, as we have seen, is emanationist. He claims that the universe was not created *ex nihilo* at a particular moment in time, but rather that it exists out of necessity, emanating in manifold forms from God's divine nature.

It is easy to see why such a conception would not have pleased al-Ghazali. It seems to do away with God as a free agent. Al-Ghazali's response to all this is to argue that the Qur'an is quite clear that the universe was created by God. If God is an agent, able to act according to his own will, then it is perfectly reasonable to suppose that he created the world *ex nihilo*, and that he could eliminate it again should he so choose. In effect, then, al-Ghazali defends a particular conception of divine agency: God is all-powerful, therefore he can act to create and destroy worlds.

Ibn Rushd

This tension between philosophy and religion, and in particular al-Ghazali's attack on the Hellenization of Islam, provides the context within which Ibn Rushd (known as Averroes in the West), the greatest of the Islamic philosophers of the Middle Ages, wrote what was probably his most important work of original philosophy, *The Incoherence of Incoherence* (*Tuhafut al-Tuhafut*). It's a defence of philosophical reason against its critics.

Ibn Rushd's critique of al-Ghazali's view of divine agency is exemplary in terms of the kinds of argumentative techniques that he employed. He argues that al-Ghazali goes wrong by mixing up the temporal and the eternal. It is quite reasonable to suppose that temporal beings (such as humans) can decide to embark upon some course of action, then delay doing so, then begin, then stop, and then start again, but it doesn't work that way for God. Consider, for example, what follows from God's omniscience and omnipotence. God will always know the best arrangement for the universe, and He will always be able to instantiate it, so it doesn't make sense to think that He might choose not to instantiate it at a particular moment in time. To put this another way, there is nothing internal or external to His nature that might lead him to delay the moment of creation. Indeed, it isn't clear that there will even be different moments in time for God, especially if one thinks that God is present at all times.

Similar kinds of difficulties afflict al-Ghazali's position if one reflects upon God's perfection. God is eternal and unchanging. This makes it problematic to suppose that He has desires that He might act upon in the same way as human beings have desires that they act upon. The idea of desire suggests some kind of perturbation in God, which is then annulled when the desire is fulfilled. But this makes no sense, since it implies a change in God's nature – and as we have seen, God's nature is eternal and unchanging. It seems to follows then that God's acts must simply be a manifestation of His nature, and that they are not willed in the same way that human beings will their acts.

It is easy to see why this kind of argument might get an Islamic philosopher into trouble. As al-Ghazali suggested, it does seem to do away with God's agency, His freedom to choose. Although Ibn Rushd denied this particular criticism, he was aware that there was a general issue about the impact of philosophical arguments on less sophisticated believers. In his work *Decisive Treatise*, he argues that it is clear from the Qur'an that there is an obligation to attempt to understand the world through the study of philosophy.

> That the Law summons to reflection on beings, and the pursuit of knowledge about them, by the intellect is clear from several verses of the Book of God, Blessed and Exalted, such as the saying of the Exalted, 'Reflect, you have vision': this is textual authority for the obligation to use intellectual reasoning, or a combination of intellectual and legal reasoning. Another example is His saying, 'Have they not studied the kingdom of the heavens and the earth, and whatever things God has created?'. . . this is a text urging the study of the totality of beings.

However, Ibn Rushd did not think that the arguments of philosophers were suitable for general consumption. In particular, where philosophy leads to conclusions that conflict with the apparent meaning of scripture, then it should be kept from the ordinary masses. He was quite clear that there could be no *real* conflict between philosophical truth and scripture – any disagreement simply meant that an allegorical reading of scripture was required. This had long been accepted by the Muslim community as a legitimate way of proceeding, which meant that al-Ghazali, and the other critics of philosophy, were wrong to claim that philosophers were indulging in unbelief when they questioned doctrines such as the creation of the universe or bodily resurrection.

Nevertheless, Ibn Rushd did believe that in order to serve the end of the collective well-being of the Muslim community, it was necessary for teachers to modify their arguments depending upon the audience they were addressing. To attempt to teach the ordinary faithful about a higher interpretation of scripture when they do not have the conceptual apparatus to understand it almost inevitably harms their faith, and thereby affects the happiness of the community as a whole. Philosophical enquiry is sanctioned by God, but it requires the kind of talent and rigorous training that necessarily means it will be suited only to a minority of people.

Ibn Rushd's philosophical arguments on religious matters were not entirely defensive. He also developed a number of arguments in favour of the existence of God, contending that the fact that the world fits so neatly with the purposes of human beings, and the fact that all living things are clearly the work of a designer, is proof of God's reality. However, even if it ultimately fails, it is for his defence of philosophical reason, which he mounted in the face of considerable opposition, that he is rightly celebrated.

Moses Maimonides

This emphasis on the importance of reason is also found in the work of Moses Maimonides, the standout Jewish philosopher of the medieval era. Mainmonides argued that the Bible is a complex text, even when it appears simple, and that religious truth is often hard to discern. Thus, for example, he had very little time for the Bible's tendency to anthropomorphize the characteristics of God. If the Bible talks about a prophet hearing the words of God, it is not referencing an auditory phenomenon, but rather using metaphor to describe the process whereby a prophet comes to understand God's desires. Similarly, sightings of God in the Bible are not literal sightings, but rather a poetic way to talk about a certain intellectual understanding of God.

Of course, this does raise the question as to how we're supposed to identify the truths the Bible contains and know when we're meant to take something literally, as opposed to metaphorically. In *The Guide for the Perplexed*, Maimonides' greatest work, he suggests that the key here is that the revealed will of God will always be in harmony with reason. If there's a conflict between reason and the Bible, then reason holds sway, and we need to revisit the Bible to see how we have misinterpreted the words. Thus Maimonides states that if he had come to the conclusion, with Aristotle, that matter is eternal, then he would have had no difficulty in adjusting his view of the Biblical treatment of creation.

Maimonides was aware that his views were likely to be disturbing to the average believer in the street, and would perhaps precipitate crises of faith if they were disseminated too widely. Therefore, he ensured that *The Guide for the Perplexed* would not be readily accessible to people who did not have the requisite level of intellectual sophistication. The consequence is that it is a difficult work to understand, and requires a certain technical competence to be properly appreciated. Nevertheless, Maimonides is a thinker of considerable repute, his philosophical writings retain their interest for a contemporary audience, and within the Jewish tradition he has been proclaimed the 'second Moses'.

The Scholastics

As we find ourselves somewhere in the middle of the Middle Ages, it's worth pausing to reflect on a curious fact. Medieval philosophy has an appallingly bad reputation. The term 'Middle Ages' is itself the result of a bit of unkind Renaissance spin-doctoring. A number of similar expressions were coined, which reduce centuries of human history to the significance of a mere temporal bridge – the Latin *medium aevum* among them, where incidentally we also get the English word 'medieval'.

The suggestion is that between the glories of antiquity and the wonders of the modern era lies a trivial, middle age. The spin stuck. We still think of humanity as wretched in the Middle Ages – close your eyes and Monty Pythonesque peasants slapping together mounds of 'lovely filth' should come easily to mind. All was dark, cold, leech-covered and worryingly pungent. Contemporary philosophy textbooks devote long, glassy-eyed chapters to the Greeks, only to speed past the next 15 centuries with an embarrassed cough and a sentence or two, slamming on the brakes as the more familiar territory of modern philosophy appears. You can do an entire philosophy degree almost anywhere and only glance in passing at what was, in fact, a long, complex and philosophically perfectly interesting stretch of time. Why do we neglect our medieval comrades?

Part of the problem is the sheer size of the age and the diversity of the characters within it. There's debate about where to place the start and the end of medieval philosophy, but almost no matter how you do it, you're left with centuries populated by a great variety of philosophical types. If you cast the net broadly, you might locate the start with early Christians of the second and third centuries CE, who, like Augustine, were trying to bring a fledgling and still conceptually nebulous Christianity in line with the established philosophy of antiquity. At the other temporal end, perhaps you are willing to go so far as the mystical Nicholas of Cusa in the 15th century. The intervening millennium includes, as we saw in the last chapter, Christians thinking through Neoplatonism as well as Muslim philosophers analysing and commenting on Greek thoughts. Our subject in this chapter is the new shift in philosophy that occurred between 1100 and 1400 or so: the rise of the Scholastics, yet another set of philosophers up to something different from the rest. It's hard to get a handle on so much, and perhaps as a result, few make the attempt.

A second problem has to do with the fact that even to consider wading into all this, you'll have to equip yourself not just with Latin, but with the unspeakably technical vocabulary of medieval Latin – perhaps acquaint yourself with some Arabic for good measure too. You'll also have to find a way to weather the style – tortured and technical, it's not as sunny and inviting as one of Plato's dialogues. Even if you manage all that, there's just a lot of medieval philosophy out there. You can scan a few fragments and read the whole surviving output of quite a few Presocratics. But volumes and volumes of the work of individual medieval philosophers are still being assembled by those labouring in the field – many, many works are not even available in translation. Medieval philosophers did not experience writer's block. In some cases, their output is staggering.

A third problem is the subject matter of medieval philosophy – a lot of it is straight theology, and where this comes into contact with philosophy, it is sometimes an effort to find a reason to care. Can Aristotle's talk of potentiality and actuality shed light on the sense in which God is said to be three-personed? Might some conception of essence inform our notion of Christ as essentially man and essentially divine at the very same time? Is there a way to think about form and matter that clarifies the transformation of bread and wine into the body and blood of Christ in the Eucharist? Many people, even many religious people, can live full and happy lives without concerning themselves with any of this. Whether or not it sparks your interest, the fact remains that the philosophers of this age were writing for each other, not for us or even for everyday people at the time. Monks talking to other monks about things that might be of genuine interest only to monks. It's entirely possible that medieval philosophy would not speak to you even if you could read Latin.

The last and largest problem is just that many people do not see medieval philosophy as philosophy at all. It's theology, they'll say, and little else. Where reason is brought to bear, it's always simply in the service of religion. Philosophy gets pushed back behind the shadow of superstition, marched out only to secure conclusions already believed as a matter of faith. As Russell's version of this charge has it: 'The finding of arguments for a conclusion given in advance is not philosophy, but special pleading.' In his *New History of Western Philosophy*, Anthony Kenny replies:

> It is not in fact a serious charge against a philosopher to say that he is looking for good reasons for what he already believes in . . . Russell himself spent much energy seeking proofs of what he already believed: [his] *Principia Mathematica* takes hundreds of pages to prove that 1 and 1 make 2.

Medieval philosophers operated on the basis of truths secured through revelation, but many explicitly sought to push reason as far as it could go. What can reason discover on its own?

How can philosophy help us make sense of what we take to be true? Those are two fair questions, pursued not just by Russell in the last century, but by the Scholastic philosophers of the 12th century too.

The schoolmen

The Scholastics of the High and Late Middle Ages get their name from the Latin word '*scholasticus*', itself derived from the Greek word for school. The Scholastics, then, were the men of the schools, and the schools in question were initially cathedral schools, which were set up to ensure an educated clergy. By the early 13th century, however, recognizable universities were up and running in Paris and Oxford, and all the large names of this era – Aquinas, Bonaventure, Duns Scotus and William of Ockham – had a connection to one or both places. Soon full-time faculty members were teaching full-time students, using what came to be known, unimaginatively, as the Scholastic method. It consisted of lectures and disputations.

At first, lectures were nothing more than masters reading aloud from canonical texts – scripture, some second-hand Plato and bits of Aristotle, Peter Lombard's *Sentences*, the writings of the Church fathers and so on – inserting a few explanations, while students listened. No doubt far livelier were disputations, where a student was assigned a position to defend against the objections of other students, with the master resolving the matter in the end. Some masters undertook far riskier public quodlibetal disputations and stood ready to fight their corner of a question – citing authorities and producing arguments on the fly – on any subject raised by anyone in attendance. Someone emerging from this course of study would be equipped with a line-by-line acquaintance with authoritative texts, as well as a keen feel for the flow of argumentation.

As the first universities were being established, the most philosophically momentous event of the entire medieval period occurred. The works of Aristotle reappeared in the West, and absolutely everything changed. At the start of the 12th century, the only Latin translations of Aristotle available to Western thinkers amounted to just a part of his work on language and logic, and his taxonomy of the kinds of things one might know. By the middle of that century, thanks to the rediscovery of earlier translations, translations of Arabic texts, and the efforts of one James of Venice, a lot more was recovered – including the remainder of Aristotle's logical works, his physics, a treatise on the soul, and a good bit of his metaphysics and ethics. In the second half of that century, more Arabic works were translated into Latin, and scholars finally had access to the stimulating work of Islamic philosophers, their commentaries on Aristotle and treatments of Plato.

It's hard now to conceive of what this might have been like for an unsuspecting monk, head buried in the manuscripts of some dark scriptorium. Imagine being a physicist, amazed by the insights of Einstein's theory of relativity. You've studied him all of your life, then someone shows up with 40 new books written by Einstein on entirely new topics. You've got something nearer an Einsteinian system now, as well as long commentaries on it by a number of geniuses you'd never heard of, where before you had just a tiny fraction of his thinking on one or two problems. You'd fall over.

Perhaps some Scholastics did fall over, but most recovered and quickly took sides. Some tried to integrate Aristotle into Christianity, others attempted to refute the things Aristotle said that didn't seem to fit their religious doctrine, others retreated to the comparative safety of Plato, while more took up positions for and against Aristotle's various Islamic interpreters. The great reconciler of Aristotle and Christianity was Aquinas, but before we consider him, it's necessary to reverse a little and pay homage to Anselm of Canterbury, the so-called Father of Scholasticism.

The greatest conceivable being

Anselm is a kind of intermediate figure, with part of his head in Neoplatonism and the rest immersed in the attempt to square reason and faith in the particular manner characteristic of the age that came after him. But he does not operate with the later distinction between revelatory truth and rational truth specifically in mind. In fact, famously, he blends the two, claiming that understanding requires religious belief. As he puts it, 'I do not seek to understand that I may believe; but I believe that I may understand. For I believe this too, that unless I believe, I shall not understand.'

Anselm wrote about truth, free will, evil, the Trinity, logic, God's attributes, as well as the question of why God had to become a man, but he's most famous for inventing a unique kind of proof of the existence of God, called the ontological argument. The argument has had an energetic history, and, almost a thousand years later, it still won't lie down. It was recast by Descartes and again by Leibniz in the modern period, and it was even trotted out by Hegel. It has had more recent reformulations in terms of modern modal logic, the logic of possibility and necessity, notably by the mathematician Kurt Gödel and the contemporary philosopher Alvin Plantinga. Detractors include big philosophical guns as diverse as Kant and Hume, both of whom raise objections they take as decisive. Many people get the feeling that something has to be wrong with the argument, but it's not easy to point to the trouble.

The argument, in all its forms, attempts to secure the existence of God with reflection just on the idea of God. Other kinds of argument begin with the existence of something out there in the world – perhaps with such things as cause and motion, as we'll see in a moment with Aquinas. But Anselm, uniquely, starts with nothing but the idea of God. There are easy versions and hard versions of the ontological argument. We'll start with an easy one.

God is that being than which no greater can be thought. But that being than which no greater can be thought must exist not just in the mind, but also outside the mind. It is greater to exist outside the mind as a real thing than merely inside the mind as an idea. So God exists, not only as an idea, but also outside the mind.

The crucial claims here are that there are different ways to exist – merely mentally or actually out in the world – and one of those ways is somehow greater. What is greater, a bacon sandwich in your mind or a real bacon sandwich that actually exists? Similarly, if God just existed in our minds, we could think of something greater, namely God really existing out there in the world too. So if God is that being than which no greater can be thought, He must exist in reality. Poof! God is defined into existence.

Anselm's actual argument is much more tricky but stronger than this version. There are a number of interpretations, but try this one. Believers, Anselm says, hold that God is the greatest conceivable being, something than which nothing greater can be conceived. Against the believers, he lines up the Fool of the Psalms, who says in his heart, 'There is no God.' The Fool denies that God exists but still understands what he hears when he hears the expression 'something than which nothing greater can be conceived'. The atheist, in other words, admits that the notion of the greatest conceivable being can exist in the understanding but denies that there's anything more to it than that. There is no greatest conceivable being in reality.

But, Anselm argues, this being than which nothing greater can be conceived can't just exist in the understanding, because in denying its worldly reality the Fool is caught in a contradiction. Weirdly, the Fool is stuck with the preposterous claim that she can conceive of a greater being than that being than which none greater can be conceived. As Anselm puts it:

> If that than which nothing greater can be conceived exists in the understanding alone, that very thing than which nothing greater can be conceived is a thing than which something greater can be conceived. But this is impossible. Therefore it is beyond doubt that there exists, both in the understanding and in reality, a being than which nothing greater can be conceived.

The earliest and possibly the best critic of the ontological argument was a contemporary of Anselm, a Benedictine monk called Gaunilo. His reply, *On Behalf of the Fool*, aims to show that there is something untoward going on in Anselm's thinking, because by parodying his logic, one can populate the world with all sorts of great things that plainly do not exist. For example, that island than which no greater can be conceived must exist. If we deny this, we'd be stuck in the same sort of contradiction as the Fool in Anselm's argument. But there is no such island. So there must be something amiss with Anselm's reasoning. Replies are of course possible; in fact Anselm did reply to Gaunilo, and this partly explains the longevity of the debate. Most of the other long-lasting arguments of the Scholastic period are owed to Aquinas, but before we turn to him it would be a mistake to tell the story of the scholastics without mentioning what's probably the most famous love story of the times.

Abelard and Héloïse

Abelard was born into a noble family around 1079 in a small town in Brittany. He had an astonishing aptitude for logic and particularly argumentation – it's said that he never lost a verbal dispute, sometimes wiping the floor with his own teacher. He walked away from his inheritance to study philosophy, initially under Roscelin of Compiègne. Roscelin, incidentally, is credited as the founder of nominalism (from the Latin *nomen* or name), the view that universals are only names, not independently existing things.

Abelard, no doubt influenced by Roscelin, went on to defend his own brand of nominalism, arguing for a reductive view of not just universals, but nearly everything. He was not a realist about propositions, relations or events in the past and the future. But he was most at home with logic, and his *Sic et Non* (*Yes and No*) presents the logical case for and against nearly 160 propositions. He decides none of them, revelling just in lining up the arguments themselves. The book set the combative style and tone of philosophy right up to the Renaissance and beyond.

But he is remembered outside of philosophy not for all this, but for his disastrous affair with Héloïse. Abelard was an incredibly charismatic teacher, attracting crowds of students, drawn to his wit and devastating debating style. He took the post of master at the Notre Dame School and contrived to become the personal tutor to Héloïse, a budding scholar in her own right, but also a beautiful young girl – very young, in fact more than 20 years younger than Abelard. She was also the niece of a formidable canon, Flubert. Abelard and Héloïse soon formed a romantic connection. Flubert discovered the affair and, enraged, demanded that they end it. But they continued to meet clandestinely, and Héloïse became pregnant. Abelard insisted on marriage, Flubert relented, but Héloïse was against it, as she feared the scandal would wreck Abelard's career. They secretly married and had a child, Astrolabe, and (there are conflicting versions of the story) Héloïse retreated to a convent. Uncle Flubert, thinking that Abelard had sent Héloïse away to be rid of her, settled on an alarmingly permanent solution to the problem. As Abelard puts it in his aptly titled *The History of My Calamity*:

> Violently incensed, they laid a plot against me, and one night while I all unsuspecting was asleep in a secret room in my lodgings, they broke in with the help of one of my servants whom they had bribed. There they had vengeance on me with a most cruel and most shameful punishment, such as astounded the whole world; for they cut off those parts of my body with which I had done that which was the cause of their sorrow.

Abelard fled, becoming a monk in the monastery of Saint Denis, and Héloïse withdrew to the convent of Argenteuil, where she eventually became prioress. They continued to correspond, initially romantically but eventually on scholarly matters. There is debate about where they are buried. There is a monument to them in the cemetery of Père Lachaise in Paris, and it's likely that their bodies are there, side by side. Letters are sometimes left at the crypt, written by unrequited lovers.

The Dumb Ox

Thomas Aquinas was born into Italian nobility, and had the reasonable life of a Benedictine monk ahead of him, when he joined the Dominican order instead. His family was horrified. The Dominicans, unlike the more upscale Benedictines, were a mendicant or begging order, surviving by preaching in the vulgar vernacular and begging for alms. His parents, hoping he might change his mind, had him kidnapped and imprisoned for more than a year in the family castle. Aquinas got on with writing logical treatises, until his brothers tried to make him see the error of his ways by helpfully inserting a prostitute into his cell. He chased her out with a stick from the fire. The family realized then that he was a lost cause and released him.

Aquinas became a student of the genius and polymath Albert the Great, and it was around this time that his rotundity and shy, plodding manner led his charming fellow pupils to give him the nickname 'the Dumb Ox'. Albert, however, spotted his quiet pupil's intellect and predicted that the Dumb Ox's 'bellowing in doctrine will one day resound throughout the world'. That it did.

Aquinas wrote commentaries on the gospels, Aristotle, Boethius, Peter Lombard's *Sentences*, and long treatises in the style of disputations on nearly every theological and philosophical topic imaginable. He produced two vast *Summations*, summaries of religious doctrine. One, *Summation of the Catholic Faith Against the Unbelievers*, is written, as you might expect, for missionaries hoping to convert infidels or those in dialogue with Jewish or Islamic thinkers. The other, unfinished work is *Summation of Theology*, a kind of encyclopedic treatment of doctrine for those within the faith. It is said that Aquinas paced back and forth between three scribes, dictating three different philosophical treatises to them at the same time. He produced around eight million words – the unfinished *Summation* alone is five volumes – but then something, perhaps a mystical experience, changed him. He said, 'All that I have written seems to me like straw compared to what has been revealed to me.' He did not write another word, and died a few months later.

Unlike many other medieval theologians, reeling from the rediscovery of Aristotle, Aquinas didn't simply reject the parts of Aristotle's philosophy that didn't fit with Christianity (the so-called 'Errors of Aristotle'). He recognized, following Albert, that Aristotle's arguments were persuasive, and so he had to find a way to reconcile philosophy and faith in a manner that gives philosophy its due. As Pope Leo XIII puts it: '[C]arefully distinguishing reason from Faith, as is right, and yet joining them together in a harmony of friendship, he so guarded the rights of each, and so watched over the dignity of each.' Aquinas actually ends up defending Aristotle in many places, even where he is in conflict with religious doctrine. For example, he shows that Aristotle is right to think that the world could have been eternal – God could have set things up that way, had he so chosen – even though revelation tells us the world in fact has a beginning in time. Aristotle might have been wrong, but he wasn't being unreasonable. It's a fine line to walk, and because not everyone could follow Aquinas' thinking, it got him into posthumous trouble.

The large insight Aquinas borrows from Aristotle is his claim that, for any discipline, one must recognize the difference between what is assumed and what is proven. When engaged in theology with fellow believers, one set of premises is relevant. When arguing against the unbelievers about such things as the existence of God, however, there are still premises in common. These are deployed by Aquinas in his famous Five Ways.

The Five Ways

Aquinas argues that there are five ways to prove the existence of God, rooted in propositions, he claims, that everyone has to accept – facts about the world all around us. From these, he argues backwards to God as the reason or cause of each evident fact. The five things accepted by all are the existence of movement, causal sequences, the dependency of some things on others, the fact that some qualities can be compared on a scale of degrees (some people are less good than others, for example), and the way things in nature appear to be goal-directed. Here, for example, is Aquinas' third way:

> We find in nature things that are possible to be and not to be . . . but it is impossible for these always to exist, for that which is possible not to be at some time is not. Therefore, if everything is possible not to be, then at one time there could have been nothing in existence. Now if this were true, even now there would be nothing in existence, because that which does not exist only begins to exist by something already existing . . . Therefore, not all beings are merely possible, but there must exist something the existence of which is necessary . . . This all men speak of as God.

The idea is that the things we see around us are merely possible, contingent – they come to be and pass away. If everything were just possible, at some point everything might not be, might cease to exist. But if, at some point, there were nothing, there would still be nothing, yet plainly there are plenty of contingent things all around us. So there must be something that doesn't exist in this wishy-washy contingent way, something that exists necessarily, that cannot pass away, and that thing must be God.

The other four ways operate much the same. The things around us are moving. Whatever moves is moved by something else – there's no such thing as spontaneous motion. But this chain of movement can't go back for ever, because movement itself would become stalled in an infinite regress. Nothing would be moving now, but plainly things are moving, so there must be some first Unmoved Mover back at the start that got everything going. Similarly, reflection on the idea that all effects have a cause leads back to a first Uncaused Cause at the start of the chain. Degrees of goodness or nobility only make sense if we posit something perfectly good as a supreme standard by which all such things are judged – Aquinas concludes that such a perfect being can only be God. Finally, the Aristotelian thought that purpose is everywhere, even in unintelligent nature, leads Aquinas to an Intelligence behind all the goal-directed behaviour we see in the natural world.

Because of his affinity for Aristotle's potentially heretical philosophy, Aquinas' works were condemned for a time after his death. It wasn't until Pope Leo's fine words in his favour in 1879 that Aquinas finally became the official philosopher of Catholicism and enjoyed a revival that, although it has had some blips, is still under way. It took a while for Aquinas to be recognized, and this is partly because of the times that followed him. The Renaissance was not at all kind to the schoolmen.

4
Knowledge

Renaissance and Enlightenment

The Scholasticism of the previous chapter has not been treated well by history. Part of the problem has to do with the absurdly parochial nature of many of its concerns, which has been satirized in the idea that the Scholastic philosophers spent much of their time worrying about such things as how many angels it is possible to get on the head of a pin. Although it is likely nobody considered that precise issue, when you consider that Aquinas' *Summation of Theology* contains 358 questions and answers about angels, you can see the point of the objection. Isaac D'Israeli, an 18th-century man of letters (and father of Benjamin), made the same point by listing the sorts of questions the Scholastics concerned themselves with when wondering about the virgin birth:

Others again debated – Whether the angel Gabriel appeared to the Virgin Mary in the shape of a serpent, or a dove, or a man, or of a woman? Did he seem to be young or old? In what dress was he? Was his garment white or of two colours? Was his linen clean or foul? Did he appear in the morning, noon, or evening? What was the colour of the Virgin Mary's hair? Was she acquainted with the mechanic and liberal arts? Had she a thorough knowledge of the Book of Sentences, and all it contains? . . . But these are only trifling matters: they also agitated, Whether when during her conception the Virgin was seated, Christ too was seated; and whether when she lay down, Christ also lay down?

All pretty entertaining stuff, of course, but there is a serious point here. This concern with theological minutiae was bought at the expense of wider philosophical enquiry. Philosophy during the heyday of Scholasticism effectively became a branch of theology. This is not to say that the Scholastic philosophers were not interested in reason or rational argument. As we noted in the previous chapter, many Scholastics sought to push reason as far as it could go. But nevertheless it is true that *where* they were interested in pushing reason was determined by an almost exclusive interest in theological matters.

This was not a happy circumstance for the prospect of furthering human knowledge. If you're spending your time worrying about whether or not Jesus was a hermaphrodite, then the chances are you're looking in the wrong place if you want to discover philosophical truths. The contrast between the narrowness of focus of the Scholastics compared to the breadth of interest of the earliest Greek philosophers, for example, is striking. Russell argues that after the death of

Democritus, philosophy lost much of its vigour, independence and childlike zest, a process that was exacerbated by the re-entrenchment of popular superstition that occurred after the deaths of Plato and Aristotle. The rediscovery of Aristotle by the Scholastics meant that there was something genuinely novel about the new Catholic philosophical orthodoxy, but its obsession with theological 'truth' meant that it was, in effect, philosophy done in a straitjacket.

It is generally agreed that the high point of Scholasticism occurred in the latter part of the 13th century, at which time anything resembling a scientific sensibility was almost entirely absent from the intellectual scene. If you lived at this time, then inevitably you had very little idea about how the world actually worked. So, for example, the Ptolemaic view, espoused by Aristotle, that the Earth was at the centre of the universe was endorsed almost without exception. The idea that matter is made of the four 'classical' elements – earth, water, air and fire – was also widely accepted, at least in the Western world.

However, it would be a mistake to think that the universal acceptance of erroneous belief is synonymous with the absence of a scientific sensibility, since science is not a shopping list of correct beliefs, but rather a method of finding out about the world that emphasizes empirical observation and measurement, prediction, testability and the absolute revisability of all truth claims. It is in falling short in these terms that the intellectual atmosphere of the Late Middle Ages was most antithetical to the scientific world view. Crucially, though, as we move into the 15th and 16th centuries, things begin to change.

Renaissance humanism

Perhaps the first sign that the world was changing was the emergence in the 14th century of what has become known as Renaissance humanism. This was not humanism in the sense that we understand the term in the present day. The Renaissance humanists were not by any stretch of the imagination secularists, and although they were much more focused on the practical affairs of individuals than their Scholastic contemporaries, they certainly wouldn't have believed that human beings were the *only* source of value in the world, as many present-day humanists do. Renaissance humanism properly understood was a reaction against Scholasticism that stressed the importance of the 'humanities' – grammar, rhetoric, poetics, moral philosophy and history – in the education of a citizenry. In general, the early humanist thinkers favoured a much less technical and regimented approach than that of the schoolmen, valuing literary flair and rhetorical brilliance rather than strict deductive reasoning.

Perhaps the defining characteristic of humanism was its celebration of the prose and poetry of classical antiquity. This led the humanists to rediscover many Greek classical texts, which they translated into Latin, thereby reintroducing them to a Western audience. This precipitated a general broadening out of the hitherto narrow Aristotelian focus of Scholastic philosophy, and in particular to a renewed interest in Platonism, Stoicism and Epicureanism.

The fact that the humanists were steeped in classical Latin and Greek also led them to be highly critical of the late-medieval translations of Aristotle (and others) that the Scholastics relied upon. These were denounced variously as barbaric, arid and incomprehensible, and new translations were produced, written in a deliberately elegant style, many of which, for better or worse, amounted to new interpretations.

The combined effect of these developments was to loosen the grip the Church had on intellectual life, with the consequence that a space opened up for philosophers to challenge the established orthodoxy. Thus, for example, under pressure from arguments advanced by Renaissance philosophers such as Pomponazzi, one finds Church theologians in the 14th century abandoning the terrain of philosophy when it came to issues such as the immortality of the soul. This marked the start of a process that saw philosophy becoming detached from theology, and beginning to establish itself as a relatively autonomous discipline.

Machiavelli's Prince

If the humanist philosophers were able to carve out a space for the emergence of an independent philosophy, then it is fair to say that Niccolò Machiavelli did the same for political science. Prior to his arrival on the scene, it was generally accepted that the virtuous political leader had to behave morally at all times, embodying the virtues of justice and mercy in his conduct. This meant politics could in some aspects be treated as a subset of moral philosophy: if you wanted to know how political leaders *should* behave then you had only to consider the morality of their actions. Machiavelli rejected this view, arguing instead that a political leader, or prince, 'must not mind incurring the scandal of those vices without which it would be difficult to save the state'. By separating out issues of morality and leadership in this fashion, he took the first steps in establishing political science as an independent discipline.

Machiavelli was born in Florence on 3 May 1469, and first came to notice as a youthful Florentine diplomat. His world was that of grubby politics, and he had close-up and personal experience of the strengths and weaknesses of some of the major political figures of his day. This put him in a great position to write what is now seen as his signature work, *The Prince*, which is a study in the art of leadership.

The Prince was first published in 1532, some seven years after Machiavelli's death, and it was initially well received. However, it wasn't too long before people began to grumble about Machiavelli's claim that the decision-making of political leaders should not be governed by considerations of morality. This claim was a little shocking, since it suggested to many that Machiavelli was some kind of amoralist, that he wasn't really interested in what political leaders ought to do, but only in identifying those strategies that would maximize their chances of securing and maintaining political power and glory.

There is certainly an element of truth to this view. It is not mere happenstance that Machiavelli quite happily professed admiration for the brutal cunning that Cesare Borgia employed in disposing of his political adversaries, citing with approval how Borgia used deception in order to lure the leaders of the Orsini, a faction that had been plotting against him, to the town of Sinigaglia, where he promptly murdered them all. Machiavelli was quite clear that he did not accept the traditional conception of political leadership – as, for example, outlined in Cicero's *De Officiis* – which held that a rational person will always act virtuously if they want to secure honour and glory:

> . . . there is such a gap between how one lives and how one ought to live that anyone who abandons what is done for what ought to be done learns his ruin rather than his preservation: for a man who wishes to make a vocation of being good at all times will come to ruin among so many who are not good. Hence it is necessary for a prince who wishes to maintain his position to learn how not to be good, and to use this knowledge or not to use it according to necessity.

The basic thesis Machiavelli is advancing here is that people are no good; therefore, virtuous or not, certain styles of leadership just aren't going to work. If it is true, as he believed, that people are 'ungrateful, fickle, simulators and deceivers, avoiders of danger, greedy for gain', then this imposes a limit on what strategies a leader can expect to be effective. Thus, for example, the prince who builds his power entirely on what he sees as the people's love for him is almost certainly going to be abandoned when the going gets tough:

> . . . men are less hesitant about harming someone who makes himself loved than one who makes himself feared because love is held together by a chain of obligation which, since men are a sorry lot, is broken on every occasion in which their own self-interest is concerned; but fear is held together by a dread of punishment which will never abandon you.

However, though there is something right about the charge that Machiavelli's views on leadership are amoral, there is also something wrong about it. Not least, Machiavelli seems to suggest that if you do the moral calculus right, you'll notice that *effective* leadership has more going for it in moral terms than supposedly virtuous leadership. For example, when considering whether it is better for a prince to rule by mercy or by cruelty, he argues that the merciful prince will often bring greater harm to his people by tolerating disorder than the cruel prince who scares his people into harmony. He employs a similar kind of argument to show that excessive generosity is counterproductive: while an extravagant display of spending might bring popularity in the short term, in the long term it will entail higher taxation, and a prince will end up resented and disliked as a result.

There is also a more general way in which Machiavelli is innocent of the charge of amoralism. He actually *did* think that leaders should strive for honour and glory, in the sense that he believed they should aim to create a legacy that would be justly celebrated. It's just that he didn't think this was attainable by always acting virtuously. In fact, it is precisely a measure of a prince's *virtú* that he is willing to do whatever it takes to achieve his goals. However, this does not mean that absolutely anything goes: cruelty for cruelty's sake is ruled out, for example:

> Well used are those cruelties . . . that are carried out in a single stroke, done out of necessity to protect oneself, and are not continued but instead converted into the greatest possible benefits for the subjects. Badly used are those cruelties which, although being few at the outset, grow with the passing of time instead of disappearing.

History hasn't yet quite figured out how to view Machiavelli. From the 16th century onwards, he has been condemned by many as an advocate of evil and supporter of tyranny; Cardinal Pole, for example, said of *The Prince* that it was written with 'the finger of the Devil'. Other people, however, take a different view: some praise him for realizing that politics isn't about the merits of competing conceptions of virtue, for example, but rather about real political actors playing out their roles in real situations with all the messiness that this implies; and others see him as an almost revolutionary figure, standing up against the strictures of authority and established morality. There is no doubting his influence, of course, and even today he is both celebrated and condemned as the man who insisted that successful political leaders need both the strength of a lion and the cunning of a fox.

The scientific turn

Part of the novelty of Machiavelli's approach was his insistence that political ideas have to be rooted in a proper understanding of what actually occurs on the ground. It doesn't matter how complex a theory of political leadership you construct, or how subtle an analysis of virtue you develop, if your ideas are not responsive to the way people actually live their lives and to the lessons of history, then it's likely that your conclusions are going to be wrong. This turning back towards the world after the extreme rationalism of the Scholastics was funda-mental to the emergence of the new scientific sensibility, and it found its most important and systematic expression in the work of Francis Bacon.

By all accounts, Bacon, who was born into minor nobility in Elizabethan England, was not an easy personality. His political career was hampered in its early stages because Queen Elizabeth apparently did not relish his company, and he was known for his rapacious ambition, which was driven at least in part by the fact that he was always in debt as a result of his fondness for a lavish lifestyle. Nevertheless, despite his personality quirks, he not only rose to the position of Lord Chancellor, but also developed what is probably rightly considered the first proper statement of the scientific method.

Bacon outlines his ideas about science, or 'natural philosophy' as it was termed then, in *Novum Organum*, the second part of a planned six-part work, *Magna Instauratio* (*Great Instauration*), which remained unfinished at his death. His aim is to establish the foundations for 'sure proven knowledge', and his hope is to acquire mastery over nature. This is worth emphasizing. Bacon is not motivated by the idea that there is intrinsic value in finding things out about the world. He does not believe that knowledge should be pursued for its own sake. Rather, his aim is to get us into a position where we are able to transform the world in the interests of the common good – hence the catchphrase commonly attributed to him, 'knowledge is power'. Moreover, there seems to have been a religious dimension to his ambition. With the fall of Adam, mankind had forfeited its dominion over nature. Natural philosophy, properly conducted, could regain it.

Bacon begins *Novum Organum* by detailing four sorts of errors, the 'false idols' that we tend to fall into when we attempt to understand the natural world: idols of the tribe, idols of the cave, idols of the marketplace and idols of the theatre. These errors sound remarkably familiar, even today.

The idols of the tribe are errors rooted in human nature itself, affecting everybody equally. Bacon means such things as the tendency of the human intellect to impose order on sensory experience where there is no order to be found in nature; what modern psychologists call 'confirmation bias', which is the tendency to focus selectively on evidence that supports one's ideas; and wishful thinking, that is, believing things to be true because one wants them to be. Bacon cautions us:

> It is not true that the human senses are the measure of things; for all perceptions . . . reflect the perceiver rather than the world. The human intellect is like a distorting mirror, which receives light-rays irregularly and so mixes its own nature with the nature of things, which it distorts.

The idols of the cave are errors that we are prone to make as individuals, based on our particular physical and mental make-up. This is a bit of a catch-all category, including such things as the tendency to overgeneralize a theoretical approach or explanation; the fact that we find it difficult to steer a middle ground between a fondness for tradition and a fondness for novelty; and the problem of striking a balance between focusing on differences and focusing on resemblances. We have a tendency to prefer our own familiar view of the world, which consequently blinds us to other possibilities.

The errors of the marketplace are the distortions that

language imposes on our thinking. Bacon argues that words have a power of their own, which infects the intellect, thereby rendering philosophy and the sciences 'sophistical and idle'. He points specifically to the fact that there are words that refer to things that do not exist; and words that have multiple and ambiguous meanings.

Finally, there are the idols of the theatre, which are errors derived from traditional and corrupt philosophical systems. He attacks, in particular, philosophies that are sophistical, inadequately empirical and, worst of all, superstitious.

Happily, there is a ready solution at hand:

> The course I propose for the discovery of sciences is such as leaves but little to the acuteness and strength of wits, but places all wits and understandings nearly on a level. For as in the drawing of a straight line or a perfect circle, much depends on the steadiness and practice of the hand, but if with the aid of a rule or compass, little or nothing; so it is exactly with my plan.

Bacon's eliminative induction

The course that Bacon proposes science should follow relies on induction, which is the practice of drawing one general conclusion from the observation of many specific instances. However, he does not have in mind the sort of simple induction that had characterized natural philosophy up to this point – which he declared puerile. He has something much more sophisticated in mind. A simple example will suffice to illustrate how induction can vary in its level of sophistication.

Imagine you are a budding scientist in the prehistoric world, and you're interested in what causes water to boil. You travel from camp to camp, and you notice that boiling water is always associated with the presence of fire. You conclude, therefore, that fire is the cause of boiling water, and you're hailed as a brilliant scientist. This is a very simple example of induction: you observe multiple instances of a phenomenon, and you draw a general conclusion.

However, one day you're travelling slightly further afield and you come across a previously undiscovered tribe. While visiting their camp, you notice they have a large metal contraption they call an 'electric cooker', upon which a large receptacle is placed, which turns out to contain boiling water. As far as you can tell, there is no fire present, which means that your previous conclusion that fire is the cause of boiling water was in a certain way flawed, since it is possible for water to boil in the *absence* of fire. You conclude, therefore, that there must be something common to both fire and the cooker that causes the water to boil.

This is also a fairly simple kind of induction, but it shows that if you add a layer of complexity, in this case the fact that water can boil in the absence of what previously appeared to be a necessary condition of its boiling (the presence of fire), then you get a more finely grained understanding of the phenomenon in question. Bacon's idea is that a highly sophisticated form of induction, which takes account of the circumstances in which a particular phenomenon appears, and the circumstances in which it does *not* appear, can function as the bedrock of a reliable science. In particular, it should be possible to identify all the circumstances in which a particular phenomenon occurs (listing these on a table of presence); the most significant circumstances in which it does not occur (totted up on a table of absence); and the circumstances in which it increases or decreases (written down on a table of comparison). In this way, one should be able to uncover the cause-and-effect relationships that govern the things that make up the natural world.

Bacon illustrates his point using the example of heat. Suppose we have noticed that water is normally inert, but it boils at high temperatures and freezes at low temperatures. On the basis of these observations, we might hypothesize that other liquids will behave in the same way in the presence and absence of heat. So we could try boiling oil. Or freezing mercury. After a while, given enough observations, we'd hopefully be in a position to construct a general law describing the behaviour of heat in liquids. Bacon argues that the laws of nature form a kind of pyramid of increasing coverage, and our understanding and control of things increases the more laws we discover. This is not science as we know it today, which in a way is less ambitious. But it is much more than the chaotic investigations characteristic of Bacon's day. And it is certainly recognizable as something well on its way to science as we understand it.

Galileo's trial

It would be remiss to talk about the emergence of the new scientific sensibility without saying something about one of the signature events of the rise of modern science, namely, the 1633 trial of Galileo Galilei.

The background to this trial was a dispute over whether the Earth or the Sun is at the centre of the universe. The Catholic Church, at this time overwhelmingly the dominant force in large parts of Europe, was committed to the Ptolemaic view, endorsed by Aristotle, that the Sun, and all the stars, rotated around a stationary Earth. This view had come under pressure in the middle of the 16th century, when Nicolaus Copernicus published *On the Revolutions of the Celestial Orbs*, in which he argued that the Sun was at the centre of the universe, and the Earth, rotating on its own axis, orbited around the Sun once every year.

At first, Copernicus' theory was not taken too seriously, but with the invention of the telescope in 1609, Galileo was able to make a series of observations that seemed to confirm Copernicus' idea, and he began to argue for it in public. Not everybody was happy about this. In 1615, a Father Lorini alerted the Roman Inquisition to Galileo's activities, claiming that his ideas were 'suspicious' and 'presumptuous', and needed to be investigated. The eventual consequence was that the Catholic Church declared the Copernican model to be 'heretical' and Galileo was formally admonished.

For a while, the issue died down: Galileo busied himself with other matters, and the wider Copernican movement was pretty much intimidated into silence. However, things began to change in 1623, when a new pope, said to be sympathetic to the sciences, was elected. This provided the impetus for Galileo to begin work on *Dialogue Concerning the Two Chief World Systems*. This was finally published in 1632, and it featured a debate between Salviati, who argues for the Copernican view, and Simplico, who remains obstinately committed to the old Ptolemaic model. It is clear that Salviati is the mouthpiece for Galileo's own views, and the reader is supposed to conclude that the Copernican model accurately describes the universe.

This did not go down well with the Catholic Church. Pope Urban VIII commissioned an investigation, which came down against Galileo, and then passed the case on to the Inquisition. In April 1633, Galileo, now nearly 70 years old, travelled to Rome to appear before Father Firenzuola, the Commissary-General of the Inquisition. He was found 'vehemently suspect of heresy', required to 'abjure, curse and detest' his heretical opinions, and sentenced to house arrest for the remainder of his life. His book, *Dialogue Concerning the Two Chief World Systems*, was added to the Church's list of prohibited publications.

A popular legend has it that Galileo, on being confronted by the Inquisition, muttered the phrase, 'And yet it moves' (about the Earth). Unfortunately, there is no reason to think this actually occurred. It is much more likely that he was intimidated into acquiescence. Indeed, his own words testify to the outcome:

I affirm, therefore, on my conscience, that I do not now hold the condemned opinion and have not held it since the decision of the authorities . . . I am here in your hands – do with me what you please.

The Catholic Church did not formally drop its general opposition to heliocentrism until the 1820s; and it wasn't until late into the 20th century that it finally apologized for the wrong it had done to Galileo Galilei.

Reason

There are at least two ways to come to know something. Maybe most of what we know depends on our sensory experience of the world. You know what the weather is like where you are, you know about the contents of the room that you're in, and you might have an idea of what's going on next door – all because of what you can see, hear, smell, touch and, if you're adventurous, taste all around you. But sometimes you can know something just by thinking about it. Good examples of this slightly weird sort of knowledge are logical laws, and perhaps the most famous one is the law of non-contradiction. Here's one of Aristotle's versions of it: opposite assertions cannot be true at the same time. Think about that for a moment. Is it true?

It almost has to be true, doesn't it? Bear in mind that Aristotle doesn't mean subjective opposites like hot and cold, where maybe you can imagine someone finding a bucket of water hot and another person finding it cold – so in a sense the bucket is both hot and cold. He means that for any positive proposition (p), there's some opposite proposition that asserts its negation (not p). There's a light in the window. There is not a light in the window. These sentences can't both be true at the same time. It looks like any p and not p can't both be true at once.

But how do we know this? What evidence might we muster for it? Sensation just doesn't seem up to it. You need to have seen some windows to understand the sentences, but that's not the point. The question is, how do you know that the law of non-contradiction is true? Some people say that they can tell that it's true just by thinking about it – by thinking about what a contradiction is, what a proposition is, and maybe what truth means. It's hard to think that any other sort of evidence could possibly count. Would it make sense to try to prove this law by going out and looking at a lot of windows?

Maybe you just thought about the law of non-contradiction and 'saw' that it was true, you had a kind of rational intuition, and all this happened independently of any particular experience. That's not to say that experience is entirely irrelevant to your seeing that the law of non-contradiction is true – maybe someone born with no capacity for sensation at all could never have the law of non-contradiction in mind. But the evidence you have for this law, the way you can just 'see' its truth, seems to have nothing at all to do with real seeing or with anything your senses might convey to you. Reason does the job on its own.

Rationalism is a catch-all for views that hold, to one degree or another, that some truths can be known independently of experience in this way. Empiricism is the contrasting view that everything we know ultimately originates from our experience of the world. Modern philosophers are usefully divided into rationalists and empiricists, and we'll take up the rationalists in this chapter and the empiricists in the next. We'll start with and focus on René Descartes, who is rightly called the father of modern philosophy. He had something to do with the birth of modern science too.

Modern philosophy itself really is a new phase in human thinking. The modern philosophers, particularly Descartes, perhaps buoyed up by humanism and the new science of their day, deliberately distanced themselves from medieval riffs on Plato and Aristotle. They did so sometimes discreetly, anonymously and often posthumously – the Church could make things extremely unpleasant for heretics – but for all the caution, the moderns were striking out in new directions. Even so, in departing from the ancients, there's a sense in which modern philosophers were doing exactly what the ancients themselves did. For the first time since Aristotle, philosophers tried to understand the world afresh, building up whole philosophical systems, setting out what they actually thought instead of merely trying to understand those who preceded them. This new age produced some of the greatest philosophers in history: among them the rationalists René Descartes, Baruch Spinoza and Gottfried Wilhelm Leibniz, and the empiricists John Locke, George Berkeley and David Hume. As Scholasticism faded into the background, philosophers had the freedom to think in a way not enjoyed since antiquity. Conceptually, the good times were rolling once again.

The proper method

Descartes was born in 1596 in a town that's now named after him, just south of Tours in France. He was instructed by Jesuits and received a thoroughly Scholastic education, but emerged unsatisfied. The teachings of the Jesuits 'contained no point that was not disputed and hence doubtful'. Doubt bothered Descartes. He would have hated sitting through a Scholastic disputation. You can think of his philosophy as an attempt to be free of doubt, and to secure, once and for all, certain knowledge of the world.

Descartes prepared for life as a lawyer but quickly saw that it wasn't for him. He became a soldier and then something of a wanderer, 'mixing with people of diverse temperaments and ranks, gathering various experiences, testing myself in the situations which fortune offered me'. Fortune offered him a number of testing situations with people of diverse ranks, including the experience of running up impressive gambling debts and fighting a duel over a romantic connection. After all this excitement, he sequestered himself in Holland for many years, pursuing mathematics, science and philosophy. His work in mathematics was particularly fruitful, and among other things he paved the way for analytical geometry. Cartesian coordinates are named after him.

The culmination of his efforts is a large treatise called *The World*, which lays out a general system that Descartes hoped might supersede Aristotle's physics and metaphysics, securing a firm foundation for the new sciences. Among other things it defends a heliocentric view of the solar system. But just as he was about to publish, Galileo came under censure for propounding the same view, and with great reluctance Descartes put the project on hold. Instead, he published a sample of his work from the book, prefacing it with a 'Discourse on the Method of Properly Conducting One's Reason and of Seeking the Truth in the Sciences'. The sample chapters and *The World* have since faded in the shadow of that preface, which has become the free-standing *Discourse on Method*. It's among the most agreeably readable of philosophy's classic texts, written to interest and convince not just theologians and scientists, but the powdered and cultured frequenters of Parisian salons. For the first time since antiquity, a philosopher made an effort to speak to everyday people. The book is a page-turner. You're swept up by Descartes' hope and enthusiasm – you're right there with him in his search for the truth.

Careful reasoning is the essence of his method, and his model is mathematics. The idea is that if one proceeds carefully, slowly, from a secure foundation, bit by bit, truth by truth, in the manner of a mathematical proof from definitions and axioms to theorems, reason alone will free us from uncertainty and lead us to all the truths there are to know. He identifies four rules for the direction of thought:

> The first was never to accept anything as true that I did not know to be evidently so . . . to include in my judgements nothing more than what presented itself so clearly and so distinctly to my mind that I might have no occasion to place it in doubt.
>
> The second, to divide each of the difficulties that I was examining into as many parts as might be possible and necessary in order to solve it.
>
> The third, to conduct my thoughts in an orderly way, beginning with the simplest objects and the easiest to know, in order to climb gradually . . .
>
> And the last, everywhere to make such complete enumerations and such general reviews that I would be sure to have omitted nothing.

Through long chains of careful reflection, accepting only propositions revealed by 'the divine light of reason', Descartes holds that there is no truth so hidden or distant that we won't eventually uncover it. Here, then, is the rationalist's method for discovering everything there is to know about the world and our place in it.

Unshakeable foundations

Four years after publishing *Discourse on Method*, Descartes produced *Meditations on First Philosophy*, a book aimed not at those in the salons but at theologians and men of letters. It's an attempt to use his method 'to establish something firm and lasting in the sciences'. The book is not so much a break from the philosophy that came before it as a demolition job, an attempt to begin afresh by blasting away everything and starting again from scratch. It's written as a series of meditations over six days, which read like diary entries. Each night, as Descartes sits beside the fire, he carries on a few steps further.

He begins by seeking an indubitable truth that might serve as the secure foundation for a new metaphysics and, built on top of that, a new science. If he can find any grounds for scepticism, the belief in question cannot be beyond doubt, and therefore it cannot serve as a proper foundation. Since the stakes are so high, what might be ridiculous speculation in another context counts as solid ground for doubt now. After all, nothing less than absolutely indubitable truths can serve as a foundation for certain knowledge.

The place to start, he argues, is with sensation. Almost everything he believes has come to him from his senses, but sometimes the senses deceive us – oars appear bent in water, for example. If the senses sometimes deceive us, how can we be sure that any of our sense-based beliefs are true?

The possibility of perceptual error bothers him, but it's not enough to force him to jettison all his sensory beliefs. Maybe there's ground for doubting the senses in less than optimal conditions, like trying to see through water, yet he can't doubt that he's sitting by the fire, writing his book, just because his eyes sometimes play tricks on him. But he has to admit that he's had vivid dreams, even dreamed that he was sitting by the fire when he was actually lying in bed. He's forced to conclude that 'there are no conclusive signs by means of which one can distinguish clearly between being awake and being asleep', largely because he could simply be dreaming any such sign. But even if he is dreaming, even if that's not his hand there writing down notes in his journal, even if he's not sure he's got a hand, there still must be 'simple and universal things' that make up his dreams. Dreams have to be built up out of something basic that's real. So perhaps heads and hands and eyes are figments of a dream, but still, there must be corporeal nature in general, and things like quantity, size, number, place and time as such. Whether one is awake or asleep, simple truths are simple truths: two plus three is five and triangles have three sides. What could possibly shake belief in such things?

God certainly could. 'Who can give me the assurance that God has not arranged that there should be no earth, no heaven, no extended body, no figure, no magnitude or place, and that nevertheless I should have the perception of all these things?' And if something less than God created Descartes, perhaps some chance sequence of events, then he's in even more epistemic trouble, because his origins are therefore much less than perfect. He can't quite accept that God would deceive him in this way – after all, God is supposed to be perfectly good – so instead he imagines a sinister adversary, an evil demon of great genius and power, making every effort to lead him astray. That finally does it. Such a creature might exist, so there's a sliver of a reason for doubting all his beliefs. He concludes, 'Of all the opinions that I once accepted as true, there is not one which is not now legitimately open to doubt.' Not bad for about five pages of philosophy.

Mind, body and God

Descartes then discovers that one proposition is immune to all of the sceptical doubts that he has raised. If his senses lead him astray, if he can't tell whether he's awake or asleep, if there's an evil demon deceiving him, there's still a 'him'. Even if he's led astray and deceived, he still has to exist. As he puts it:

Having thought carefully about it, and having scrupulously examined everything, one must then, in conclusion, take as assured that the proposition: I am, I exist, is necessarily true, every time I express it or conceive of it in my mind.

This is a version of philosophy's most famous punchline. In Latin, *cogito, ergo sum*: I think, therefore I am. But what

213

exactly does it mean? What is this 'I' that exists? Descartes says that he used to think of himself as a man, as being made up of flesh and bones – as having a body. He also thought of himself as having feelings and thoughts, and these he attributed to his soul. But if he thinks about the demon again, can he be sure that all these things are really 'in' him, genuinely part of his nature? He might not have a body, but the one thing that cannot be 'detached' from his essence, one thing he can't be wrong about, is the fact that he thinks. 'I am, therefore, precisely speaking only a thing which thinks.'

In trying to work out what he actually is, Descartes introduces to philosophy what has become known as Cartesian dualism, the view that the mind and the body are two fundamentally different kinds of substances. Minds are thinking things. Bodies are things extended in space. It is among philosophy's most influential ideas. We'll return to Descartes' theory of mind in the chapter on Mind and Matter.

Given that his nature is thinking, what sorts of things does he think about? He has, he says, ideas of other finite substances, like himself, but he also has the idea of an infinite, eternal, independent, omniscient and omnipotent substance. Could a finite, imperfect thing create the idea of an infinite, perfect thing? Recall Scholastic arguments that run from the idea that all effects have a cause back to a first Uncaused Cause at the start of the chain. There has to be something other than just another cause back there that explains all the ordinary causes – something somehow more real, able to cause itself, able to explain all the ordinary causes. Similarly, Descartes argues that causes have to have at least as much reality in them as the effects they produce. So how could something imperfect create something perfect? There's not enough 'reality' in the imperfect cause to create something as monumentally real as perfection. So a finite being like himself couldn't have created the idea of a perfect being. Descartes is led to the thought that God must exist.

The existence of God, a good God who is no deceiver, does a lot of heavy lifting for Descartes. If he's created by God, then he knows that God would not set him up to go systematically wrong when he applies his mind to a problem. If he only assents to what he clearly and distinctly perceives to be true – if he takes care to use his God-given faculties properly and apply his method scrupulously – he'll steer clear of error. On the basis of this firm foundation and rationalist method, he thinks, humanity need only get on with piling up the truths about the world.

The Cartesian circle

Does Descartes actually manage to escape the sceptical doubts he raises at the start of the *Meditations*? Recall that his efforts depend on two propositions: God exists and is no deceiver, and whatever is clearly and distinctly perceived is true. He certainly was aware of one of the largest objections to his project, because it was raised by Antoine Arnauld and considered by Descartes himself. Arnauld says:

THE STORY OF PHILOSOPHY

I have one further worry, namely how Descartes avoids reasoning in a circle when he says that it's only because we know that God exists that we are sure that whatever we vividly and clearly perceive is true. But we can be sure that God exists only because we vividly and clearly perceive this; so before we can be sure that God exists we need to be able to be sure that whatever we perceive clearly and evidently is true.

Isn't this circular? If so, then Descartes is not entitled to the conclusion that God exists or the thought that whatever he perceives clearly and distinctly is true. If he doesn't have any of that, he's stuck just with the truth that he exists.

Descartes' reply depends on a distinction between perceiving something clearly and vividly and remembering that one has perceived something in this way. The first time he reflects on God's existence, carefully attending to each thought and seeing it all clearly is what is required. After the fact, though, all he needs is the memory of seeing the proof clearly and distinctly. But if he didn't know that God exists and is no deceiver, that memory would not be enough. Clarity and distinctness, in a way, stand up for themselves. After all, Descartes did find out that he exists before he established the existence of God, so clear and distinct ideas are good enough to get us truth on their own. God is only needed to shore up our other faculties, for example memory.

The real trouble, some argue, is not with circularity in

Descartes' thinking, but in the unwarranted introduction of an 'I' at the start of his recovery of knowledge. When he discovers the truth of the *cogito* – 'I think, therefore I am' – isn't it a leap to suppose that there's an 'I' doing the thinking? Given the enormous sceptical hole he's dug for himself, is he really entitled to conclude anything more than 'Thinking exists, therefore there's thinking'? Bringing an entire self along for the ride might well be going too far.

Under the aspect of eternity

Taking Descartes' geometrically inspired method to heart, the second rationalist we'll consider, Spinoza, actually cranks out philosophical theorems in the style of a mathematician, and the result is a strangely compelling conception of morality and freedom.

It's worth mentioning in passing that Spinoza occupies a place near Socrates in the hearts of many philosophers – like Socrates, he stuck to his guns no matter what. He was born into a Portuguese family of Jews who hoped to escape discrimination by emigrating to a tolerant Holland. If his infamous book of biblical criticism, the *Theologico-Political Treatise*, is anything to go by, the Jewish community was right to excommunicate him in 1656. In it, he treats the Bible as a historical document, full of the prejudices of ordinary, occasionally slightly stupid human beings. Despite being a scholar of acute insight and no small renown in his lifetime, he lived entirely frugally, earning a modest living as a lens grinder. The dust probably killed him. He refused an academic post at Heidelberg so that he could retain his intellectual independence. For a time 'Spinozism' was synonymous with atheism, yet Romantic poets would later call him a 'God intoxicated man'. There's enough going on in his subtle writing to warrant a number of interpretations of his thought.

His masterpiece is *Ethics Demonstrated in Geometrical Order*. The writing is at times haemorrhage-inducing: a spare Euclidean series of definitions, axioms, propositions, demonstrations, postulates and corollaries. But its five books – 'Concerning God', 'On the Nature and Origin of the Mind', 'Concerning the Origin and Nature of the Passions', 'Of Human Bondage' and 'Of Human Freedom' – build up a strikingly original picture of ourselves and our place in the universe, culminating in an account of human morality and happiness reminiscent of Stoicism.

The first large conclusion of the book is that there is just one substance, which might be called God or Nature. It's open to different interpretations, but the argument starts with the thought that a substance is a free-standing thing: 'that whose concept does not require the concept of another thing'. There cannot be two or more substances 'of the same nature or attribute'. But there's also the notion of God, defined as 'a substance consisting of an infinity of attributes'. If substances can't share attributes, and God has all attributes, there must be just one substance. 'Except God, no substance can be or be conceived.'

Then what is all this diversity we see around us in nature, and what, for that matter, are we? Spinoza's God does not create everything in a separate act – instead everything that exists follows necessarily from God's nature; better, everything that exists is a mode of God's nature, a way of its being or existing. Just as a person might exist as happy or annoyed (those are two possible modes of existing), everything around us is a mode of God, a way that God is. Spinoza thinks that in fact God has an infinite number of attributes, but only two are known to us, the two identified by Descartes: thought and bodily extension in space. They're the same thing, comprehended in two different ways.

The point about everything flowing necessarily from God's nature is actually the key to our freedom, according to Spinoza. He claims that 'all things have been determined from the necessity of the divine nature to exist and produce an effect in a certain way' – and that includes us. All of our feelings and emotions 'follow from the same necessity and force of nature as the other singular things'. And like every being, our aim is self-preservation. Our emotions or, as Spinoza calls them, 'affects', reflect our see-sawing ability or inability to survive and flourish. Passions like fear, anger and joy are emotions directed outwards, at causes outside of us, which tend to hinder or increase our attempts to preserve ourselves. The point is that for most of us our happiness depends on causes that are actually entirely beyond our control. As Spinoza puts it, 'Man's lack of power to moderate and restrain the affects I call Bondage. For the man who is subject to affects is under the control, not of himself, but of fortune.' The trick is to understand exactly what is going on, and thereby take control of one's responses.

We put ourselves in charge of the passions by owning them and making them our actions. An affect, Spinoza says, 'ceases to be a passion as soon as we form a clear and distinct idea of it', as soon as, in other words, we understand its place in the unfolding necessity of God's nature. The better we know God, the more virtuous we become. Perhaps your hatred of your neighbour and her new interest in playing the banjo late at night will diminish once you see that her acts, like all things, are determined by nature. Your anger at the thief who steals your car will fade once you see that you could never have held on to it anyway. If we see things 'under the aspect of eternity', not simply from our tiny points of view, we are no longer slaves to our passions. We find the only kind of freedom that is possible for us by understanding and accepting our place in nature – or, what is the same thing for Spinoza, we find salvation in the intellectual love of God.

Leibniz's windowless mirrors

We come finally to the third of the modern rationalists, Leibniz. The first thing to notice is that his output is rather alarming – in breadth, depth and size. This is partly explained by the fact that his father was a philosopher with an impressive library, and Leibniz gained access to it at a young age.

He taught himself Latin before he was in his teens, quickly mastered Greek, and soon worked his way through his father's books. As an adult, he made contributions to nearly every discipline going, particularly philosophy and mathematics. He never collected his philosophical views into a single magnum opus, but he did write a lot that is philosophically interesting. In 1923, a project was launched to prepare a complete collection of his works. Efforts are still under way – there are more than 80,000 manuscripts to analyse and identify.

Not since Aristotle has a philosopher turned his attention to so much. He discovered calculus independently of Newton – the debate over who got there first raged for years. The Leibniz Stepped Reckoner, a machine of his own devising, is the first mechanical calculator capable of addition, subtraction, multiplication and division – some think of it as at least an ancestor of the computer, if not a computer in its own right. It took a number of disciplines decades and decades to catch up with him. As the Enlightenment philosopher Diderot concludes, 'When one compares the talents one has with those of a Leibniz, one is tempted to throw away one's books and go die quietly in the dark of some forgotten corner.'

Leibniz argues that there must be some fundamental substance out of which the aggregates we see all around us are made: he calls this unit a 'monad'. Whatever is simple in this sense can't be divided up or broken down further – otherwise monads would turn out to be made of something yet more simple and basic. Therefore monads are indivisible and without parts. But whatever is extended in space has parts, so monads, like Descartes' notion of mind or soul, must not be extended, must not exist in space. As they have no parts to change, they can't be changed by other created things – there's no way into them. There's no way out of them either, so they can't have effects on anything else. As Leibniz puts it, 'The monads have no windows through which anything may come in or go out.'

But they have to have properties, because everything that exists has properties. What's more, Leibniz claims that every monad has to have not just properties, but properties different from every other monad. The only way for *two things* to be *two things* is for them to have some variation in attributes. This sort of thought shows up often in Leibniz's thinking, so much so that it is called Leibniz's Law or the Identity of Indiscernibles. As he puts it, 'it is never true that two substances are entirely alike'.

So different monads must have different properties, and like all things they must be able to undergo change. But the change in question can't come from outside, and it can't be a change in a part. Instead, Leibniz argues that monads undergo unified changes in perceptual states – most monads are like little, unconscious souls, changing from one state to another, containing within themselves traces of their whole histories and intimations of their futures, mirroring, from their unique perspective, the entire universe within themselves. Monads reflect the world not because the world affects them, but because they change according to their own internal principles. Fortunately, all monads are synchronized by God in a state of 'pre-established harmony', such that everything ticks over in perfect accord with everything else. Your toe hurts when you stub it not because of the stubbing, but because all the monads involved are purring along in perfect, divinely ordained harmony.

Descartes made do with multiple instances of two substances, Spinoza reduced all the world to just one vast substance, but for Leibniz, the universe is packed with little soul-like monads. The extravagance of his metaphysics is just too much for some. As Voltaire moans, 'Can you really believe that a drop of urine is an infinity of monads, and that each of these has ideas, however obscure, of the universe as a whole?'

It wasn't this doctrine, though, that most annoyed Voltaire. Leibniz argues that God had a choice when bringing our universe into being, and given his goodness, power and wisdom, this must be the best of all possible worlds. Following the horrors of the Lisbon earthquake in 1755, Voltaire lampooned Leibniz in his story *Candide*. In it, a caricature of Leibniz, Pangloss, continues to insist that despite their long catalogue of misfortunes, all is for the best in this, the best of all possible worlds. Candide, at the book's end, finds what peace he can in resignation:

And sometimes Pangloss would say to Candide:

'All events form a chain in the best of all possible worlds. For in the end, if you had not been given a good kick up the backside and chased out of a beautiful castle for loving Miss Cunégonde, and if you hadn't been subjected to the Inquisition, and if you hadn't wandered about America on foot, and if you hadn't dealt the Baron a good blow with your sword, and if you hadn't lost all your sheep from that fine country of Eldorado, you wouldn't be here now eating candied citron and pistachio nuts.'

'That is well put,' replied Candide, 'but we must cultivate our garden.'

Experience

It's not easy to believe that scientific experimentation had to be invented. We learn naturally by trial and error, and it seems obvious that a reasonable way to find out about the world is to test hypotheses against observations. Reining in our thoughts, tying them only to what the world teaches us, seems the best way to get on with working out what's true. If you're of a certain frame of mind, you might think that the metaphysical speculations of the rationalists are nothing more than philosophical flights of fancy. Our conclusions have to be grounded in experience, limited by what our senses tell us – otherwise, as Voltaire worries, we end up with windowless souls in our urine.

The view that knowledge originates in experience has a long history, going back via Bacon and Avicenna to Aristotle and possibly further. Even so, it's taken us a while to think it through. Plato certainly got in the way by insisting that we can't really have knowledge of what we see all around us – instead we can only really know the forms through a kind of intellectual apprehension. Some Scholastics claimed that God imprints truths on the soul, so we're born with a kind of divinely guaranteed innate knowledge. As we saw in the last chapter, the rationalists insist that the careful application of our rational faculties alone is the only secure way to truth – indeed, for Descartes, the senses lead us astray.

Some might argue that we're still coming to grips with understanding the relation between observation and knowledge. We're refining our notions of evidence, taking more and more care with research, understanding the social aspects of scientific enquiry, and further cultivating our notion of what counts as a good trial or experiment.

Still, we are some way from the scientific pioneers of the 17th century, when even the great minds of the day engaged in experimentation that might be described, charitably, as fractionally less than illuminating. It was not the sort of thing that would make it past an ethics committee now, much less peer review. Many seemed content to poke around for no better reason than to see what might happen. Newton himself quite literally poked around in his own face with a bodkin, a long sewing needle, in an effort to discover something about vision:

I Took A Bodkin & put it betwixt my eye & bone as near to [the] backside of my eye as I could: & pressing

my eye [with the] end of it . . . There Appeared severall
white darke & colored circles . . . Which circles plainest
Were When I continued to rub my eye [with the] point
of [the] Bodkin, But if I Held my eye & bodkin still,
Though I continued to presse my eye [with] it yet [the]
circles would grow faint & Often disappeared UNTIL I
removed [them] by moving my eye or [the] bodkin.

In the interests of thoroughness he tried this in both a dark
and a light room.

Perhaps partly despite themselves, the budding scientists
of the Enlightenment made great advances in nearly every
direction – physics, chemistry and biology in particular took
off. The philosophically inclined thinkers of the time were,
like everyone else, impressed by the extraordinary results of
the new 'experimental method'. But what does it mean to say
that knowledge originates in experience? What's the right way
to think about the relationship between our sensory images
and objects in the world? How do we know that our senses
really do represent physical things? We consider the three
great empiricists in this chapter – Britain's finest: Locke,
Berkeley and Hume – and we'll try to unpack their answers
to those questions. While empiricism begins in the hope and
excitement characteristic of the early scientific age, it ends up
very quickly confronting a kind of scepticism that stalks
empirically minded philosophers to this day. The boundaries
described by the limits of sensory experience are a kind of
mental prison, as we'll see.

The limits of knowledge

Although Thomas Hobbes has a claim to be the first modern empiricist, Locke is the true father of empiricism because he fleshed out the view, making it a full-blooded theory of knowledge, in his masterpiece *An Essay Concerning Human Understanding*. It took him 20 years, on and off, to write the book. He put the finishing touches to it as a political exile, on the run in Holland. Locke was in the service of Anthony Ashley Cooper – officially as physician, but unofficially he was a friend and confidant. Cooper was a leading politician of his day, but when his religiously motivated political manoeuvring got him into trouble over the succession to the English throne, he judiciously and rapidly fled the country. His associates, including Locke, slunk away too. In the Netherlands Locke became acquainted with Prince William of Orange and Princess Mary, and when they took power in England, he was invited to sail back aboard Princess Mary's ship. After the Glorious Revolution, Locke's political views were finally in fashion, and he had profound effects on our understanding of government – we'll take up his political views in the next chapter. For now, though, we turn to his *Essay*.

Locke says that his work was motivated by a late-night conversation between friends on a topic that had nothing much to do with human understanding – one report has it that morality and revelation were being discussed. They reached an impasse. Doubts arose on every side. Locke decided that before they or anyone else could make progress on such matters, 'it was necessary to examine our own abilities and see what *objects* our understandings were, or were not, fitted to deal with'. But that's not to say that Locke is in the system-building business, in the style of Descartes. He's not doing 'first philosophy', securing a philosophical foundation for science. Instead, he thinks of scientists like Newton and Boyle as the real architects of the edifice of knowledge. The philosopher is employed as an 'under-labourer in clearing the ground a little, and removing some of the rubbish that lies in the way to knowledge'. It's enough for him to give an account of the understanding, and in so doing work out where its ideas come from and how far it can take us. Then we'll be able to recognize what we can know, take care when we have only goodish guesses, and finally 'sit down in a quiet ignorance of those things which, upon examination, are found to be beyond the reach of our capacities'.

Locke's principal target, the rubbish he aims to sweep away, is the rationalist notion that some ideas are innate, 'stamped upon the Mind of Man, which the Soul receives in its very first Being; and brings into the world with it'. The existence of innate ideas is proven, proponents claim, by the fact of universal agreement. Everyone, not just Descartes and Anselm, has the idea of God. But Locke argues that 'children and idiots' do not. Newly minted human beings, in particular, don't seem to have any ideas at all. They do eventually, which is a point in favour of the notion that they're learning ideas from experience. Locke dismisses the rationalist reply that certain ideas are still innate but somehow dormant, capable of being perceived eventually, under the right conditions. If that were right, every last one of the ideas the mind might ever be capable of perceiving would count as innate too, but that's preposterous.

If ideas are not innate, how do we get them? Locke lays out his position succinctly:

> Let us then suppose the mind to be, as we say, white paper, void of all characters, without any ideas; how comes it to be furnished? . . . Whence has it all the materials of reason and knowledge? To this I answer, in one word, from experience.

Locke introduces a raft of distinctions to clarify this view. Steel yourself, because we'll have to work through a number of them in order to make sense not just of Locke, but of Berkeley, Hume and Kant too. Ideas, Locke says, are the objects of thought, and his first distinction concerns the source of ideas. All ideas come from either sensation or reflection. When our sense organs encounter objects in the world, we have sensory ideas. When the mind operates on the ideas we already have – by thinking, doubting, believing, reasoning and so on – we can reflect on the results through a kind of inner sense, and thus acquire still more ideas. For Locke, that's it: these two outer and inner experiences are the ultimate source of all of our ideas.

There's also a distinction between types of ideas: all of our ideas are either simple or complex. Simple ideas are associated with a single sensory experience – the blue of the sky and the sweetness of an apple are each a simple idea. Complex ideas are built up out of simple ideas, as when we have a complex sensory experience – the fully rounded sensation of tasting, touching, smelling and seeing a muffin, for example. We can also produce complex ideas of our own by combining the ideas we have in reflection. Simple ideas, however, can never be created by us.

What is the relationship between the sensory ideas we have and objects in the world? Locke introduces another distinction, this time between the qualities of objects. Something's primary qualities are 'utterly inseparable from the body' and endure throughout all changes that physical things undergo – Locke's list is solidity, extension, figure and mobility. Whatever you do to an object, it still has these properties, and in that sense these properties are primary, are really out there in objects themselves. But secondary qualities 'are nothing in the objects themselves, but powers to produce various sensations in us by their primary qualities' – Locke's list of these properties includes colours, sounds and tastes. In other words, the bitterness of coffee is not really 'in' the coffee, not really a feature of coffee. It's produced by something out there, but the bitterness is only in here, in the mind of the perceiver.

What else can we say about objects? We notice that sometimes certain collections of simple ideas always appear together, and we suppose that they belong to one thing. For example, a certain collection of sensory ideas of roundness, redness, sweetness and juiciness always show up together, and we end up calling this group by a single name, 'nectarine'. We do something else too: 'not imagining how these simple ideas can subsist by themselves, we accustom ourselves to suppose some *substratum* wherein they do subsist, and from which they do result; which therefore we call substance'. The trouble is that the idea of substance just seems to be something we introduce to make sense of objects. We don't have a simple idea of substance; we don't experience substances as such, so strictly speaking we can't know a thing about them. Instead, as Locke puts it, substance is 'nothing but the supposed, but unknown, support of those qualities we find existing'. It's a slightly suspicious something, and we don't really know anything about it.

What, to cut finally to the chase, are the limits of knowledge? Locke believes that the mind has no other 'immediate object but its own ideas', so knowledge can only be knowledge of our own ideas. 'Knowledge then seems to me to be nothing but the perception of the connexion and agreement, or disagreement and repugnancy of any of our Ideas.' There are four kinds of agreement or disagreement: identity or diversity, relation, co-existence, and real existence. We can, for example, know that 'blue is not yellow' (diversity); that 'two triangles upon equal basis between two parallels are equal' (relation); that 'Iron is susceptible of magnetical impressions' (co-existence); and that 'God is' (real existence).

Further, human knowledge admits of three degrees. The most certain is intuitive knowledge, which happens when the mind compares ideas and just 'perceives' a truth about them, without the intervention of any other idea – blue is not yellow, for example. Second, there is demonstrative knowledge, where the mind reasons and sees a truth about two ideas by means of one or more ideas, that is to say, the mind proceeds by steps to a truth, as in a mathematical proof. This is not as certain and immediate as intuition, but it is a kind of knowledge. Whatever falls short of these two sorts of knowledge is 'but faith or opinion' and not knowledge at all, with one exception. Locke says that we have sensitive knowledge of the existence of things when we perceive them. This is not as secure as intuition or deduction, but he thinks that it goes beyond mere probability, just squeaking past the post and into the category of knowledge. We don't think, when we look around and see the objects in the room, that they're only *probably* there. We know it.

But *how* do we know it? By now you must feel the icy fingers of scepticism on your shoulder. If Locke says that the objects of human knowledge are confined to our ideas, how on earth can we know about anything outside our heads? How do you know that the real nectarine out there is anything at all like your idea of it? Locke has admitted that substance – the unknown whatever-it-is that supports the properties we experience – is forever beyond us. He's argued that a lot of the properties we perceive, the secondary ones, aren't really in the objects out there at all. Even if we accept the slightly dubious notion of sensitive knowledge, we're still stuck with the idea that we can only know about the existence of objects we happen to be looking at right now. Do we therefore not know about anything unless we're staring right at it?

If we say that all knowledge begins in experience, as we seem to have to if we want to avoid letting our rationalist fantasies rip, we're stuck in solitary confinement, in the prison of our minds, unable to move beyond our ideas. Doesn't the empiricist project lead, almost instantly, to sceptical doubts? This possibility was studiously avoided by Locke, but it was taken very seriously by both Berkeley and Hume. Before we get to them, however, it's worth pausing over one of Locke's largest contributions to philosophy.

Personal identity

Locke introduced into modern philosophical reflection the question of personal identity. What is it that makes a person the same person over time? We want to say that the child in the photograph is, in some sense, the same person who grows up and grows old, but what is it about the baby then and the grown-up now that makes them both the same? Locke argues that a person is 'a thinking intelligent Being, that has reason and reflection, and can consider it self as it self, the same thinking thing in different times and places'. But just what is it that makes that 'thinking intelligent Being' the same in different times and places? Locke's answer is worth quoting in full:

Since consciousness always accompanies thinking, and 'tis that, that makes every one to be, what he calls *self*; and thereby distinguishes himself from all other thinking beings, in this alone consists *personal Identity*, i.e. that sameness of a rational Being. And as far as this consciousness can be extended backwards to any past Action or Thought, so far reaches the Identity of that *Person*; it is the same self now as it was then.

Locke claims that memory is the criterion of identity, not body or even soul. It's the coherence of conscious life, chained back to previous incarnations through memory, which makes a person the same person over time.

Hume is sceptical about the self. He argues that if we want to keep out of philosophical trouble, every genuine idea must be traced back to some original sensory impression or complex set of impressions. Otherwise we really don't know what we're talking about, or worse, we might not be talking about any actual thing at all. Is there an impression corresponding to our idea of the self? 'If any impression gives rise to the idea of self,' Hume argues, 'that impression must continue invariably the same, through the whole course of our lives.' But there is no such continuous impression. Instead, there's just a riot of changing impressions, a bundle of perceptions, but no self. As he puts it, 'For my part, when I enter most intimately into what I call myself, I always stumble on some particular perception or other, of heat or cold, light or shade, love or hatred, pain or pleasure. I never can catch myself at any time without a perception, and never can observe any thing but the perception.' The idea of a self, he concludes, is nothing but a philosophical fiction.

To be is to be perceived

Berkeley, a bishop born near Kilkenny in Ireland, is best known for holding the jolting thesis that matter does not exist. The only things that exist, he says, are ideas and the minds that perceive them. The view has been subject to more than its fair share of mockery. The diarist James Boswell reports the famous response of an exasperated Samuel Johnson:

> After we came out of the church, we stood talking for some time together of Bishop Berkeley's ingenious sophistry to prove the nonexistence of matter, and that every thing in the universe is merely ideal. I observed, that though we are satisfied his doctrine is not true, it is impossible to refute it. I never shall forget the alacrity with which Johnson answered, striking his foot with mighty force against a large stone, till he rebounded from it – 'I refute it thus.'

Berkeley's position seems outlandish to almost everyone, but it follows in a straight line from Locke's claim that all knowledge is knowledge of ideas, not of objects in the world. What Berkeley does, in a sentence, is remove the dubious notion of substance from Locke's empiricism, and he does so masterfully. His arguments are ingenious and spectacularly clear. He gets his conclusion up and running in about a page and a half.

Following Locke, Berkeley argues that the objects of human knowledge are ideas – ideas imprinted on the mind by sensation, perceived by looking in on the operations of the mind, or formed by memory and the imagination. In addition to ideas, there are minds that perceive them. Here's the rub: ideas cannot exist outside of minds. As Berkeley puts it, their *esse* is *percipi*: for ideas, to be is to be perceived. 'There was an odour, that is, it was smelt; there was a sound, that is, it was heard.' The sound of waves crashing on the shore cannot exist unheard, the blue of the sky cannot exist unseen, and the feel of sand underneath your feet cannot exist outside your mind. The existence of an idea consists just in its being perceived.

Yet there is this opinion, Berkeley notes, 'strangely prevailing amongst men', that such things as houses, mountains, rivers and other sensible objects somehow exist outside of the mind that perceives them. Isn't that a contradiction? 'What are the aforementioned objects but the things we perceive by sense? and what do we perceive *besides our own ideas or sensations*? and is it not plainly repugnant that any one of these, or any combination of them, should exist unperceived?'

But isn't it right to think that our ideas are caused by and somehow represent real things out there in the world? Berkeley asks whether those things out there are perceivable. If so, then they are ideas in your head and you agree with him. If not, he writes, 'I appeal to anyone whether it be sense to assert a colour is like something which is invisible; hard or soft, like something which is intangible, and so on for the rest.' How can an idea be like anything other than another idea? How could an idea of a cow be like something invisible, untouchable, unsmellable and so on?

But what happens to the world when it is not being perceived? If you shut your eyes for a moment, does the room wink out of existence because it's no longer in your mind? And if it does, how does it come back when you open your eyes again? Fortunately, Berkeley argues, God, in his benevolence, is good enough to keep everything in his infinite mind, so the whole show stays put, even when you're not looking at it.

The point Berkeley presses is just this: why should we posit anything over and above the contents of our minds? By doing so, by insisting on a Lockean substance underlying our sensory impressions, we're opening the door to scepticism. If Locke is right, then there's plenty of room for questions about how we know that our ideas match up to the real things in the external world. There's room to wonder whether or not tables and chairs are really real. But by trimming things down to just ideas and minds, there's no space at all for sceptical doubts. Berkeley insists that his view is, therefore, a defence of common sense.

I do not argue against the existence of any one thing

that we can apprehend either by sense or reflection. That the things I see with my eyes and touch with my hands do exist, really exist, I make not the least question. The only things whose existence we deny is that which *philosophers* call matter or corporeal substance. And in doing of this there is no damage done to the rest of mankind, who, I daresay, will never miss it.

Sceptical doubts

We come finally to Hume, certainly among the greatest philosophers who ever lived. He follows Locke's empiricism to its logical limits, casting doubt on our knowledge of external objects, an enduring self, inductive inference, the existence of God, causation, miracles, and the role of reason almost everywhere, particularly in moral judgements. His arguments almost sparkle with clarity. Hume's writing is often wonderful, and sometimes it seems to convey a connection to the man himself. David Pears got it exactly right when he said that Hume makes for excellent philosophical company. He's almost in the room when you read him.

Born in Edinburgh to a well-to-do family, he prepared for a career in law but gave it up, then dabbled in business but walked away from that too. He had 'an insurmountable aversion to anything but the pursuits of Philosophy and General Learning', which is good news for us, because he locked himself away in a little town in France to produce a philosophical masterpiece, *A Treatise of Human Nature*. It was Hume's attempt to create a 'science of man' by employing the new experimental method. Just as Newton discovered universal laws of motion, Hume hopes to discover universal principles of human nature. The *Treatise* was ignored at first – as Hume lamented, the book 'fell dead-born from the press, without reaching such distinction, as even to excite a murmur among the zealots'. He rewrote it, toning down some bits and amplifying others, and the more popular and agreeably shorter *An Enquiry Concerning Human Understanding* finally did get a hearing. We'll take up just one strand of it, a particularly powerful part of Hume's treatment of causation.

Hume argues that 'all the objects of human reason or enquiry may naturally be divided into two kinds, to wit, *Relations of Ideas*, and *Matters of Fact*'. Relations of ideas correspond to Locke's intuitive and demonstrative knowledge. We can apprehend their truth just by thinking about them. Hume has in mind mathematical propositions, like 'three times five is equal to the half of thirty'. Truths like these are necessary, definitional truths, propositions that are true just because of how the ideas involved are related to one another. Matters of fact are much more interesting, but much less secure. Hume here means truths like 'the Sun will rise tomorrow' or 'it's raining in Paris'. There's nothing about the ideas involved that makes them true. To discover whether or not they're true, you have to have some experiences – you have to wait until tomorrow or go to Paris and take a look.

You can spot the difference between these two kinds of

truths by noticing that the denial of a relation of ideas implies a contradiction, but the denial of a matter of fact is still possible. It's a contradiction to say 'triangles do not have three sides'. Given what the ideas in play mean, that claim is self-contradictory. But there's no contradiction implied in denying a matter of fact, in thinking, for example, that the Sun will not rise tomorrow.

So the interesting question, for Hume, concerns the evidence we can have for matters of fact that go beyond the present testimony of the senses. How do we move past what we can see and hear now to all the other things we think we know about the world? Hume argues that 'all reasonings concerning matter of fact seem to be founded on the relation of *Cause and Effect*'. How do you know that your friend is in France? You produce a letter from him with a French post-mark on it – you point to a present effect that itself points back to a hidden cause. So what is the foundation of our reasoning about causal relationships? How do we know that French postmarks are caused by French post offices? Hume argues that all of our knowledge of cause and effect comes from experience, from seeing a cause regularly followed by an effect. We can't work out what effects a new thing might have just by looking at it or thinking about it. We need repeated experiences of things of a certain sort causing things of a certain sort. Once you see a lot of matches being struck, it drives an inductive inference from particular experiences to a general conclusion: all struck matches produce flame.

Then Hume asks the killer question: how do we know that

the cause-and-effect pairs we've observed in the past will carry on together in the future? In other words, what justifies inductive inferences? He points out that 'These two propositions are far from being the same, *I have found that such an object has always been attended with such an effect, and I foresee, that other objects, which are, in appearance, similar, will be attended with similar effects.*' What's needed is a linking premise, a principle governing inductive inferences, something like 'the future will be like the past'. But what's your reason, your argument for thinking that the future will be like the past?

According to Hume, only two kinds of reasoning can secure this principle – relations of ideas and matters of fact. Is the claim that the future will be like the past a relation of ideas? There's no contradiction implied in the thought that the future will not be like the past, so the claim can't be a relation of ideas. Is it a matter of fact that the future will be like the past? If we tried to secure the principle of induction from past experience, we'd be arguing in a circle – we'd be saying that we have inductive grounds for believing in the principle of induction. Circular arguments can't be rational grounds for belief.

So what's the basis of all our conclusions concerning experience? Hume's alarming answer is mere custom or habit, as opposed to reason or sound argumentation. He writes, 'after the constant conjunction of two objects, heat and flame, for instance, weight and solidity, we are determined by custom alone to expect the one from the appearance of the other'.

Reason just does not figure in what is now looking like our very tenuous grip on the world. When we examine the nature of human understanding with empiricist principles, we discover a dark, irrational inner core. We are literally creatures of habit, not rational beings with good reasons for our beliefs. Our inner operations, Hume says, 'are a species of natural instincts, which no reasoning or process of the thought and understanding is able, either to produce or prevent'. Without a reason for your belief that your friend is in France – without an argument for that conclusion, just a kind of instinctive leap in the dark – can you really say that you *know* where he is? Can you really say you know much of anything, at all, beyond what's right in front of you?

It's sometimes thought that scepticism is a depressing doctrine. Some people believe that humanity never will answer the questions we started asking so long ago in ancient Greece. Maybe we are doomed to wonder but never really know much of anything. In thinking through this depressing possibility, it's worth keeping in mind one of the best responses to scepticism, Hume's own. In a celebrated passage, he lets us in on his resolution to the sceptical doubts he's raised.

Most fortunately it happens, that since Reason is incapable of dispelling these clouds, Nature herself suffices to that purpose, and cures me of this philosophical melancholy and delirium, either by relaxing this bent of mind, or by some avocation, and lively impression of my senses, which obliterate all these chimeras. I dine, I play a game of backgammon, I converse, and am merry with my friends. And when, after three or four hours' amusement, I would return to these speculations, they appear so cold, and strained, and ridiculous, that I cannot find in my heart to enter into them any farther.

5
Modern Matters

Politics

Imagine you're the king of England, sometime in the Middle Ages, and your subjects are getting a bit uppity. Maybe you've hanged a few too many of them for stealing sheep, or they don't much like the fact you've been spending their tithes on fast horses and loose archbishops. You are, of course, well versed in Machiavelli's rules for leadership, but unfortunately it appears you have the cunning of a lion and the strength of a fox. In this situation, it would be very useful if you could appeal directly to God in order to legitimize your rule: after all, if you've been put on the throne by God, then it stands to reason that only He could remove you from it again.

Something like this idea is at the root of the theory of the divine right of kings. This holds that a sovereign derives his right to rule directly from the will of God, which means that he is subject to no earthly power. As Shakespeare puts it in *Richard II*, a king is: ' . . . the figure of God's majesty, His captain, steward, deputy elect, Anointed, crowned, planted many years'.

It follows from this that any move to unseat a ruler, or to curtail his powers, runs contrary to God's will, and is therefore disallowed on religious grounds. Moreover, some versions of the theory also assert that a sovereign cannot be judged to have erred, since only God is in a position to make such a judgement.

The idea of the divine right of kings is perhaps most notably associated with the French philosopher Jean Bodin, who believed that sovereignty was absolute and indivisible; and that a king's subjects were excluded from resisting his authority, since it was against the law of God to resist an authority that was accountable only to God.

This sort of idea would likely have been persuasive for most of the Middle Ages, when the Church and its traditions would have loomed large in the lives of a king's subjects, and the idea that a king's rule was divinely ordained would have been easily accepted by both the sovereign and his people. However, it doesn't fit so easily with the rise of individualism that characterized the early modern era, and with what the sociologist Emile Durkheim identified as the shift in societies from mechanical to organic solidarity – that is, social solidarity based upon the interdependence of people rather than their brute similarity.

To put it simply, as people cast off the fetters of tradition, as individualism comes to the fore, and as the Church begins to retreat at least somewhat from the domain of everyday life, the idea that there is an immutable preordained order to which everybody is subject – the rich man at his castle, the poor man at his gate – becomes much less plausible. This means that a number of rather troubling questions begin to make themselves felt. If the authority of a sovereign is not divinely sanctioned, wherein lies the legitimacy of his rule? If the basis of the old social order is breaking down, on what basis can a new social order be established? If people are throwing off the shackles of tradition and religion, what is to prevent society from descending into anarchy? It is at this juncture that Thomas Hobbes steps on to the stage.

That great Leviathan

Thomas Hobbes was not optimistic about our ability to rub along nicely with each other in the absence of a visible power to act as a restraint on our natural passions. The problem, he tells us, is that we are inclined to appropriate to ourselves 'the use of those things in which all others have a joint interest'; in other words, we're unfailingly avaricious. In his classic text, *Leviathan*, in which he discusses the nature of political authority and obligation, he makes use of the idea of a 'state of nature' in order to examine what our lives would be like if there were no constraints upon our activities.

In a state of nature, we are at liberty to fulfil all our ambitions to the maximum. We are free to possess anything we can find a way to possess; and no behaviour in the service of protecting our possessions is ruled out. The trouble is, this applies equally to our neighbours, and in a situation of scarcity and competition, this is a recipe for disaster. In particular, there is no constraint upon violence, and no security, since in a state of nature even the weak are quite capable of killing the strong, perhaps, for example, by devious means or by banding together. The natural condition of human beings, therefore, is to be at war, every man against every man. In a state of nature there is

> . . . no knowledge of the face of the earth; no account of time; no arts; no letters; no society; and which is worst of all, continual fear, and danger of violent death; and the life of man, solitary, poor, nasty, brutish, and short.

The good news, however, is that this is not the end of the story. It is Hobbes' claim, contra Epicurus, that we are also predisposed to fear death, which means necessarily we want to avoid a war of all against all. From this premise, Hobbes is able to deduce three laws – which he thinks are just as binding as the laws of geometry – that hold true in a state of nature. The first is that we must desire and seek peace. Living in a state of nature means continual fear and danger of death. Therefore, given that we're afraid of death, we have no other choice but to try to establish peace.

Peace, though, isn't possible if we insist on retaining our natural right to complete liberty, and in particular our freedom to possess literally anything we're able to possess. Therefore, Hobbes' second law is that we must give up some part of our liberty, and be content with as much liberty against others as we're prepared to allow others to have against ourselves. This means, in effect, a social contract: we agree to transfer our absolute right to liberty to a single other entity (a person or group), which then uses the power it thereby accrues in order to keep the peace and ensure that security is enjoyed by everybody. As Hobbes puts it:

> . . . it is as if every man should say to every other, 'I authorize and give up my right of governing myself to this man or assembly of men, on this condition, that thou give up thy right to him, and authorize all his actions in like manner.'

Here we run into a little difficulty. Agreeing that we are going to submit to the authority of a man or assembly of men is one thing, but actually obeying laws that are handed down and honouring agreements is quite another. Hobbes' third law of nature, therefore, is that people must keep their covenants. Unfortunately, rationality on its own won't be enough to ensure compliance, so we need a powerful incentive. As Hobbes puts it, covenants 'without the sword are but words'. Therefore, to avoid slipping back into the nightmare of a state of nature, we must submit to a single, absolute power, which will guarantee our peace and security:

This is the generation of that great *Leviathan*, or rather, to speak more reverently, of that mortal god to which we owe, under the immortal God, our peace and defence. For by this authority, given him by every particular man in the Commonwealth, he hath the use of so much power and strength conferred on him that, by terror thereof, he is enabled to form the wills of them all, to peace at home, and mutual aid against their enemies abroad.

Hobbes' *Leviathan* has the considerable merit of being the first fully worked-out treatment of how a social contract between individuals can provide the foundations of legitimate political authority. It is also novel in the sense that it is an attempt to derive a conception of political obligation by means of a deductive argument from first principles that are rooted in a non-religious understanding of the psychology of human beings. However, it is not without its problems. Perhaps most significantly it seems to constitute something of a Faustian bargain: it's true that the horrors of a state of nature as conceived by Hobbes are something to be avoided, but it is much less clear that our fears in this respect justify us giving up all our rights to an unlimited, unitary power.

Mutual preservation

John Locke, some 30 years later, is much less sanguine than Hobbes about the dangers of absolutism. In his classic work on the nature of government, *Second Treatise*, in which he sets out his version of the social contract idea, he asks fairly incredulously whether men are 'so foolish that they take care to avoid what mischiefs may be done them by polecats or foxes, but are content, nay think it safety, to be devoured by lions'. Locke rejects the idea that a ruler's power is absolute and unconditional, arguing instead that a failure on the part of a ruler to govern in the interests of the people creates the right of rebellion. In contrast to Hobbes, he argues that the social contract imposes obligations on the ruler as well as the ruled.

Locke, like Hobbes, begins his analysis with a description of the state of nature, where people exist in

> ... a state of perfect freedom to order their actions, and dispose of their possessions and persons as they think fit, within the bounds of the law of Nature, without asking leave or depending upon the will of any other man. A state also of equality, wherein all the power and jurisdiction is reciprocal, no one having more than another, there being nothing more evident than that creatures of the same species and rank ... should also be equal one amongst another, without subordination or subjection ...

He is at pains to make it clear that he conceives of the state of nature as being not merely an abstraction upon which to build a theory of government, but also a historical reality, in which many people have actually lived. Although the state of nature is defined by the absence of government, it does not follow that people have the right to do just anything they please. Rather, we are subject to a law of nature, divinely rooted, but rationally discoverable, that is based upon the injunction that just as we are required to preserve ourselves, so we are required to 'preserve the rest of mankind', which means that 'no one ought to harm another in his life, health, liberty or possessions'.

Locke's state of nature is not anything like as dark as Hobbes' version. The spectre of war, all against all, looms much less large, partly because people will be held back 'from doing hurt to one another' by the fact that everyone has the right to punish the transgressors of natural law, and to seek reparation for any harm that occurs as a result of such transgressions, and also because any malign effect of our natural passions will not inevitably overwhelm the moderating influence of our rational faculties. This being the case, it isn't immediately clear why people living in a state of nature would want to subject themselves to the dominion and control of a governing power.

Locke's answer comes down to a series of thoughts about the insecurity of living in a situation where there is no government. In particular, the constant threat that we will be deprived of our liberty and property makes us willing to quit the state of nature, which, although free, 'is full of fears and continual dangers'. So human beings naturally seek out and join in a 'society with others who are already united, or have a mind to unite for the mutual preservation of their lives, liberties and estates, which I call by the general name – property'. The main function of government, therefore, is to establish a system of settled law in order to preserve property, and to regulate its use, distribution and transfer. It comes into existence when people give up their 'executive power of the law of nature, and . . . resign it to the public'. A person's consent to live within such a commonwealth can either be explicit or implicit, but in both cases it obliges obedience to the law and ultimately to the supreme law-making body, the legislative.

Locke's preferred form of government is a constitutional monarchy with executive power in the hands of the monarch, and legislative power in the hands of a periodically elected parliamentary assembly. The key point, though, is that sovereignty ultimately lies in the hands of the people, and any government is obliged to govern in accordance with natural law and to the end of preserving the lives and property of its subjects. Locke did not believe that governments have an unconditional right to rule, recognizing that a monarch or, indeed, an assembly might exercise tyrannical power over their own subjects. In this situation, a state of war in effect exists, and the people, who remain the proper locus of sovereignty, have the right to rebel.

Property

Locke's account relies heavily on the idea we have a natural right to dispose of our property as we see fit. His justification of property rights is roughly speaking as follows: the stuff of the natural world has very little value until it is worked and shaped into the things we require for our subsistence (and more). This is achieved through our labour, which is an extension of ourselves. We have sole rights of ownership over ourselves; therefore, we have sole rights of ownership over the things we produce by means of our labour.

In a state of nature, there are limits to property rights. For example, it is not permissible to deprive other people of their means of subsistence by claiming too much in property; and people can only claim what they can use and improve. However, the existence of money as a medium of exchange significantly complicates this picture. Money doesn't spoil, and therefore acts as a store of value. This means there's an incentive to produce more goods than it is possible to use, since any excess can be exchanged for money. As a result, large disparities in wealth become possible and, according to Locke, morally permissible.

However, there are layers of complication here that this sort of argument leaves untouched. For example, suppose you're born into wealth, with the consequence that you start off with a huge advantage in life through no merit of your own. Is your wealth, and the advantages it brings to you, and presumably also to your children, morally justified? Or suppose through no fault of your own you happen to live in a place where nothing will grow. You work your fingers to the bone, and at the end of growing season you end up with a couple of sprouts. Your neighbour, on the other hand, living in Fertile Crescent, only has to scatter a few apple pips in his garden, and by the next weekend he has an orchard. Again, it just isn't clear that any large disparities in wealth that emerge out of this sort of situation are morally justified.

There are further thoughts to be had here. If there are questions to be asked about property rights, then there are also questions to be asked about systems of government that support property rights. For example, if it's the case that the vast inequalities of wealth that characterize most extant societies are morally suspect, then it is at least arguable that the political systems that ensure the health of such societies are also morally suspect. If a constitutional monarchy functions to prop up an iniquitous social order, then so much the worse for constitutional monarchy.

Rousseau and the general will

The Genevan philosopher Jean-Jacques Rousseau caused something of a stir in mid-18th-century France by arguing, in a neat reversal of the orthodox view of his age, that in various ways the advent of civilization had corrupted the natural goodness of humankind. Departing from the Hobbesian line that people are relentlessly avaricious and that their lives in a state of nature would be 'nasty, brutish and short', Rousseau claims instead that human beings were originally 'noble savages', largely solitary, peaceful, preoccupied with the demands of securing their immediate needs. They had little use for language, foresight or any of the other accoutrements of civilization. The problems faced by humanity are actually those of social existence and the inequality it inevitably engenders. Thus at the beginning of *The Social Contract*, his most important work, he famously states that 'Man is born free; and everywhere he is in chains'.

Rousseau argues that it was primarily the emergence of private property that spelt the death knell of the noble savage. As soon as the first person enclosed and then claimed ownership of a piece of land, we were on a downward spiral. Civil society necessarily followed because of the need to justify and regulate ownership and the inequality it inevitably created. And, of course, once you have inequality, then any incipient competitiveness, jealousy and aggression, which first emerges when people begin to enjoy fixed relations with each other, will inevitably be magnified.

In *The Social Contract*, Rousseau considers how we are best able to manage this state of affairs. There's no going back to a state of nature, so we've got to find some way of keeping in check the moral degeneracy that comes with the iniquities of civilization. The solution he puts forward makes use of a concept of 'the general will'. He argues that once people live in social groups, in fixed relations with other people, they are no longer absolutely free to pursue their own selfish interests. The only way they can retain a modified sort of freedom is by agreeing to a social contract, which establishes that every individual member of the group forms part of that group's sovereign body. Freedom then consists in acting in accordance with the 'general will' of the group.

This, of course, is a highly circumscribed kind of freedom, and some people have argued that Rousseau's conception comes dangerously close to fascism, in that it valorizes the group rather than the individual. It also faces the practical difficulty that it requires people to set aside their own personal interests in favour of the common good, which isn't something that we seem generally inclined to do. Nevertheless, in locating sovereignty in the will of the people, Rousseau's idea of the 'general will' marked a significant moment in the history of democratic thought, and secured his reputation as an important, if somewhat paradoxical, Enlightenment thinker.

The rights of women

The late 18th century fell a long way short of the Enlightment ideal which held that society should be organised so as to enable people to fulfil their potential as rational, autonomous beings. In particular, as Mary Wollstonecraft, champion of the rights of women, pointed out, women suffered from systematic disadvantages that were woven into the very fabric of the social system: they were raised in a way that extinguished their intellectual and rational capabilities; they learned to give way, and to develop a docile and flattering sexuality designed only to be alluring to men. Wollstonecraft argued that men as well as women suffered from this situation. Women would be much better placed to cultivate desirable virtues if they enjoyed the same rights as men.

In Wollstonecraft's view, the primary barrier preventing women from fulfilling their potential was the way they were educated. In the introduction to *A Vindication of the Rights of Women*, she writes that she had looked at the 'various books written on the subject of education, and patiently observed the conduct of parents and the management of schools . . . what has been the result? – a profound conviction that the neglected education of my fellow-creatures is the grand source of the misery I deplore.' The only possible solution is a change in women's education. In particular, Wollstonecraft thought that women should be encouraged to develop their rational capacities in broadly the same way as men. The best education, she claims, 'is such an exercise of the understanding as is best calculated to strengthen the body and form the heart. Or, in other words, to enable the individual to attain such habits of virtue as will render it independent.'

Wollstonecraft's feminism is not of the modern kind, of course, and some of her views seem anachronistic. For example, it was her belief that a woman had a duty to become a mother, even if this should not involve her subjugation to a man. Nevertheless, she remains an inspiration to

21st-century feminists; and although she was not the first person to take up the cudgels on behalf of women, her importance is such that it is right to consider her the first feminist.

Workers unite!

There are not many philosophers who can claim they were at least partly responsible for the way the history of an entire century unfolded. But this is the position Karl Marx enjoys in relation to the 20th century. The revolutions that took place in that century in Russia and China were both inspired by his writings; and the Cold War saw Western capitalist countries fronting up against societies that identified themselves as being socialist or communist.

Marx wrote with the intention of affecting history, of course. In the *Communist Manifesto*, written with his friend Friedrich Engels, one finds the following call to arms:

> The Communists disdain to conceal their views and aims. They openly declare that their ends can be attained only by the forcible overthrow of all existing social conditions. Let the ruling classes tremble at a communist revolution. The proletarians have nothing to lose but their chains. They have a world to win. Workers of all countries, unite!

This overt political aspect does raise the question as to whether

Marx can properly be considered a philosopher. The most plausible reply is that he wasn't a pure philosopher, but there's enough of philosophical interest in his work to earn the attention of philosophers.

The best entry point into Marx's ideas is probably the issue of how he sees the nature of human beings. The first thing to say is that most Marxist scholars deny he has a theory of human nature as such, arguing instead that he is broadly committed to the 'blank slate' view that a human mind is constructed in the context of an individual's lived experience in a particular social and material reality. Nevertheless, although Marx doesn't think of human nature in the same terms as, say, a contemporary evolutionary psychologist, he does have certain ideas about the nature of human beings that inform his wider political analysis.

Perhaps most significantly, he claims that it is in the nature of human beings to cooperate with each other in a process of freely chosen labour. Part of the importance of this idea is that it stands against the Hobbesian view that the relationships between human beings are necessarily antagonistic. Indeed, it is Marx's claim (along with Engels) that the earliest hunter-gatherer societies were relatively free of conflict, largely because the absence of any surplus production meant there was no private property to create a division between the haves and have-nots.

But the possibility of freely chosen, cooperative labour is also important, because Marx suggests that in a certain sense we realize our humanity through our labour. Roughly speaking, the thought here, which runs through Marx's earlier work and has antecedents in the philosophy of Georg Hegel (more of whom later), is that we can come to full self-realization in the process of transforming the world in our own image. Think perhaps of a team of engineers admiring a newly constructed bridge, and gaining a sense of their collective humanity as they gaze upon their creation.

Alienation

The concept of alienation, which provides the moral force to Marx's critique of capitalism, is linked to this idea that we realize our humanity through our labour. Simply put, people are alienated when they are separated from the products of their labour and from the labour process itself, which occurs when they have no control over their productive situation. Alienation is always self-alienation: to be alienated is to be separated from one's essential humanity, and it means being unable to live a fully human life. All class societies, which are defined in terms of the division between those who own and control the means of production and those who do not, feature some level of alienation. However, it is in capitalist societies that alienation is most pronounced.

Capitalism is characterized by a fundamental conflict between two ineluctably opposed classes, the bourgeoisie, the owners of factories, machinery and so on, and the proletariat, the workers, who own only their own labour power, which they are forced to sell to the bourgeoisie in circumstances they do not choose. The proletariat are alienated because they have next to no control over the labour process, and because their productive energies are expended in the service of a class that exploits them. The proletarian

> . . . does not fulfil himself in his work but denies himself, has a feeling of misery rather than well-being, does not develop freely his mental and physical energies but is physically exhausted and mentally debased. The worker, therefore, feels himself at home only during his leisure time, whereas at work he feels homeless. His work is not voluntary but imposed, forced labour. It is not the satisfaction of a need, but only a means for satisfying other needs.

Happily, the proletariat have a way out of this situation. Capitalism is rife with contradictions, which means it's inherently unstable. The proletariat, as the bearers of the emancipatory potential of humankind, are in a position to take advantage of the crises that inevitably befall capitalist societies in order to bring about the downfall of capitalism. Specifically, it is the destiny of the proletariat, as a class-for-itself, a class aware of its own reality and situation, to abolish all class distinctions, instituting a new form of society, communism, based on collective ownership. In doing so, they will end the alienation of people from the products of their labour, from the labour process itself, and from their essential humanity.

Where's the revolution?

The problem with making predictions about how history is going to unfold is that history has a habit of doing its own thing. Capitalism, though it has been enveloped by periodic crises, is still going strong; and the 'communist' experiments of the 20th century were for the most part spectacularly unsuccessful and often brutally repressive. So it seems that Marx just got it wrong.

Not surprisingly, Marxists have offered countless explanations for this state of affairs. Marx himself was certainly aware that capitalism is able to draw upon many resources in order to counter the destabilizing effects of its internal contradictions. Thus, for example, you'll find that Marxists talk a lot about things such as 'ideology', 'hegemony' and 'false class consciousness' in order to explain why the proletariat hasn't yet come to the realization that it has a historic role to play in bringing down capitalism. The basic idea is that as a result of their dominance in the economic sphere of society, the bourgeoisie control what might be termed, following Louis Althusser, the ideological state apparatus of society, which includes such things as the educational system and the mass media. As a result, they are able to manipulate the dissemination of ideas so that the proletariat are bombarded with pro-capitalist messages, thereby keeping them blind to their real situation. So the proletariat never make the transition from being a class-in-itself to a class-*for*-itself, and capitalism continues on its merry way.

The other possibility is that Marx was right about the inherent instability of capitalism, but wrong about how long this would take to play itself out. This sort of analysis tends to be coupled with an argument about how capitalism has been successful in exploiting new markets, particularly in the developing world. However, this kind of argumentative move raises the spectre of unfalsifiability: one can imagine a 25th-century Marxist insisting that revolution is just around the corner, and that Marx was right about the fundamentals but had just underestimated the ability of capitalism to exploit the new intergalactic markets.

It's only fair to point out that Karl Marx is by no means the only political theorist to have been embarrassed by future events. Thomas Hobbes, for example, though probably more right than wrong about the propensities of human beings in a state of nature, would likely find it hard to maintain his confidence in the wisdom of absolutism in the face of the horrors of the 20th century. Even John Locke, though fabulously prescient in his advocacy of the separation of powers, would perhaps regard the wild disparities of wealth that characterize modern capitalist societies, and the gulf between the riches of the first world and the abject poverty of large parts of the developing world, as at least evidence in favour of the proposition that governments need to do more than simply secure property rights.

However, the significance of these philosophers, and others like them, is not that they have always got things right. It is rather that they have shown how the tools and techniques of philosophy can be employed to shed light upon issues that affect the lives of millions of people – something that is still relevant today. The issue of the legitimacy and scope of government remains a hot topic, as has recently been shown both by the 'Arab Spring' and by the furore over the activities of the WikiLeaks website. If a modern philosopher is going to look at this issue, then almost inevitably they will have to take into account both social-contract theory and the radical possibility that the basis of the legitimacy of government in the modern world is not clear.

Idealism

The developmental biologist Lewis Wolpert doesn't think much of philosophy. He concedes that it is 'clever', but this doesn't stop it being 'totally irrelevant'. As far as he is concerned, philosophy has made no real contribution to the sum total of human knowledge: 'If philosophy hadn't existed – apart from Aristotle – what would we not know? The answer is that it wouldn't have made the slightest difference.'

This sort of thing can perhaps be dismissed as an amusing piece of knockabout, a scientist getting a few friendly blows in at the expense of his philosophical colleagues. But there is a suspicion that maybe there's a kernel of truth in the claim that philosophy hasn't delivered a whole lot. Consider, for example, how much the natural sciences have progressed even in the last 150 years when compared to philosophy over the whole duration of its existence. It just isn't obvious that there's a philosophical equivalent to the discoveries in quantum physics, for example, let alone Einstein's special and general relativity.

Things seem particularly bleak if one looks at what's been going on in the field of metaphysics, roughly speaking that branch of philosophy that concerns itself with fundamental questions of existence. Take the issue of free will, one of the standard topics in this area. It is probably fair to say that we're no further forward in determining whether free will exists, or even what it entails, than we were when Hobbes was thinking about the issue in the 17th century. The arguments between libertarians and determinists, compatibilists and incompatibilists, rage on pretty much as they have always done. Likewise with the issue of the existence of God, where there is simply no consensus among philosophers about what the weight of evidence tells us.

There is a puzzle here, which Immanuel Kant first drew attention to in his classic work *The Critique of Pure Reason*. Let's assume that philosophy can be divided into two broad camps: the rationalists and the empiricists. As we saw in the chapter on Reason, rationalists think that it is possible to find out certain metaphysical truths simply by means of rational reflection, without reference to sense experience. But reason leads rationalists to all sorts of different, conflicting conclusions. Perhaps there's just one substance, maybe there are two, or then again the world might be packed with individual monads. The empiricists, as we saw in the chapter on Experience, think that all knowledge is ultimately dependent on sense experience. But this led some to posit a self and others to deny it, some to stand by the notion of material substance and others to reject it. So reason leads rationalists and empiricists into metaphysical contradictions. And in the case of empiricism, it points uncomfortably in the direction of scepticism.

But it is easy enough to see that both the rationalist and empiricist approaches have been very successful in non-philosophical areas of enquiry. Mathematics, for example, is rationalist in character, requiring no reference to sense experience; and the natural sciences, though of course thoroughly bound up in reason, depend for their success on empirical data, which is often straightforwardly rooted in sense experience. So the puzzle is this: why have rationalism and empiricism been such failures in metaphysics, when the tools they employ are clearly up to the job in other fields of enquiry?

Kant and the Critique of Pure Reason

This is the question Immanuel Kant set out to answer in *The Critique of Pure Reason*, a work that was the product of more than a decade's reflection, but which took only four to five months to write. The first thing to say here is that attempts to read the book tend to result in panic-stricken incomprehension. J. M. D. Meiklejohn, in a translator's preface, had a few trenchant things to say about Kant's writing style:

He wearies by frequent repetitions, and employs a great number of words to express, in the clumsiest way, what could have been enounced more clearly and distinctly in a few. The main statement in his sentences is often overlaid with a multitude of qualifying and explanatory clauses; and the reader is lost in a maze, from which he has great difficulty in extricating himself.

However, the difficulty is not only a matter of style; it also relates to the subject matter of the work. Kant argues that neither rationalism nor empiricism is up to the task of rescuing metaphysics from confusion, and, even worse, the spectre of scepticism looms. What is actually required is for reason to make itself the object of its own enquiry in order that its proper scope and limits might be determined. This is a

> . . . call to reason again to undertake the most laborious of all tasks that of self examination and to establish a tribunal which may secure it in its well grounded claims while it pronounces against all baseless assumptions and pretensions not in an arbitrary manner but according to its own eternal and unchangeable laws. This tribunal is nothing less than the Critical Investigation of Pure Reason.

A critical investigation of reason itself is bound to get a little tricky, so don't worry too much if what follows is at times rather confusing. Furrowed brows and deep sighs are a quite normal response when one first comes across Kant. Perhaps the best jumping-off point to get a sense of how his investigation proceeds is with two distinctions.

The first is between analytic and synthetic propositions. Analytic propositions are definitional truths. To put this precisely, a proposition is analytic if its predicate is contained within the concept of its subject. So, for example, the proposition 'All bachelors are unmarried adult males' is analytic, since the concept 'bachelor' contains the ideas of 'unmarried', 'adult' and 'male' within it. Given what the concepts mean, these truths are necessary. Other propositions, however, introduce information that isn't contained within its subject concept. These are synthetic propositions, because the subject and predicate come together to form (synthesize) an informative truth. An example would be the proposition 'All boys play football', where it is clear that playing football is no part of the concept 'boy'. It's clear that such truths are not necessary – they depend for their truth on how the world is.

Kant operates with one more distinction, this time between how propositions are known. There are a priori and a posteriori propositions – from the Latin words meaning 'prior to' and 'after'. We don't need to have any particular experience to know the truth of an a priori proposition. It's known 'prior to' or independently of experience. A priori truths are necessary truths, like '2 + 2 = 4' and 'triangles are three-sided'. Knowledge of the truth of an a posteriori proposition, on the other hand, *does* depend on experience. You won't know that grass is green unless you've seen some grass.

The terminology employed here is perhaps a little disconcerting, but the ideas themselves are not too complex. Basically, it seems we're left with four types of propositions: (a) analytic a posteriori; (b) synthetic a posteriori; (c) analytic a priori; and (d) synthetic a priori. It is fairly clear that analytic a priori propositions and synthetic a posteriori propositions are unproblematic. Rationalists are interested in analytic a priori propositions and empiricists in synthetic a posteriori propositions. It's the other two possibilities that are weird. The idea of an analytic a posteriori proposition doesn't make much sense – why would you need experience to know something that's true by definition? This just leaves synthetic a priori judgements, which is the point at which things become really rather strange and unfortunately a good deal more complicated.

Kant's Copernican revolution

It is Kant's claim that not only are synthetic a priori propositions possible, they are in fact the condition of possibility of metaphysics itself. The oddness of this claim becomes clear as soon as one begins to think about what a synthetic a priori proposition would involve: it would have to be necessarily true, known independently of experience, and yet add something to our understanding of a subject concept that cannot be derived through an analysis of the concept itself. It is extremely difficult to see how such a thing could exist. Kant's task, then, is to show that our intuitions about the implausibility of synthetic a priori propositions are mistaken, something he claims will take a Copernican revolution in the way we think about metaphysics and the nature of the mind.

Kant's Copernican revolution is centred on the relationship between the mind and the world of experience. Prior to Kant, the orthodox view was that this works in just one direction: the mind simply records whatever happens to be occurring in the world. The metaphors to describe this conception are familiar: the mind is a 'blank slate' upon which experience writes itself, or it's a lump of wax awaiting the impression of the world's signet ring. According to this view, we can be said to have knowledge of the world to the extent that the impressions in our mind mirror the way the world actually is.

Kant reverses this conception – swapping things around as dramatically as Copernicus' reordering of the solar system – by arguing instead that the mind actively constitutes the world of experience. The mind shapes and organizes sensory input, turning it into the world of objects situated in space and time, and further moulding it in terms of categories such as substance and causality. The mind creates the familiar, everyday world that we inhabit. Far from it being the case that the mind conforms to the world, the world in fact conforms to the mind. Or, as Anthony Kenny puts it, 'through the senses, objects are given us; through the understanding they are made thinkable. Experience has a content, provided by the senses, and a structure, determined by the understanding.' It is reasonably easy to get a handle on the basic idea that the mind has a role in shaping the world of our experience. For example, one might think about the sudden shifts in perception that occur when one stares for long enough at the ambiguous figure illusions that are popular among gestalt psychologists. But the trouble is that Kant is talking about something much more profound and subtle than mere optical illusions or hallucinations.

Consider, for example, his claim that our sensory experience is ordered into relations of space and time by the activity of the mind. According to this view, space and time are not something out there in the world, but rather are subjective, a part of the structuring apparatus of perception. It is precisely this that guarantees that everything we experience will have the character of being in space and time. Bertrand Russell illustrates this point by noting that if we always wear blue-tinted spectacles, then we can't help but see the world as being blue; and likewise, if we always wear 'spatial spectacles' in our mind, then we can be certain that we'll experience everything as existing in space.

In addition to space and time, which are forms of 'intuition', Kant identifies 12 'categories' that further function to shape and categorize our sensory experience. These are: unity, plurality, totality, reality, negation, limitation, substance, causality, reciprocity, possibility, existence and necessity. As with space and time, the nature of the mind is such that we cannot help but experience the world in terms of these categories.

It is by reflecting on the categories that Kant gets the synthetic a priori propositions he needs to make metaphysics possible. His argument is that we can only have the experience of the world we actually have if certain metaphysical propositions – synthetic a priori propositions – are true. For example, the concept of cause only works if it is true that *every event has a cause*. The concept of substance only makes sense if it is true that *substance endures through all change*. These metaphysical propositions are a priori because they're necessarily true, but crucially they're also synthetic because they add information that isn't contained in their subject concepts. So, for instance, the idea that every event has a cause is not contained within the concept of cause; we can think of an uncaused event without entertaining a contradiction.

Unfortunately, as far as the complexity of the argument is concerned, we're not out of the woods yet. Although the categories are the condition of possibility of objects in general, they apply only to the world of experience. Kant argues that we cannot know what the world is like beyond its appearance to the mind. The world of objects, the empirical world, is the experienced world. What the world is like in itself, what objects-in-themselves (noumena) are like, is beyond the reach of our understanding.

This explains why metaphysics has got itself into difficulties. Kant argues that metaphysics only works if it is mindful of the proper scope of reason and the limitations attached to the categories of understanding. To put it simply, contradictions arise in metaphysics when it attempts to apply concepts associated with categories such as causality and substance to the world as it is in itself, rather than to the world of appearances. Kant illustrates the dangers of reason stepping beyond its proper bounds by setting up an antinomy between the claim that 'the world has a beginning in time and is limited in space' and the claim that 'the world has no beginning in time and no limits in space'. He then shows that it is possible to prove both claims, not in order to demonstrate that we should embrace contradiction, but rather to show that reason has no business concerning itself with the universe *as a whole*.

Metaphysics, when it confines itself to the world of experience, is a perfectly respectable activity, likely to reward careful enquiry. Speculative metaphysics, which looks at the world as it is in itself, is an example of reason going beyond its proper limits, and will inevitably end in confusion and contradiction.

Mind and reality

Philosophical idealism in its broadest sense is the view that mind is the most basic reality and that the world is in some sense dependent upon the mind. The proper contrast here is not with rationalism or empiricism, but rather with materialism, which holds that matter is all that exists and that the mind is in some way dependent upon matter.

The term 'idealism' is not used in a consistent way, and there are a number of different sorts of idealism floating around the philosophical world. For example, Berkeley's view that physical objects are just collections of sense impressions tends to be called 'subjective idealism'; Kant's notion that the mind actively constitutes the world of experience has attracted the label 'transcendental idealism'; and Hegel's philosophical system, more of which later, is termed 'absolute idealism'.

A useful way of classifying the various idealisms is in terms of a distinction between ontological and epistemological idealism. The British idealist philosopher Timothy Sprigge defines ontological idealism as the view that it is *absolutely true* that the physical is mind-dependent, and common-sense or scientific notions that depart from this view are simply wrong. Epistemological idealism, on the other hand, affirms only that the most acceptable view of the physical world, including the claim that it is mind-independent, is *true only for us*, but that truth-for-us is the only sort of truth it is sensible to seek.

In terms of this distinction, Kant's philosophy is a kind of epistemological idealism. The world of empirical objects is created by the mind's unconscious attempts to understand sense data that stream in from unknowable things-in-themselves. The operations of the mind remain opaque to us in terms of their fundamental nature; as do the unknowable things-in-themselves that in some mysterious way constitute the ground of all experience.

There is a curious, and rather troubling, aspect to this picture. It isn't clear that one loses anything by entirely doing away with the noumenal world, the world of things-in-themselves. In other words, it seems possible to deny the existence of the noumenal world without losing the world of physical objects. The thought here is that if the mind is able to create the forms of sensible intuition, space and time, as well as the categories of understanding, then there is no reason why it could not also create the 'external' world *tout court*.

This suggests a much more radical form of idealism than Kant intended, and he would have been horrified by it, but it's not immediately clear why we should favour Kant's transcendental idealism over this version, which holds that there is nothing that isn't the creation of the mind. Indeed, Johann Fichte, one of the fathers of German idealism, was committed to precisely this kind of more radical view, arguing in essence that the external world is the creation of the mind, or ego, and that it is posited in order to provide the ego with a setting within which to act out a kind of morality play as part of a process of self-discovery or self-becoming.

Of course, there are objections to the more radical view. For example, it seems to threaten solipsism, the possibility that only oneself exists. If there is nothing more fundamental than the world of appearances, then what grounds do we have for assuming that the other people who inhabit this world have minds such as our own? Moreover, if we think there are good reasons to think that other people have minds, then how do we explain why it is that we all seem to inhabit the same shared world? In other words, why does each individual ego share the same world with all the other egos?

Fichte offered a striking solution to these sorts of problems. He postulated that our individual egos are in fact merely aspects of a single absolute mind that is working out its moral destiny through an apparent multiplicity of lives. This idea is an example of what has become known as absolute idealism, which received its most powerful – or notorious, depending on your perspective – statement in the work of G. W. F. Hegel.

Hegel's absolute idealism

Hegel has been described by at least one philosopher as 'unspeakable', and it has to be said that many would agree with this characterization. Hegel's magnum opus, *The Phenomenology of Spirit*, is so difficult to understand, it makes Kant's first *Critique* look like a textbook example of the application of the rules of style of Strunk and White. Theodor Adorno, who once wrote a study of the work, insisted there were parts of it that were literally incomprehensible, which might explain why there are as many different interpretations of Hegel's ideas as there are of Heraclitus' fragments.

It should be said that part of the difficulty of the work has to do with its subject matter. Hegel is a system builder, and conceived the *Phenomenology* as being the final word in philosophy. There are also issues to do with the difficulty of translating the text from German that don't help if you're trying to read the book in English. Nevertheless, it seems very unlikely that Hegel could not have managed to write it more clearly had he wished, and there is the suspicion, sometimes expressed, that the impenetrability of the work is part of its point. Having ideas so complex they cannot be expressed in clear words sometimes impresses in a world that values displays of intellectual virtuosity.

The central thesis of the *Phenomenology* is that reality comprises a single, absolute mind (or consciousness), which Hegel terms 'Spirit', that is engaged in the project of trying to understand itself as *reality* through the various stages of its development. Like Fichte, Hegel is committed to the view that individual minds, or consciousnesses, are merely aspects of a single consciousness, which comprises the totality of existence. This radical and highly counterintuitive thesis entails that the various apparently discrete objects of reality, including individual consciousnesses and the objects of consciousness, are in fact aspects of a single, absolute consciousness.

This probably all sounds rather baffling, so it's worth narrowing the focus a little to look at how Hegel deals with one particular aspect of the way that Spirit comes to understand itself as reality. By narrowing the focus, we will lose something in terms of getting to grips with his overall thesis, but gain a deeper understanding of a number of his more specific arguments and of the way he does philosophy.

Part B of the *Phenomenology*, which contains some of its most renowned sections, deals with the way that an individual consciousness journeys towards 'self-certainty'. The idea of self-certainty is a complex one; however, it seems to be most clearly expressed by the notion of 'belongingness'. According to the philosopher Charles Taylor, Hegel has in mind that self-consciousness aims towards:

> . . . integral expression, a consummation where the external reality which embodies us and on which we depend is fully expressive of us and contains nothing alien . . . It is the longing for total integrity which for Hegel underlies the striving of self-consciousness, at first after crude and unrealizable versions of the goal, then when man has been educated and elevated by conflict and contradiction, after the real thing.

Hegel argues that self-consciousness emerges when conscious-ness recognizes the reflection of itself in the objects towards which it is directed:

> Consciousness of another, of an object in general, is in fact necessarily self-consciousness, reflectedness in self, consciousness of oneself in one's other.

Somewhat ironically, however, self-consciousness is threat-ened precisely by those objects it requires to become aware of itself. The external object is foreign to the self; it is an otherness in the face of which self-consciousness is unable to attain self-certainty. Self-consciousness, therefore, seeks to negate the otherness of the external object by annulling it.

But there is a predicament here. Self-consciousness cannot

destroy the external object, since to do so would be to deprive itself of the foundations of its own existence. Self-consciousness requires an object whose foreignness can be annulled without the object itself being destroyed. Hegel argues that only another self-consciousness fulfils this requirement, since only another mind is able to effect its own negation, and yet remain an external object. Specifically, a self-conscious being needs the acknowledgement and recognition of other self-conscious beings; only in this way can it attain the self-certainty it desires. This leads us to the famous dialectic of Master and Slave.

Although mutual recognition between two self-conscious beings will ultimately bring the self-certainty that both seek, this will not be easily won. At first, neither self-consciousness is certain of the truth of the other (as self-consciousness), and hence both are deprived of the source of their own certainty. Consequently, each will try to attain the recognition of the other without reciprocating. The resulting struggle for one-sided recognition is necessarily to the death, since in risking their own lives, each self-consciousness demonstrates to the other, and to itself, that it is not a slave to its particular bodily form and has the status of a *being for itself*. However, it is clear that the death of either participant in this situation is self-defeating, since it would deprive the survivor of recognition altogether. Hence, the solution to a struggle that must put the life of each participant in danger is the enslavement of one and the mastery of the other:

> The one is independent, and its essential nature is to be
> for itself; the other is dependent, and its essence is life
> or existence for another. The former is the Master, or
> Lord, the latter the Bondsman.

This is not the end of the matter, of course. This resolution is unstable, partly because the Master only attains the recognition of the Slave on pain of death; but also because the Slave labours and transforms the world at his master's behest, and as a result becomes aware of his own freedom and creativity in the things that he produces. This provides the impetus for self-consciousness to move forward to the next stage of the journey towards self-certainty and self-realization as absolute Spirit. This process only comes to an end when the distinction between consciousness and its objects is dissolved, and consciousness recognizes that it is identical with the sensible world.

Hegel's dialectic

The term 'dialectic' originated in ancient Greece, where it was exemplified in Plato's Socratic dialogues, which featured a question-and-answer-based discussion that aimed at teasing out the truth about a subject. In Hegel's hands, the term keeps its sense of involving a tension or exchange between opposing parties, but now refers to a system of logic or reasoning.

Hegel's dialectic relies on the concepts *thesis*, *antithesis* and *synthesis*. Put simply, the idea is that any given phenomenon (thesis) contains within itself contradictory aspects (antithesis) that require a movement towards resolution (synthesis); and that historical progress occurs as a result of a dynamic that has this dialectical form.

We can see this kind of reasoning in operation in Hegel's treatment of the dialectic of Master and Slave. The relationship between Master and Slave (thesis) is unstable. This is partly because the Master is unable to gain what he most desires, the freely given recognition of the Slave, precisely because he has subjugated the Slave; and it is partly because the Slave is able to get a sense of his autonomy and freedom in the things he creates at the behest of the Master. The relationship, then, contains the seeds of its own downfall (the antithesis). Resolution occurs only when the situation is transcended, and self-consciousness moves on to a new stage of development (synthesis).

Marx also employed Hegel's dialectical method, in his case with the intention of showing how conflicts in the material base of society function as the motor of history. Marx famously argued that the history of all hitherto existing societies is the history of class struggle. Society is built on top of a material base (thesis), which refers primarily to the way in which production is organized. In all hitherto existing societies, this has meant a division between the owners and non-owners of production. This situation is inevitably unstable (antithesis), and in the right circumstances will erupt into open conflict. The resolution of this situation will only occur when society moves to a new form of production, organized along different lines (synthesis). In this way, Marx was able to explain the transition between ancient (slavery-based), feudal and capitalist societies.

Hegel's influence

Hegel's philosophy, despite its baffling esotericism, has been tremendously influential in a number of different directions. Perhaps most significantly, the ideas of Karl Marx were heavily influenced by Hegel's dialectical reasoning. In fact, it is probably not too much of a stretch to say that Marxism can be understood as a sort of inverted Hegelianism. Marx expresses this point as follows (italics added):

> To Hegel, the life process of the human brain . . . which, under the name of 'the Idea' he even transforms into an independent subject, is the demiurgos of the real world, and the real world is only the external, phenomenal form of 'the Idea'. *With me, on the contrary, the ideal is nothing else than the material world reflected by the human mind, and translated into forms of thought.*
>
> The mystification which dialectic suffers in Hegel's hands, by no means prevents him from being the first to present its general form of working in a comprehensive and conscious manner. With him it is standing on its head. It must be turned right side up again . . .

Hegel was also influential in more straightforwardly philosophical circles. The Anglo-American idealism of philosophers such as T. H. Green, F. H. Bradley and Josiah Royce, for example, which was probably the dominant philosophical approach right up until the beginning of the 20th century, owes a debt to Hegel's legacy. Even philosophers not particularly inclined towards idealism have incorporated Hegelian themes into their work. One thinks of Friedrich Nietzsche, Edmund Husserl, and existentialists such as Martin Heidegger and Jean-Paul Sartre, for example. Thus, writing in the middle of the 20th century, Maurice Merleau-Ponty felt able to say that 'All the great philosophical ideals of the past century, the philosophies of Marx, Nietzsche, existentialism and psychoanalysis had their beginning in Hegel'.

Hegel's ideas today, however, do not enjoy anything like the same stellar reputation. Under the onslaught of analytic philosophy, Hegelianism fell into disrepute in the middle part of the 20th century, and it is fair to say that it hasn't yet recovered. Hegel is the last of the great system builders, and it is unlikely that we will see his like again, at least not in the foreseeable future.

Right and Wrong

Imagine that you're happily married, and you share everything with your partner. Although you agree about most things, you're currently arguing about the merits of a large charity donation. Your view is that the money will make a lot of difference to the lives of other, less fortunate people, and that you're affluent enough to be able to give the money away without missing it. Your partner accepts your point, but thinks you both already give enough through the taxation system to make a large charity donation inappropriate. You have, for now, undertaken not to make the gift.

However, you've just been told by your employer that you're due a very large bonus. It would be possible to get a proportion of this diverted to a charity. Confidentiality would be guaranteed, which would mean it could happen without your partner ever finding out. You're aware that any benefits your family would gain from the money would be nothing compared to the benefits gained by the people helped by your gift. However, you're also aware that your partner would never agree to make the donation, which means if you want to give the money away without risking your marriage, you're going to have to do so secretly. Of course, this also means you're going to have to lie about the size of your bonus and break your agreement not to make a donation. The question is, if you make the gift without telling your partner, are you doing something morally wrong?

There are a number of different ways you could think about this issue. For example, maybe your initial reaction is to question what is meant by the idea of a 'moral wrong', or to wonder how it might be possible to justify some particular moral judgement – such as 'pain is bad'. If so, then you're thinking about what are called 'meta-ethical' issues. Meta-ethics is the branch of moral philosophy that concerns questions such as 'Are there moral facts?', 'If there are moral facts, where do they come from?' and 'What do words such as "right", "wrong", "courage", and "justice" actually mean?' These sorts of questions have been discussed throughout the history of philosophy – so, for example, you'll remember we looked at the nature of 'the good' when we discussed the Euthyphro dilemma in the chapter on Plato and Socrates. But it is really only in the last hundred years, since the publication of G. E. Moore's *Principia Ethica*, that meta-ethics has been considered in a systematic fashion.

Or maybe your immediate reaction to this scenario is to wonder what sort of arguments can be marshalled for and against the proposition that it would be morally wrong to make the donation. If so, you'll be thinking about issues that fall under the rubric of normative ethics, which is the branch of moral philosophy dealing with the questions that arise when considering whether certain things are right and wrong, or whether particular actions are good and bad. It doesn't take much reflection on this dilemma to see that things can quickly become very complex once one starts thinking about these sorts of first-order questions.

Perhaps, for example, you think the key issue here is whether or not the world will be a happier place if you make the donation. If so, your moral approach is 'consequentialist' – you think outcomes are what count – and probably you'd conclude that making your donation in secret is morally justified (and if not in this particular circumstance, then at least in some circumstances). Of course, this also means you have to accept that lying, or, at the very least, deception, is not always morally wrong. This is not actually a particularly counterintuitive thought, and it would be a brave philosopher who claimed that lying is never justified, not even in a situation where the effect of not lying would be the occurrence of some large harm.

Kant is just one such brave philosopher. He does not believe that actions are justified (or not) by their consequences, but rather by whether they are undertaken in accordance with the demands of moral law, and in these terms, he claims, lying is always morally wrong. Later on, we'll look in more detail at what he has to say about morality, but for now it is enough to recognize that if outcomes are discounted in a moral calculus, then, arguably at least, our scenario takes on a very different character. Not least, it brings into sharp relief the fact that part of what is going on here is that you're considering breaking an undertaking and using deception in order to secure an outcome you desire (namely, making a donation to charity without risking marital strife).

Ethical theories that emphasize duty or obligation, and that look at whether an action adheres to moral rules rather than at its consequences, are known as deontological ethical theories. Kant's moral philosophy is an example of deontological ethics, as is divine command theory, which holds that an action is obligatory (or prohibited) simply by virtue of the commands by God. There is, of course, a danger in making sweeping statements, but it is probably fair to say that people attracted to deontological ethics are less likely to think that it might be morally justified to make the donation in the situation described here than people attracted to consequentialism.

A final point worth mentioning is the possibility that in focusing on particular actions, in this case whether a charitable donation in a very specific situation is morally justified, we're rather missing the point in terms of what is ethically important. Consider, for example, that a virtue-ethics approach holds that what we should be focusing on is the character of the moral agent, whether their actions are directed towards cultivating virtue and what their choices tell us about their moral behaviour. Virtue ethics does not provide a rulebook for action in the same way as some other moral frameworks. Rather, it asserts that people should behave in a way that is most likely to cultivate a virtuous character. Therefore, if you continually lie to your partner, then almost certainly a virtue ethicist will conclude that your behaviour is wrong, even if on any particular occasion your intention is good.

It is entirely possible that there is no definitive answer to the question of whether you would be wrong to make a donation in the situation described here. In fact, whether you think a definitive answer is even *possible* will depend upon your meta-ethical commitments. However, there is a strong sense in which the point of these sorts of scenarios is not to suggest definitive answers, but rather to illustrate the sorts of arguments philosophers engage in when thinking about moral issues. It is now time to do this in a more systematic fashion by looking at some of the main approaches favoured by moral philosophers.

Divine command theory

Matthew's Gospel reports that when a lawyer asked Jesus which of God's commandments was the greatest, he replied as follows: 'Thou shalt love the Lord thy God with all thy heart, and with all thy soul, and with all thy mind. This is the first and great commandment. And the second is like unto it, Thou shalt love thy neighbour as thyself.'

This is a perfect illustration of the sorts of commands that divine command theory says have an obligatory character.

They clearly express God's will and, therefore, obedience is morally required. In general, divine command theory asserts that things are morally good or bad, and actions are obligatory, permitted or forbidden solely because of God's will or commands. Or, more formally, it holds that actions are wrong, for example, if, and only if, and solely because, they are forbidden by God.

The obligatory character of divine commands flows from the sovereignty of God. The idea here is straightforward enough (certainly in the Abrahamic tradition): God is the Supreme Being, the creator of everything, and as a result, he has absolute authority over all of his creation. It follows, then, that if he tells you to jump, you jump; if he forbids you from coveting your neighbour's ox, then it would be morally wrong to covet your neighbour's ox.

The main advantage of divine command theory is that it seems to provide an objective basis for morality. The thought is that while it is very difficult for somebody who embraces a naturalistic world view to explain how there can be moral properties in the world, it's a lot easier if you think the world is created and sustained by a moral being. However, the trouble is that divine command theory suffers from weaknesses that severely undermine its credibility as a moral account.

Probably the most talked-about difficulty is one we've already come across in the guise of the Euthyphro dilemma. This arises out of the following question: does God command what is good because it is good; or is it good simply because it is commanded by God?

The problem is that whichever way you answer this question, you run into difficulty. If you respond that God commands what it is good *because* it is good, then you risk ending up with a diminished God, because the response seems to imply that there are moral standards independent of God's will. This threatens both God's authority, since he will not have control over the domain of morals, and his independence, because his own goodness is dependent upon the extent to which he conforms to independent moral standards. Moreover, further problems emerge if one digs a little deeper. For example, it's possible that God's omnipotence is threatened, because the existence of independent moral standards would seem to imply that he can't command what is evil and thereby make it good, which arguably at least is a limit on his power.

Given these difficulties, you might be tempted to suppose that one ought to respond to the dilemma by saying that the good is good just because God commands it. However, this response leads to its own, equally troubling, set of problems. In particular, it seems to make morality arbitrary, just a matter of God's whim. Consider, for example, that God might wake up one morning and decide that adultery is now obligatory. If the good is good just because God commands it, and God has freedom of will, then it seems there is nothing to rule this out. The 17th-century philosopher Ralph Cudworth makes the same point in a slightly different way:

. . . nothing can be imagined so grossly wicked, or so foully unjust or dishonest, but if it were supposed to be commanded by this omnipotent Deity, must needs upon that hypothesis forthwith become holy, just, and righteous.

There are other problems too with claiming that the good is good just because God commands it. For example, it seems to make the claim that God is omnibenevolent – of unlimited benevolence – rather empty, because if the good is merely that which God commands, then saying that God is good seems to be just a matter of saying that he exercises his will. As C. S. Lewis puts it:

. . . if good is to be *defined* as what God commands, then the goodness of God Himself is emptied of meaning and the commands of an omnipotent fiend would have the same claim on us as those of the 'Righteous Lord'.

It is probably not quite true to say that there is no escape from the Euthyphro dilemma, though avoiding its clutches certainly requires some fancy intellectual footwork. Perhaps the most sophisticated escape route depends upon drawing a distinction between God's essence and God's will. If God's goodness is a matter of his essential nature, then this acts as a constraint upon what He can will. It seems possible, then, for a divine command theorist to argue that it is both true that the good is good simply because it is commanded, and also that God can't command literally anything, since he is constrained by his own nature from doing so. However, it is by no means certain that this argument works as an escape route, and the debate over the Euthyphro dilemma, unsurprisingly, is ongoing.

Although many thinkers, including Augustine, Aquinas, Duns Scotus, Martin Luther, John Calvin and John Locke, have endorsed versions of divine command theory, the approach enjoys only limited support in the present day. A large part of the story of its declining influence has to do with the advent of modernity and the desire to separate out philosophy from theology. If divine command theory is even going to get off the ground, then the larger theistic world view of which it is a part has to be philosophically defensible, and, of course, it is not at all clear that it is. Therefore, it is no surprise that with the Enlightenment and the declining influence of religion, philosophers began to look elsewhere when thinking about morality.

Consequences

Jeremy Bentham, the English jurist and philosopher, who was born in the middle part of the 18th century, was clearly a diverting sort of fellow. In life, not only was he a renowned legal and social reformer, but he also designed the infamous 'panopticon' (a kind of prison), a central heating system, a scheme for reducing the national debt, a system for detecting forged banknotes, a refrigerator, a rudimentary telephone and a canal that was to be dug through the middle of Nicaragua. In death, he had his body preserved and put on display in the cloisters of University College London (where you can still view it), and on one occasion even managed to get his head kidnapped. Stolen by students from King's College, it turned up eventually in a locker at Aberdeen railway station.

However, despite all this merriment, what Bentham is probably most famous for is the first systematic statement of what has come to be known as 'utilitarianism', which holds, roughly speaking, that an action is right to the extent that it maximizes overall happiness.

Bentham's utilitarian thinking rests on what he takes to be a fundamental psychological fact about human beings.

> Nature has placed mankind under the governance of two
> sovereign masters, pain and pleasure. It is for them alone
> to point out what we ought to do, as well as to determine
> what we shall do. On the one hand the standard of right
> and wrong, on the other the chain of causes and effects,
> are fastened to their throne. They govern us in all we do,
> in all we say, in all we think . . .

From this it follows that if we want to maximize human well-being in general, we should seek to achieve as great a balance of pleasure over pain as possible aggregated across all people. This results in a Principle of Utility, or a General Happiness Principle, that is thoroughly consequentialist in character.

> By the principle of utility is meant that principle which approves or disapproves of every action whatsoever, according to the tendency which it appears to have to augment or diminish the happiness of the party whose interest is in question.

The idea that we should seek to maximize general happiness has intuitive appeal. It makes psychological sense to us that pleasure is morally significant: certainly, we tend to want it for ourselves and for our loved ones, and it's easy enough for us (most of the time) to extend this desire to other people. However, a number of rather tricky problems emerge as soon as one begins to think about Bentham's principle more closely.

The first thing to say is that it isn't clear that pleasure and pain are quantifiable in the way that Bentham supposes. Consider (or imagine!), for example, what it feels like to run a marathon. In one sense, it's clearly pleasurable, otherwise people wouldn't do it, and claim to enjoy it, but in another sense, it obviously isn't, because it hurts like hell. More confusingly, it doesn't seem implausible to suggest that it can be both pleasurable and painful at the same time. How one might even begin to factor all that into a calculus that aims at establishing an objective measure of the balance of pleasure and pain isn't at all obvious.

Bentham, though, insists that such a 'hedonic calculus' is possible. He identifies the sorts of factors, including the intensity of pleasure and its duration, that would have to be part of such a calculation, and also considers the relative merits and demerits of different sorts of pleasure and pain. He is also good enough to provide a mnemonic in case we have difficulty remembering the various stages of the calculation.

Let's grant that Bentham's hedonic calculus, or something like it, is possible. Where does that leave his kind of utilitarianism? The answer is that it faces a whole set of problems, the discussion of which has helped to drive the development of utilitarianism as a moral philosophy over the centuries since Bentham's death, and which still engage the interest of philosophers in the present day. We'll look at two of these problems here.

The first has to do with the consequences of specifying the *quantity* of pleasure as the morally significant fact. The problem here is that it leaves open the possibility that rampant hedonism is the best way for human beings to live. If we're at our happiest blissed out on a soma-type drug, then, in terms of Bentham's theory, it seems this is how we should encourage people to live. John Stuart Mill, a one-time student of Bentham, recognized the force of this objection. In his classic essay, *Utilitarianism*, in which he advances his own consequentialist theory, he distinguishes between lower and higher pleasures, arguing, contra Bentham, that the quality as well as the quantity of a pleasure has to be taken into account. As he famously claims, it's better to be Socrates dissatisfied than a pig satisfied.

Mill's argument in favour of the superiority of higher pleasures – which are, in effect, those associated with the higher faculties – is that those people who are equally acquainted with and equally capable of enjoying both higher and lower pleasures have a marked preference for the former. However, this argument is not decisive. Not least, it lacks empirical warrant: it just isn't obviously true that people capable of enjoying both kinds of pleasure, and familiar with both, would rather give up lower than higher pleasures.

The second problem has to do with the moral status of scapegoating. Consider the following scenario. There has been a brutal, sexually motivated murder of a child in a particular town. Although the police are certain it was just a random attack, it has led to an outbreak of vigilantism within the community that has resulted in injuries to a number of innocent people. During the course of their investigations, the police learn that there is a person living in the area who has a previous conviction for downloading child pornography. They know that he isn't responsible for the murder, but they also know that if they plant incriminating evidence, they will be able to secure his conviction. They reason that the outbreak of vigilantism will end with his punishment, and therefore, to the extent that it promotes the greatest balance of happiness over unhappiness, the punishment is justified.

The difficulty here is that it isn't obvious that this sort of thing is ruled out by a straightforward utilitarian account, and yet at the same time it seems that punishing an innocent man in this fashion is a clear injustice. A further complication arises from the fact that there are occasions where we tend to think it is justified to sacrifice the lives of a few people in order to save the lives of many. For example, most of us will accept that on occasion it may be necessary to seal off a geographical area in order to prevent the spread of a disease, even if people currently healthy will fall ill and die as a result.

The Trolley Problem

Some of the complexities of thinking about morality from a utilitarian perspective are neatly illustrated by what is known as the Trolley Problem. This was first described by Philippa Foot, and has the following standard form:

> A trolley is running out of control down a track. In its path are five people who have been tied to the track. Fortunately, you can hit a button, which will send the trolley down a different track to safety. Unfortunately, there is a single person tied to that track. Should you hit the button or do nothing?

Most people will respond that you should hit the button to divert the trolley so that it kills one person rather than five. Certainly, if you're committed to a consequentialist ethic, then it is very likely you'll think the right thing to do is to divert the trolley.

However, things get rather interesting when you add some variation into the scenario. The philosopher Judith Jarvis Thomson posed the following variation of the Trolley Problem:

A trolley is running out of control down a track towards
five people. You are on a bridge under which it will pass,
and you can stop it by dropping a heavy weight in front
of it. As it happens, there is a very fat man next to you
– your only way to stop the trolley is to push him over
the bridge and on to the track, killing him to save five.
Should you push the fat man on to the track?

The moral calculation here seems to be the same as it was
in the original version of the problem. You can sacrifice the
life of one person – the fat man – in order to save the lives of
five other people. However, we tend to have very different
intuitions about the fat-man scenario: most people think it
would be *wrong* to push him off the bridge.

So why do we have these different intuitions? A possible
explanation is that there is a genuine moral difference between
the two scenarios. In the original Trolley Problem, we can save
the five people on the track without *intending* to do any harm
to the single person tied to the other track: our intention is
simply to divert the train away from the five people it is running
towards. This is permissible under what is termed the doctrine
of double effect, which asserts (among other things) that so
long as we don't intend a bad effect, *even as a means to a
good effect*, then an action is justified if the good effect sufficiently outweighs the bad effect. Significantly, it is clear that
pushing the fat man off the bridge doesn't pass this test: here

we're specifically using the fat man in order to achieve the good effect, namely, saving the five people.

However, the idea that the difference in our intuitions about these two scenarios has to do with whether we're using somebody as a means to an end is thrown into doubt by the loop-back variation of the Trolley Problem.

> As before, a trolley is hurtling down a track towards five people. As in the first case, you can divert it on to a separate track. On this track is a single fat person. However, beyond that person, the track loops back on to the main line towards the five, and if it weren't for the presence of the fat person, who will stop the trolley, hitting the button would not save the five. Should you hit the button?

In this variation, the success of our plan *depends* on the presence of the fat man on the track. If he isn't there, the five people die anyway. It's only by running him down that we get to save them. So, just as in the case of the fat man on the bridge, this is ruled out by the doctrine of double effect. However, when presented with the loop-back variation, and unlike in the case of the fat man on the bridge, people tend to reply that diverting the trolley is morally justified.

If you're feeling perplexed by all this, then it might be a comfort to know that there isn't really a right answer here.

The importance of the Trolley Problem, and its variants, is precisely that it shows that the reasons for our moral intuitions are not always obvious.

The categorical imperative

Kant rejects the sorts of means-to-an-end reasoning that leads utilitarianism into difficulties when it comes to issues such as scapegoating. For Kant, doing the right thing is not a matter of good character, or moral intuition, or calculations about outcomes, it is rather about acting out of a duty of respect for the moral law. The moral law is categorical, rather than conditional, in form. Kant had no time for moral reasoning that relied on a calculus to the effect that if you want to achieve some good outcome x, in circumstances y, then you should do z. Rather, the moral law is expressed in terms of categorical statements of the form 'do this' or 'don't do that', hence his contention, noted earlier, that lying is always wrong.

According to Kant, the moral law can be stated in terms of what he called the categorical imperative: 'Act only in accordance with that maxim through which you can at the same time will that it become a universal law.' This is not quite as complicated as it sounds. Roughly speaking, it means you should ask yourself whether the maxim, or principle, of your action could be used to establish a universal rule of behaviour, governing not just your particular action, but the actions of everybody else who happened to be in the same situation. If you can imagine the maxim being universalized, then you're acting morally; if you can't, then you're not. Thus, the moral value of an action lies 'not in the purpose to be attained by it, but in the maxim in accordance with which it is decided upon'.

To make this more clear, let's consider one of Kant's own examples. It is Kant's claim that if the maxim of your action is inconceivable in a world such as ours then you have a 'perfect duty' to refrain from acting upon it. His illustration of what's involved in such a perfect duty concerns a promise that you have no intention of keeping.

Suppose you approach a friend to ask for a loan to help pay your rent. She agrees, but says that she needs the money back by next week. There's no way you can pay her back in this time frame, but you consider taking the money anyway in the full awareness that if you do, you'll be misleading her about when you'll be able to return it. Kant argues that actions take place under maxims, or principles, and the maxim you're thinking of acting upon here – as indeed was the case in the scenario with which we began this chapter – is something to the effect that 'I will make lying promises when it helps me get what I want'.

So what's the problem? Well, imagine that you try to universalize this maxim so that all rational agents must lie if it helps get them what they want. Kant argues that such a notion is not even conceivable. If everybody lies, then the whole idea of promising would soon become impossible: nobody would ever believe a promise, so there would be no point in making promises. In such a world, there could be no such thing as giving your word that you'll pay some money back, since the idea of somebody 'giving their word' would make no sense. It follows, then, that universalizing the maxim of your action results in a contradiction, and, as we noted earlier, if a maxim isn't conceivable when universalized, then there exists a 'perfect duty' to refrain from acting upon it. It follows, then, that you should never promise to pay back money knowing full well that you'll not be able to do so.

There is something rather appealing about the idea that there are moral duties that we simply must uphold. So, for example, a second version of Kant's categorical imperative, sometimes known as the humanity formulation, has it that we should never treat humanity as a means only but always as an end in itself. This idea fits very closely with a common moral intuition that at least partly explains why we find the idea of scapegoating, which seems to be justified in straightforward utilitarian terms, so difficult to handle. Perhaps, then, it would be easy enough to get people to agree that we have a duty always to consider someone's humanity and autonomy in our dealings with them. The trouble is, it is one thing to agree with something in principle, it is quite another to live consistently in terms of that principle. Kant readily concedes we don't find it easy to act morally, indeed mostly we fail at it, but nevertheless he argues that conformity to the categorical imperative is a prerequisite of rational agency.

However, the demands of duty come at a high cost. Consider, for example, the following scenario. It's the Warsaw

Ghetto, 1943, the Nazis are rounding up Jewish people for deportation, and you've got a gun in your face. Your children are hidden in the cellar, but you know that if the soldiers search the place, they're going to be found. Rather than searching every house they enter, the soldiers have taken to intimidating people into revealing whether there are other occupants. So they ask you the question: are there any other people in the house?

What price now Kant's categorical imperative?

The rediscovery of virtue

Virtue ethics is said to have been rediscovered as a result of an article published in 1958 titled 'Modern Moral Philosophy' by the English philosopher Elizabeth Anscombe. In this article, she argues that 'the concepts of obligation and duty – moral obligation and moral duty – and of what is morally right and wrong, and of the moral sense of "ought", ought to be jettisoned if this is psychologically possible'. This is clearly a radical proposal, since it would seem to do away with both consequentialist and deontological approaches to moral philosophy. Anscombe, however, argues that it is necessary because the language of 'moral ought' only has meaning within religious frameworks that reference a lawgiver, which are no longer generally accepted.

Although philosophers have not found her specific criticisms of the language of 'moral ought' to be persuasive, her argument that moral philosophy should turn away from talk of duty and obligation, and look instead, or again, at moral character and the 'virtues' that are linked to human flourishing has struck a chord. Thus, as Robert Louden notes, philosophers such as Alasdair MacIntyre, Philippa Foot and Edmund Pincoffs have all argued for a third option in normative ethics; namely, one that is concerned with the traits of character that make up the morally good person.

The emphasis on virtue makes a difference to how moral agents and their actions are viewed. For a utilitarian, what counts is whether an agent, when faced with a particular choice, seeks to maximize welfare or utility. If she does, then regardless of considerations of character, she acts morally. A virtue-ethics approach, in contrast, encourages a far deeper engagement with the character of the moral agent. Acting virtuously is not simply a matter of aiming at some specific goal; it is rather about cultivating a particular sort of character, rooted in virtuous traits such as kindness, honesty and courage, and then instantiating these in a life lived well.

The virtue-ethics approach is still a minority position in the sphere of normative ethics. The field remains dominated, as it has been for more than 200 years, by the struggle between consequentialist and deontological approaches. However, virtue ethics does constitute an interesting alternative to approaches that focus exclusively on notions such as duty, obligation and morally right and wrong actions, and likely we have not heard the last of it.

6
Current Concerns

Nihilism and Existentialism

In his famous lecture 'Existentialism is a Humanism', published in 1946, Jean-Paul Sartre tells the story of a dilemma faced by one of his students: 'His father was quarrelling with his mother and was also inclined to be a "collaborator"; his elder brother had been killed in the German offensive of 1940 and this young man . . . burned to avenge him. His mother was living alone with him, deeply afflicted by the semi-treason of his father and by the death of her eldest son, and her one consolation was this young man.'

Sartre's student had a choice between joining the Free French Forces, or staying near his mother and helping her to live. He was aware that his mother would be plunged into despair if he left and also that there was no guarantee that leaving to fight would make any difference to anything.

Consequently, he found himself confronted by two very

different modes of action; the one concrete, immediate, but directed towards only one individual; the other an action addressed to an end infinitely greater, a national collectivity, but for that reason ambiguous – and it might be frustrated on the way.

The question Sartre poses is 'What could help the student choose?' The answer he gives is that there is nothing. Not Christian doctrine, since it just isn't obvious to whom the student owes more brotherly love – his mother or his country; not the Kantian imperative never to regard a person solely as a means to an end, since either decision requires that he treats *somebody* as a means and not as an end; not feelings because, although feelings are formed and confirmed by one's actions, they are not in themselves guides to action; and not by seeking counsel, since any counsel he seeks – a priest or professor, for example – would indicate that he has already made his choice, since he's bound to know in advance roughly what sort of advice he is going to be given. Sartre concludes that what the student is left with is simply the freedom to choose, to invent himself through his choice.

This story exemplifies one of the key themes of existentialism, a philosophical approach and cultural movement that came to prominence in the middle part of the 20th century; namely, that we are absolutely and radically responsible for all our actions. As Sartre puts it, we are alone in the world, without excuse.

That is what I mean when I say that man is condemned to be free. Condemned, because he did not create himself, yet is nevertheless at liberty, and from the moment he is thrown into the world he is responsible for everything he does.

There is no divine lawgiver to issue commands; no *felicific calculus* to tell us what to do; and no obligations or duties that we are required to perform. Nor is our behaviour determined by our past, passions or nature. Rather, we are thrown into the world, abandoned by God, and forced to create ourselves through the free choices we make, for which we bear absolute and unavoidable responsibility.

The 'knight of faith'

Although the term existentialism tends to be associated with 20th-century thinkers such as Jean-Paul Sartre, Simone de Beauvoir and Albert Camus, and though it conjures up images of the Left Bank, Parisian cafés and Gitanes cigarettes, its antecedents actually lie in the 19th century, and in particular in some of the themes explored by the philosophers Søren Kierkegaard and Friedrich Nietzsche.

Kierkegaard, who was born in Copenhagen in 1813, was the quintessential philosopher of the individual. Rather than indulging in the sort of abstract theorizing popular among the then dominant German idealist philosophers, he focused instead on subjective experience, highlighting the importance of personal choice and commitment. It is this emphasis on the subjective dimensions of lived experience that can be seen as a precursor of existentialism. However, it would be a mistake to think that Kierkegaard would necessarily have had much time for 20th-century existentialism. Not least, whereas the existentialism of Sartre and his colleagues was thoroughly atheistic, Kierkegaard's was suffused with religious themes and imagery.

This can be seen most clearly in his idea of the 'knight of faith', which he explores primarily in his book *Fear and Trembling*. In this work, Kierkegaard argues that conventional Christians fall a long way short of authentic Christianity in their faith. They tend to be born into the religion, and maybe turn up at church once a week, but that's pretty much it. He also argues that Christian philosophers, such as Aquinas, have misunderstood the nature of true faith in thinking that it's a matter of developing proofs for the existence of God or working out how scripture is supported by reason.

In fact, a believer's Christianity is only authentic if she makes a profound leap into a realm of unqualified religious commitment – hence Kierkegaard's idea of a *leap to faith*. To the extent that such a 'knight of faith' accepts divine authority in all its paradoxical irrationality, she is able to live outside the sphere of ordinary morals, beyond good and evil, as it were. Kierkegaard, through the voice of Johannes de Silentio, the pseudonymous author of *Fear and Trembling*, uses the biblical figure of Abraham to illustrate this idea.

314

In Genesis, God commands Abraham to sacrifice his only son. 'And he said, Take now thy son, thine only *son* Isaac, whom thou lovest, and get thee into the land of Moriah; and offer him there for a burnt offering upon one of the mountains which I will tell thee of.'

In moral terms, it is very hard to see any good reason for Abraham to obey this command. Certainly, Immanuel Kant thought Abraham should tell 'God' that he wasn't going to do any such thing:

Abraham should have replied to this supposedly divine voice: 'That I ought not to kill my good son is quite certain. But that you, this apparition, are God – of that I am not certain, and never can be, not even if this voice rings down to me from (visible) heaven.'

Kierkegaard, however, disagrees, arguing that the 'story of Abraham contains . . . a teleological suspension of the ethical'.

The idea here is roughly that God has temporarily suspended the sphere of morality in order to test Abraham's faith. From Abraham's perspective, absolutely alone before God, there is nothing to do except to make a choice: either to remain wedded to the ethical sphere, or to make a leap, and thereby put his faith in a higher authority than that constituted by the moral order. Having made the leap, this 'knight of faith' does not remain in the religious sphere. Rather, as he descends the mountain, he returns once again to the sphere of ethics. But crucially, he now knows that its obligations and rules are not binding. His loyalty is to a higher authority, and in this sense he lives with the permanent possibility of moving once again beyond good and evil.

Übermensch

As is well known, Friedrich Nietzsche does not share Kierkegaard's enthusiasm for Christianity, labelling it a slave morality and declaring that it is 'essentially and fundamentally, life's nausea and disgust with life, merely concealed behind, masked by, dressed up as, faith in "another" or "better" life'. Nevertheless, according to Nietzsche, Christianity, for better or worse, has played an important part in keeping the spectre of nihilism at bay. In particular, by constructing a world of intrinsic value and certain truth, it functions as a buttress against the meaninglessness that nihilism threatens.

In the modern era, however, Nietzsche argues that Christianity has crumbled, partly as a result of its own internal drive towards truth, which has shown it up to be merely a human construct, and partly as a result of the onslaught from science and reason. The consequence is that the basis of people's belief in transcendent values has ceased to exist, and nihilism now holds sway. Nietzsche writes:

One interpretation of existence has been overthrown, but since it was held to be the interpretation, it seems as though there were no meaning in existence at all, as though everything were in vain.

This is what Nietzsche is getting at in his most famous aphorism:

> God is dead . . . And we have killed him. How shall we comfort ourselves, the murderers of all murderers? What was holiest and mightiest of all that the world has yet owned has bled to death under our knives: who will wipe this blood off us?

Nietzsche's madman, in whose mouth he puts these words, tells us that the source of a transcendent realm of objective values that we once believed in is no more. We have come to recognize that the divine will, Plato's forms, Enlightenment values, the Kantian imperative and so on are nothing but human constructions now scattered to the wind.

This raises a question that is properly existentialist in character: how do we live now we have given up our belief in absolutes? Nietzsche's answer is embodied in the figure of the Übermensch, the Superman: 'The noble type of man experiences *itself* as determining values . . . it knows itself to be that which first accords honour to things; it is *value-creating*.' Nietzsche's Übermensch is the measure of all things, a creator of new values in the vacuum of nihilism. It is able to cast off the metaphysical fictions characteristic of the herd mentality, and to embrace its freedom to create new and better forms of being. The 'death of God' therefore opens up the possibility of a higher ethic based on the creative power of humanity.

At this juncture, it is worth making a general point about the philosophical style of both Kierkegaard and Nietzsche. They are not systematic philosophers in the manner of a Hume, for example. Kierkegaard employs pseudonymous characters in order to make his points, Nietzsche has a penchant for aphorism, and they both enjoy storytelling. The consequence is that the meaning of what they say is often obscure and ambiguous. So, for example, Nietzschean scholars do not agree about how exactly the figure of the Übermensch should be interpreted, or indeed about the function it performs in Nieztsche's philosophy. This problem of interpretation means you should treat the outlines above as being merely a certain take on some of the ideas in their work that resonate with 20th-century existentialism. If you explore their thinking in more detail, you'll find that their interests range far beyond the issues we've covered here.

Is Nietzsche a nihilist?

The other issue worth briefly considering here is whether Nietzsche is properly regarded as a nihilist. Nihilism is not an easy term to define. It first came into usage in Russia in the middle part of the 19th century to refer to a certain sort of revolutionary, anarchic sentiment. However, fairly quickly the term began to be used in the dual sense that it has today: on the one hand, to refer to the view that there are no objective or rationally defensible moral standards against which we can judge our behaviour; on the other hand, to mean the despair and anguish that is said to flow from our awareness that the human condition is essentially meaningless.

Friedrich Nietzsche is one of very few philosophers to make widespread use of the term nihilism. In particular, he uses it to refer to the disintegration of the realm of (apparently) transcendent values that occurs with the collapse of Christianity and the growing awareness that all our value systems are human creations. However, where he departs from at least some traditions of nihilism is in rejecting the idea that this is a matter for despair. For Nietzsche, the collapse of Christianity, and its attendant slave morality, is necessary if there is to be any hope that humanity will be able to create new and superior forms of value.

This is suggestive of the sense in which it is *not* accurate to characterize Nietzsche's philosophy as nihilistic. While it might be true that Western societies in the immediate aftermath of 'the death of God' are nihilistic, Nietzsche certainly didn't believe this was the end of the story. Rather, his figure of the Übermensch is testament to his belief that from the ashes of the destruction of old forms of value, humanity might be reborn. The Übermensch is the future of humanity, 'the lightning out of the dark cloud of man'. Its destiny is to renounce the current disintegrating framework of values, and to mark down its own place in the world according to its 'will to power'.

Being and Nothingness

Jean-Paul Sartre's standout work of pure philosophy, *Being and Nothingness*, is a large tome, which was first published during the Second World War. It is by no means an easy work, and is certainly not written in a clear style. Sartre's prose might not be as alarming as Hegel's, but at times it certainly heads in that direction, and at the very least it is likely to provoke moments of choking or spluttering. There is, after all, a limit to the number of times it is possible to read that something is not what it is and is what it is not – more of which later – without suspecting that perhaps the normal rules of communication do not apply. Nevertheless, it is worth persevering with the book, since beneath the hyperbole and the linguistic pyrotechnics, it contains moments of genuine insight, particularly as it deals with the relations between self and others.

Most introductions to existentialism tend to skip quickly past *Being and Nothingness* to focus instead on Sartre's more popular works, perhaps, for example, the essay 'Existentialism is a Humanism', which we discussed at the beginning of this chapter, or the novel *Nausea*. This approach has the advantage of being an easy way into some of the core concepts associated with existentialist philosophy; however, it tends to come at the expense of philosophical sophistication. It is one thing to know that Sartre thinks we are condemned to be free, and that we tend to spend our lives in flight from our freedom; it is quite another to understand the philosophical underpinnings of these ideas, which are rooted in a very particular view of the nature of consciousness. If you want philosophical sophistication, then you've got to look at *Being and Nothingness*, so that's what we're going to do here.

Sartre's starting point is simple enough. 'There can be no other truth to take off from than this: I think, therefore, I exist. There we have the absolute truth of consciousness becoming aware of itself.' This notion of consciousness as self-aware is reflected in the terminology that Sartre employs: he calls consciousness 'Being for-itself' (the For-itself); and everything else – the world of things – 'Being in-itself' (the In-itself).

This is a fairly standard conception: in essence it is Descartes updated for the mid-20th century. But things take a novel turn as soon as Sartre begins to flesh out his ideas about consciousness. He argues that the For-itself is defined by its *emptiness*, by the lack of that which is necessary for its completion. In his words, 'Consciousness is a being, the nature of which is to be conscious of the nothingness of its being.' This will no doubt sound like gobbledegook to the uninitiated. However, it is possible to gain a sense of what Sartre is getting at here by looking at some of the issues raised by what is termed the *intentionality* of consciousness.

Intentionality refers to the directedness of consciousness:

consciousness is always consciousness *of* something. This basic idea is easy enough to understand. Consciousness, in its various aspects, is necessarily directed towards an object. Thus, for example, a person might perceive a dog; desire an ice cream; judge a contest; remember a birthday party; or contemplate a sunset.

Franz Brentano, who first developed the idea in the late 19th century, put it like this:

> Every mental phenomenon is characterized by what the Scholastics of the Middle Ages called the intentional (or mental) inexistence of an object, and what we might call, though not wholly unambiguously, reference to a content, direction toward an object . . . Every mental phenomenon includes something as object within itself . . . In presentation, something is presented, in judgment something is affirmed or denied, in love loved, in hate hated, in desire desired and so on.

Sartre develops this idea by noting that the intentionality of consciousness implies a *gap* between thought and its objects – for example, between desire and the desired, hate and the hated, contemplation and the contemplated, and so on. The nothingness of consciousness consists in the inescapable awareness that it is *not* the object towards which it is directed.

This idea is closely tied up with Sartre's famous dictum

that we noted a moment ago, that man is condemned to be free. Freedom is a function of the separation of consciousness from the given order of things. It is detachment, the permanent possibility that things might be otherwise. Perhaps a useful way to think about this is to imagine consciousness as free floating: in the absence of constraint, the For-itself is able to adopt any number of attitudes towards its objects, and in that sense, it is absolutely free. Thus, the British philosopher Mary Warnock notes that in Sartre's conception, 'at the very centre of the For-itself, right at the beginning we discover both freedom and an emptiness'.

The For-itself, then, lacks an essence, hence the defining idea of existentialism that 'existence precedes essence'. Or, to express this idea in Sartrean language, it lacks the coincidence of itself with itself that would turn it into an In-itself. It is this that lies behind Sartre's statement that the For-itself is not what it is and is what it is not. Human beings are permanently separated from the past they are no longer, and at the same time also from the totality of their unrealized possibilities, which may or may not come to pass. It is in this detachment, in this absence of constraint, that the absolute freedom of the For-itself is to be found.

Anguish and bad faith

As we saw, it is Sartre's view that we are in perpetual flight from our freedom. He argues that we experience *anguish* to the extent that we are aware that we are fundamentally free, that we must continually make choices, but that having done so we can rely on neither their permanence nor their validity. Sartre famously introduces the term *bad faith* to designate the strategies we employ in the attempt to deny the freedom that is inevitably ours. To get a better sense of what is involved in the concepts of anguish and bad faith, it's worth having a look at his analysis of the character of vertigo.

Sartre states that vertigo is anguish to the extent that 'I am afraid not of falling over the precipice, but of throwing myself over'. Consider, for example, the experience of walking along a narrow path with a sheer drop to one side. In this situation, you might experience some fear. You will be aware that human beings are objects in the world, and, therefore, subject to physical laws. It is possible that you might slip and fall to your death. Consequently, unless you are suicidal or peculiarly reckless, you will take steps to minimize the risk, perhaps by walking as far away from the drop as possible. You thereby escape your fear by imposing your own future on the situation; or, to put this in Sartrean language, you replace mere objective possibility – that you might fall to your death – with your own possibilities.

However, as a conscious being, you are separated by a *nothingness* from both your past and your future. Therefore, the fact that you have at one moment taken the decision to pursue the course of action necessary to avoid falling over the edge in no way guarantees that you will not at the next moment decide to throw yourself over instead. As Sartre puts it:

I am in anguish precisely because any conduct on my part is only *possible*, and this means that while constituting a totality of motives *for* pushing away that situation, I at the same moment apprehend these motives as not sufficiently effective. At the very moment when I apprehend my being as *horror* of the precipice, I am conscious of that horror as *not determinant* in relation to my possible conduct.

Anguish, then, is rooted in a recognition that the future is always in doubt. In general terms, it can be described as a kind of monumental and perpetual uncertainty; a lack of definiteness, which is the consequence of the emptiness that exists at the centre of being.

Sartre argues that bad faith is the typical response to anguish. It constitutes a striving for fullness of being, which is achieved to the extent that we are able to appear to ourselves as thing-like; that is, to the extent that we are able to take on the definiteness of an In-itself, thereby fixing our possibilities and releasing ourselves from the uncertainty of freedom. *Being and Nothingness* contains a number of striking illustrations of bad faith, including a very famous example of a café waiter who strives to identify himself with his role as waiter, but who betrays the illusory nature of this identification by being just a little too perfect in his performance. However, rather than looking at these specific examples, we're going to consider more generally how Sartre treats a particular kind of bad faith – what he terms 'the spirit of seriousness' – and illustrate what it involves by using an example from *Nausea*, his great existentialist novel.

According to Sartre, the serious attitude 'involves starting from the world and attributing more reality to the world than to oneself . . . the serious man confers reality on himself to the degree to which he belongs to the world'. In particular, he attributes an independent and objective reality to the beliefs and values that seemingly govern his behaviour. He is enshrined within a network of rights and duties in terms of which he defines himself. The serious attitude is strikingly illustrated in Sartre's description of the Burghers of Bouville in *Nausea*:

Jean Pacome, the son of the Pacome of the Government of National Defence . . . had always done his duty, all his duty, his duty as a son, a husband, a father, a leader. He had also unhesitatingly demanded his rights: as a child, the right to be well brought up, in a united family, the right to inherit a spotless name, a prosperous business; as a husband, the right to be cared for, to be surrounded with tender affection; as a father, the right to be venerated; as a leader, the right to be obeyed without demur.

Sartre's Burghers find their reality outside themselves: in their positions as heads of households, in their business accomplishments, in their good deeds, in their morality, and in their knowledge that the world is perfectly explicable. They seek the certain identity that comes with membership of a particular privileged social class; and they obscure the demands of freedom by binding themselves to its framework of beliefs and values.

Authenticity

Unfortunately for the Burghers, and indeed for all of us who employ strategies of bad faith in an attempt to avoid the responsibilities of freedom, we cannot just cast off our awareness of absolute freedom, because, as we have seen, such awareness is inscribed in the very structure of consciousness. A waiter can pretend to himself that he is defined by his role, a man can tell himself that the reason he abuses his partner is because he becomes overwhelmed by violent impulses, but these pretences are inevitably swallowed up by the emptiness that lies at the heart of being. There is always a detachment between consciousness and its objects, always the possibility that things might be otherwise, and, therefore, we have no choice but to choose and then choose again.

This returns us to the themes that we explored right at the beginning of this chapter. If we are condemned to be free, then all we can do is to make choices in the full awareness that we are choosing for ourselves in the name of freedom. This is what it means to live authentically. It is to understand that our choices do not flow from the commands of God, or from a system of morals, or from political obligation, or from any other external source. Rather, when we choose for ourselves, we are choosing 'without excuse and without help', and to think otherwise is merely to engage in self-deception.

Simone de Beauvoir

Simone de Beauvoir, the existentialist and feminist philosopher, is perhaps as well known now for her relationship with Jean-Paul Sartre – which was important enough in both their lives for them to be buried together in Paris – as she is for her own philosophical ideas. This is more than a little ironic, since the major thesis of her book *The Second Sex*, one of the most important works of feminism ever written, is that women are often seen as being 'the Other' of men.

In common-sense terms, Beauvoir's notion of the Other is easy enough to grasp: it simply picks out the fact that women are in some sense subordinate to men. However, to understand her conception in its full complexity, one has to know a little bit about the work of both Sartre and G. W. F. Hegel.

In particular, Beauvoir's idea of the Other is strongly influenced by Hegel's famous dialectic of the Master and Slave (see the chapter on Idealism), which holds that people come to see themselves as autonomous subjects by dominating other people (the Other). Beauvoir connects this idea up with some of the arguments Sartre puts forward in his *Being and Nothingness*, in order to analyse the relations between men and women. Thus, in the introduction to *The Second Sex*, she argues that woman 'is defined and differentiated with reference to man and not he with reference to her; she is the incidental, the inessential, as opposed to the essential. He is the Subject, he is the Absolute – she is the Other.'

Beauvoir also appropriates two further Hegelian terms – transcendence and immanence – in order to analyse the relations between the sexes. Men tend to live out their lives through a series of projects, normally conducted within the sphere of the working world, which serve to constitute their transcendent relationship to the world. In contrast, women tend to be confined to the domestic sphere, which is characterized by immanence: in their roles as mothers, housewives and the recipients of male sexual desire, they merely repeat the same passive and mundane tasks of everyday existence throughout their lives.

Beauvoir, as a good existentialist, does not want to argue that women lack freedom in some fundamental sense, since people are necessarily absolutely free. Rather, her argument is that women have come to see themselves, and are seen by men, as being somehow naturally inferior. To be a woman is, in part, precisely to be the Other of man. The idea of 'the eternal feminine' has it that a woman's status as Other is identical with the meaning of womanhood. This naturalizing of the identification of woman with the Other means that women will often be complicit in their own subjugation (since they will tend to see themselves through the myth of the eternal feminine). This idea ties in nicely with the claim of Sartrean-style existentialism that we tend to be in flight from our own freedom. Beauvoir suggests that it is entirely possible that some women just prefer the security of a life defined in terms of their relationships with particular men.

Needless to say, it is Beauvoir's view that the idea of the eternal feminine is a myth. As she puts it in *The Second Sex*: 'One is not born, but rather becomes, a woman.' In order to throw off their status as Other, women must discard those illusions of womanhood that confine them to lives of endless repetition, passivity and drudgery.

Continental Philosophy

Karl Marx's tomb in London's Highgate Cemetery is adorned with a famous inscription, taken from his 'Theses on Feuerbach', which reads: 'The Philosophers have only interpreted the world in various ways; the point however is to change it.' The first part of this statement reflects a common thought about philosophy, namely, that it is an inward-looking, scholarly activity that has little to say about people's lives and the social and political circumstances in which they are lived. The second part of the statement suggests that philosophy is at least somewhat diminished by this fact.

It would, of course, be unwise simply to accept this statement at face value. Although it is true that a certain sort of Anglo-American philosophy is not especially socially engaged, it is also the case, as you'll have noticed, that there are plenty of instances where philosophers do concern themselves with social and political issues. The example of Epicurus, whose entire philosophy is directed towards improving the quality of people's lives, immediately springs to mind. Or, to give a very different example, one might note that contemporary Chinese philosophers have had some input into the development of the 'One-China' policy with respect to Taiwan, and have also advised on economic policy issues.

However, perhaps more interesting than these isolated examples is the case of what tends to be called 'continental philosophy', roughly speaking 19th- and 20th-century philosophy originating in mainland Europe, which differs in a number of ways from the mainstream Anglo-American or analytic philosophical tradition. According to the British philosopher Simon Critchley, the continental tradition is partly defined by its goal of individual and social emancipation. Certainly it is easy enough to identify an emancipatory agenda in the work of many of the figures who tend to be grouped under the rubric of continental philosophy. For example, the ideas of Karl Marx, the paradigmatic revolutionary thinker, play a significant role in the work of philosophers and theorists as diverse as Georg Lukacs, Antonio Gramsci, Max Horkheimer, Theodor Adorno, Herbert Marcuse, Jean-Paul Sartre, Maurice Merleau-Ponty, Louis Althusser and Pierre Bourdieu.

The fact that Marxist ideas are important in the work of so many of the major philosophers within the continental tradition suggests that the differences between analytic philosophy and its continental cousin are more than skin-deep. Not only is there no figure equivalent to Marx in the Anglo-American tradition, it is probably fair to say that a philosopher who placed the idea of revolution at the centre of their philosophy could *never* have played a comparable role in that tradition. While it is too simplistic to claim that there is no sense of social or political engagement in analytic philosophy, it is clear that any commitment of this sort is not at the centre of things.

An interest in social and political emancipation is not the only way that continental philosophy engages with issues of emancipation. There is also the question of *individual* emancipation. Here Sigmund Freud is perhaps the most important figure. His original motivation was a concern to develop a therapeutic technique that could be used to alleviate the suffering associated with hysteria. In a sense, his emancipatory vision was quite limited, since he believed that therapy can do no more than return people to a normal level of human suffering. Human misery just is part of the human condition. Although this is nothing like an original idea, the significance of Freud's work, as we'll see, lies in the way he locates the source of such misery in tensions that exist between different aspects of the personality. It would be hard to overestimate the importance of Freud's ideas. His work has been taken up and given much broader scope by others, and with the exception of Karl Marx, he is arguably the most influential thinker of the last hundred years. So we'll begin by having a look at his work.

Psychoanalysis

Freud was born into an age of confidence and optimism. In the middle part of the 19th century, the universe was rapidly giving up its secrets to the scientists of the day, and it seemed only a matter of time before the natural and social worlds would be brought under the governance of human reason. For the first time, people would be in full control of their own destinies. Freud, in his early life, embraced the spirit of the times, excelling at school and university, where he studied science and medicine, before opening up a medical practice in 1886. It is therefore a little ironic that perhaps his most enduring legacy is the notion that there are reasons to doubt the emancipatory power of human reason.

Freud's signature claim is that our behaviour is often motivated by impulses that are not immediately available to the conscious mind, lying instead within the province of a dynamic unconscious over which we have little control. The broad claim that our behaviour can be unconsciously motivated was not particularly novel even when Freud was writing at the turn of the 20th century. However, his innovation was to attach this idea to a specific theory of personality, and to argue that a therapist using the right techniques – the techniques of psychoanalysis – would be able to make the 'unconscious conscious', and thereby help patients attain a kind of psychological equilibrium.

Freud first hit upon the idea that peeling away the layers of the unconscious mind might lead to therapeutic benefits while using hypnosis with his patients in the late 1890s. He found it was possible to achieve an improvement in mental well-being simply by revealing the underlying causes of a person's distress. The psychoanalyst has access to a variety of tools with which to accomplish this end, the most famous of which is probably dream analysis, a technique by means of which 'every dream will reveal itself as a psychological structure, full of significance, and one which may be assigned to a specific place in the psychic activities of the waking state'.

Dream analysis involves treating the client's (or analys-and's) dream as a symbolic representation of their unconscious mind. Freud's basic idea here is that the mechanisms that keep unconscious desires at bay in a waking state are less effective during sleep, which allows the unconscious to make its presence felt in the mind of the dreamer, although in a heavily disguised form. The task of the therapist is to decode the dream in order to discover its true meaning. This involves reverse engineering the 'dream work' that originally constructed the manifest content of the dream, thereby allowing the analyst access to its latent content, and with it the repressed desires that the dream represents. In this sense, all dreams are a kind of wish-fulfilment, an attempt to solve some psychic conflict in a way that is acceptable to the conscious parts of the mind.

Freud's tripartite model

In order to understand the mechanisms of psychic conflict,

it is necessary to know something about Freud's tripartite theory of the human psyche. This holds that the psyche is made up of three parts: the id; the ego; and the superego.

The id, which comprises the basic drives of the psyche, 'is a cauldron full of seething excitations . . . striving to bring about the satisfaction of the instinctual needs subject to the observance of the pleasure principle'. The ego is the organized, rational, decision-making part of the personality, governed by what Freud calls the 'reality-principle', which, in effect, is just the requirement of survival in the real world. The superego is the moral, censorious part of the psyche.

According to Freud, many kinds of psychological distress are related to tensions between these aspects of the mind. Thus, for example, he notes in *New Introductory Lectures* that 'the ego, driven by the id, confined by the super-ego, repulsed by reality, struggles . . . [in] bringing about harmony among the forces and influences working in and upon it', and routinely 'breaks out in anxiety – realistic anxiety regarding the external world, moral anxiety regarding the super-ego, and neurotic anxiety regarding the strength of the passions in the id'.

The role of the analyst, therefore, is to bring these tensions to the surface, and thereby reduce their power to cause suffering. As we noted earlier, the idea here is that by coming to a proper understanding of the sources of psychic distress, the analysand is able to take their first steps on the road to recovery.

At this point, it is possible that you're wondering what all this has got to do with philosophy. If so, then you're not alone, since many philosophers do not accept that Freudian ideas and arguments are part of the philosophical canon. Indeed, there has been at least one internecine struggle within a prominent philosophy department precisely over a proposal to establish a chair in Freudian philosophy (which the Freudians lost). Nevertheless, there are grounds for including Freud within a survey of philosophy such as this: first, the idea that human behaviour is often driven by dynamics of which we have little idea is an important counterbalance to the notion that we are rational actors and that, in principle at least, we have access to the reasons that motivate our actions. Second, as we'll now see, Freud's ideas have been taken up and used by thinkers who sit squarely within the tradition of continental philosophy.

The Frankfurt School

To be a Marxist living in the West in the period after the Second World War was in many ways not easy. On the one hand, the world was still reeling from the discovery of the horrors of the Holocaust, which suggested that humanity was about as far away as it is possible to get from being ready to establish a society based upon the emancipatory ideals of Marxist theory. On the other hand, capitalism, far from crumbling, seemed annoyingly perky, with near full employment, rapid technological advance and rampant consumerism.

Radical social change, communist or otherwise, seemed a long way off. Marxism, if it were to remain credible, needed a fresh impetus, a new direction that would maintain its relevance in the latter part of the century.

The Frankfurt School, a group of philosophers and theorists attached to the Institute of Social Research at Frankfurt University, aimed to provide this new direction. In particular, theorists such as Max Horkheimer, Theodor Adorno, Herbert Marcuse and, later, Jürgen Habermas sought to combine what was right about Marxism with insights gained from other thinkers, such as Kant, Weber and Freud. This led them to develop novel and influential critiques of capitalism (and Soviet-style socialism), which, in particular, focused on the contradictory aspects of Enlightenment reason as it was manifest in conditions of modernity.

Perhaps the most influential work of this period by Frankfurt School authors was *Dialectic of Enlightenment*, written together by Horkheimer and Adorno, and first published in 1944. This is a complex work, and it's hard to summarize briefly. In essence, the argument of the book is that the crisis in modernity, which had resulted in large swathes of Europe's working class throwing in their lot with the Nazis, is linked to the dominance of a certain kind of reason. According to Horkheimer and Adorno, National Socialism was the outcome of a technocratic rationality that resulted in humanity becoming thoroughly dehumanized. This process was driven by a totalizing, instrumental rationality, linked to the Enlightenment vision of the triumph of reason, which had sought to incorporate everything in its path. In effect, reason had regressed into something that resembled the forms of superstition out of which it had supposedly emerged in the name of progress in the first place. The result was that human beings had become objects to be dominated in the name of social and political control, the most extreme expression of which was the gas chambers.

The authoritarian personality

Part of what made the rise of fascism so troubling for thinkers inclined towards Marxism was that it demonstrated that large numbers of people, perhaps even the majority in a particular country, were prepared to tolerate activities that to most outsiders in most eras would have seemed absolutely barbaric. This led Adorno to wonder whether there was a personality syndrome that might explain the patterns of obedience and complicity that characterized the Nazi era. The result of these thoughts was the 1950 publication of *The Authoritarian Personality*, written in collaboration with a group of Berkeley researchers.

In this work, Adorno et al. (hereafter just 'Adorno') argue that a person's social, political and economic views form an integrated pattern that reflects an underlying personality disposition. After analysing data from a study of more than 2,000 people, Adorno found that those who hold anti-Semitic views tend also to be prejudiced against other minority groups

– for example, against blacks and homosexuals. In other words, there seems to be a general predisposition towards prejudice; if you're prejudiced against one group, then you're going to be prejudiced against another.

Adorno argues that prejudice is associated with a particular constellation of attitudes and beliefs that is characteristic of what he calls the 'authoritarian personality', which can be understood as a particular cognitive style or way of thinking. Authoritarians will tend to hold rigid beliefs, have conventional values, be intolerant of weakness and ambiguity, respect authority and manifest highly punitive attitudes.

Adorno has a straightforwardly Freudian explanation for the existence of this personality type. On the basis of an analysis of interview data, he noted that authoritarians often had harsh upbringings, with little affection, plenty of punishment and a lot of judgement. As a result, they manifest unconscious hostility that is displaced on to 'inferior' minority groups, who then stand as a proxy for the frustrations of their childhood. Authoritarians also project their own unacceptable sexual and aggressive impulses on to the same groups. This functions as a form of ego-defence, in that it protects the authoritarian from having to face up to impulses from the id that would be unacceptable from the point of view of a rigid, conventional superego.

Adorno, and his fellow authors, constructed an 'F scale' in order to measure implicit authoritarian attitudes, finding that authoritarianism is strongly correlated with both anti-

Semitism and ethnocentrism, which suggested the possibility that authoritarian personalities might be predisposed to accept anti-democratic ideologies such as fascism.

Eros and civilization

Where Adorno sought to use Freudian theory in order to explain the horrors of Nazi Germany, his Frankfurt School colleague Herbert Marcuse, in his 1955 book *Eros and Civilization*, attempted to combine Marxism and Freudianism in order to develop a radical critique of capitalist society.

As we just saw, a central claim of Freudian theory is that the libidinal energies of the id are subject to a reality-principle, mediated by the ego, whereby they are repressed in the interests of self-preservation. To put this idea in simple terms, you can't spend your whole time having sex with anything that moves, because if you do, then you'll starve to death. According to Marcuse, the level of repression of libidinal energies varies according to the demands of a particular form of society. In modern capitalism, which, according to Marxist theory, is based on class exploitation, the level of repression goes beyond what is required merely for self-preservation. In other words, in the interests of the ruling class, there is 'surplus-repression' governed by the existence of what Marcuse terms a 'performance principle'.

Crucially, he does not believe it has to be this way. Capitalism, as a result of the technological advances brought about by the performance principle, has abolished scarcity. This means there is no longer any need for the surplus-repression of our libidinal energies, which opens up the possibility of a radical change in society. According to Marcuse, if we do away with surplus-repression, then the result will be a qualitatively different form of society, 'based on a fundamentally different experience of being, a fundamentally different relation between man and nature, and fundamentally different existential relations'.

However, though the message of *Eros and Civilization* is essentially optimistic, Marcuse had become much more downbeat about the possibility of radical social change by the time he came to write his second masterpiece, *One-Dimensional Man*, in the mid-1960s. In this work, he argues that capitalist superabundance has rendered the working class impotent through the production of a raft of 'false needs' – through the impact of advertising, for example – which in effect dominate people by depriving them of real choices. In this situation, a critical Marxism remains necessarily abstract: the political movements by which social change might be achieved simply do not exist.

Power, knowledge and subjectivity

A common thread running through the work of the Frankfurt School philosophers is an ambivalence about the idea that societies organized according to Enlightenment ideals of progress and reason can ever deliver genuine freedom to their citizenry. Coming out of a different tradition, one finds a similar ambivalence in the work of the 20th-century French philosopher Michel Foucault.

Foucault, though less influenced by Marx and Freud than the philosophers of the Frankfurt School, nevertheless draws upon a wide range of sources, including philosophy, history, psychology and sociology, in constructing his philosophical ideas. Like many French philosophers, particularly those working in the post-modern tradition, his work is not easy to understand. It is not at Hegel's level of difficulty, but it is up there with Kierkegaard, and sometimes even Kant (in Kant's more lucid moments). Nevertheless, Foucault has interesting things to say about power, knowledge and subjectivity, so it is worth spending a little time getting to grips with some of his more important ideas.

If there is an overarching theme in Foucault's work, it is an interest in the way that power and knowledge interact to produce the human subject, or the self. In order to get a sense of what this means, it is necessary to look at what he says about how subjectivity – the way we see ourselves, and how we see other people and are seen by them – is created in relations of power and discourse.

According to Foucault, modern Western societies are characterized by three modes of 'objectification', which function to constitute human beings as subjects. These modes are: dividing practices; scientific classification; and subjectification. This is actually a lot less complicated and esoteric than it sounds.

343

Dividing practices categorize and separate people according to distinctions such as normal and abnormal, sane and insane, and the permitted and forbidden. It is in this fashion that people are categorized as madmen, prisoners and mental patients, for example. Such categories function to provide people with identities in terms of which they recognize themselves and are recognized by others. Thus, in *Madness and Civilization*, published in 1964, Foucault looks at the processes whereby madness came to be established as a specific and recognizable category of human behaviour, one that justifies the incarceration of individuals within mental asylums.

The mode of scientific classification functions to objectify, or define, people in terms of the discourses and practices of the human and social sciences. Perhaps the most familiar example of this sort of thing is the way that people are defined as suffering from some particular mental illness on the basis of diagnostic criteria that exist in a manual such as the American Psychiatric Association's *Diagnostic and Statistical Manual of Mental Disorders*. Thus, for example, it is easy enough to see how a label such as schizophrenia can function in a totalizing way: that person is a schizophrenic. Similarly, in the *Birth of the Clinic*, Foucault shows how the emergence of the human sciences in the 19th century led to the human body being seen as an 'object' to be analysed, labelled and cured, something he claims is still characteristic of modern medicine today.

The final mode of objectification, subjectification, differs from the first two in that it refers to the way that people actively constitute *themselves* as subjects. This idea is found throughout Foucault's three-volume *The History of Sexuality*, where he examines how a desire for self-understanding leads people to confess their innermost thoughts, desires and feelings to themselves and to others.

The consequence of this is that we become enmeshed in networks of power relations with authority figures – doctors, psychiatrists, priests and the like, and, in the 21st century, perhaps even the collective authority of a social-networking audience – who claim they are in the position to make sense of our confessions and reveal the truth about us. Foucault argues that the expansion of this process of confession functions to make people the objects of their own, and other's, knowledge. This is a crucial part of the expansion of technologies that allow the control and discipline of bodies and populations in the modern world.

There is an interesting point here about how power relations at the level of the state changed with the advent of industrial capitalism. Prior to this occurrence, the state used displays of physical power – in particular, spectacularly barbaric displays of torture – in order to exercise control over its subjects. However, with the emergence of industrial capitalism, there was a move away from coercion, repression and prohibition, towards new, more effective, technologies of power that aimed to produce human subjects and foster human life. According to Foucault, a new regime of what he calls bio-power has become dominant, which aims at the management and administration of the human species or population, and the control or 'discipline' of the human body.

In *Discipline and Punish*, Foucault argues that Jeremy Bentham's conception of the panopticon, a type of prison, is a paradigmatic example of a disciplinary technology. The panopticon is constructed so that it functions effectively whether or not prison guards are actually present. Prisoners never know whether they are being observed, so they must behave as if surveillance were constant and never-ending. This means, in effect, that prisoners discipline themselves; they become their own guards. The parallels here with wider society are obvious. The state exercises its greatest control over its citizenry to the extent that people police themselves. If everybody accepts the discourses and practices of moral, sexual and psychological normality, then behaviour becomes regimented in entirely predictable ways. This is the beauty of bio-power: without resorting to the spectacle of negative power, it allows for 'the subjugations of bodies and the control of populations'.

Part of the importance of Foucault's account is that he shows that not all power is negative in the sense of being prohibitive or punitive. There is also productive power, which functions, for example, to constitute human subjectivities and to produce bodies. However, this position is not without its worries. In particular, it is haunted by the spectre of relativism. The problem is this. If power is everywhere – if for example the treatment of mental illness is all about the control of a particular population, and not necessarily about making people's lives better – then it seems to rule out the possibility of any genuinely benevolent or emancipatory impulse. Thus, for example, in Foucault's terms, it seems we cannot really claim that the move away from barbaric forms of punishment to imprisonment and rehabilitation is progress, since the latter is a manifestation of the desire to exercise more effective control over a population.

Many of Foucault's critics claim that his views lead straight to relativism about both truth and morality. For example, Patrick West has argued in the *New Statesman* that:

> The pervading theme in Foucault's philosophy is that human relations are defined by the struggle for power. Right and wrong, truth and falsehood, are illusions. They are the creation of language and the will to dominate . . . Thus, there is no such thing as benevolence: men have created hospitals, schools and prisons not to cure, educate and reform, but to control and dominate 'the Other'. The rationalism of the Enlightenment was merely a mask for this malevolent impulse.

Although there is certainly something right about this criticism, it would be unwise to dismiss Foucault's work as a whole. His importance is that he showed how power can operate; that is, to create human bodies, human subjects and populations that in various ways are surveyed, categorized, disciplined and controlled.

Jacques Derrida's deconstructionism

The British philosopher Ted Honderich once said of late 20th-century French philosophy 'that it aspires to the condition of literature or the condition of art'; that one thinks of it as 'picking up an idea and running with it, possibly into a nearby brick wall or over a local cliff, or something like that'.

It is very easy to find examples of this sort of thing in the work of Jacques Derrida, who employs an often deliberately experimental and provocative writing style. For example, in his work *Glas*, he divides each page into two columns, one of which deals with Hegel, the other with Genet, but, rather startlingly, both at the same time. Derrida also has a fondness for neologism and novel literary devices. Here's how he defines 'sign' in *Of Grammatology*, probably his most famous work:

> . . . the sign ~~is~~ that ill-named ~~thing~~, the only one, that escapes the instituting question of philosophy: 'what is . . .?'

No, the crossings-out are not a mistake. The idea here is that the erased words are inadequate to express their intended meaning, but there aren't any better words either. So they are put 'under erasure'. David Lehman, in his book about deconstruction, *Signs of the Times*, says of this technique that it very quickly becomes an annoying affectation. Many people agree with him.

The notion that language is slippery and complex, and that the relationship of language to reality is unreliable, is perhaps the central theme of Derrida's work. The standard way to approach a text is in terms of what Derrida calls a 'meta-physics of presence', which holds that words refer to things in the real world in such a way as to ensure that they have determinate meanings. The aim of a deconstructive reading of a text is to throw this idea into radical doubt. Deconstruc-tion tries to penetrate beneath the surface of a text in order to discover its hidden ambiguities and contradictions.

This all seems unobjectionable enough; after all, people have been analysing texts for hidden meanings for almost as long as they've been analysing texts. However, the radicalism of Derrida's approach is his suggestion that the meaning of words never escapes the text of which they are part, with the consequence that the only reality they tell us about is the one constructed within the text. The threat of relativism here is clear. The suggestion seems to be that the indeterminate nature of language, and the self-referential nature of texts, means that words never refer to states of affair in the world, and, therefore, that the distinction between truth and fiction is redundant. Thus, for example, in *Of Grammatology*, Derrida says that there 'is nothing outside the text'; and elsewhere he argues that the 'absence of the transcendental signified extends the domain and the play of signification infinitely'.

Philosophers trained in the analytic tradition do not have much patience for this sort of thing, which means Derrida does not enjoy a particularly good reputation in the hallowed halls of Anglo-American philosophy. However, among continental philosophers, and within the humanities more generally, things are different. Here Derrida is considered one of the 20th century's most important thinkers.

The European perspective

The story we've told about continental philosophy could easily have featured a different cast of characters. It would have been just as sensible to have talked about Hans-Georg Gadamer's hermeneutics; Jacques Lacan's psychoanalytic ideas; and Derrida's deconstructionism, for example. If we had done so, then it would have been a different story, of course; nevertheless, some of the major themes would have been the same. The issue of the scope of reason, the potential for human emancipation, and the nature and limits of the Enlightenment would all have featured in this second story as well. It is this thoroughgoing engagement with the social and political world that probably marks out continental philosophy as distinctive when compared to philosophy in the analytic tradition. It is not true that analytic philosophy is only ever concerned to interpret the world, but it is true that issues of human emancipation are simply not part of that tradition in the way that they are part of the continental philosophy.

Analysis

Working in the mathematics department of Jena University, in the last decades of the 19th century, Gottlob Frege devoted almost 30 years to a single problem: securing the foundations of arithmetic in logic. The project was doomed, as he came to realize, and he eventually abandoned it. In any case, he and his efforts went almost entirely unnoticed by the academic world in his lifetime. He planned a magnum opus called *The Basic Laws of Arithmetic*, but had difficulty finding a publisher who would touch it. In the end he had to cover the cost of the second volume himself, and, owing to the discovery of a fatal flaw, finally abandoned the project.

His books were reviewed (and panned) by only a handful of people, who, it seems, couldn't understand him anyway. We don't know much about Frege the man, but some of the little we do know is unpleasant – his diaries contain shocking anti-Semitic remarks. It's all an unlikely start to one of philosophy's most recent revolutions, but in the English-speaking world, most philosophers do what they do in large part because of Frege.

He is now regarded as the founder of mathematical logic. We're perhaps too close to him in time to see things clearly, but his work is considered by experts as the most substantial contribution to logic since Aristotle got things going 2,000 years earlier. His asides, written to supplement his main project, are now read as classics in analytic philosophy, especially the philosophy of language. If that's not enough, his influence, through Bertrand Russell and especially Ludwig Wittgenstein, marks him out as the grandfather of analytic philosophy – alongside continental philosophy, one of the two main approaches to philosophy as practised in the West today.

Around the start of the twentieth century, philosophers became very interested in language – philosophy took what is called 'the linguistic turn'. In the centuries following Descartes, philosophers delved into epistemology and metaphysics. Those preoccupations, via Kant, culminated in the ascendance of idealism in the West. In Great Britain and America neo-Hegelians largely set the agenda. The revolt against idealism was led at first by Russell and Moore, who in their own ways used the analysis of language to devastating effect. Russell's pupil, Wittgenstein, as well as Rudolph Carnap and the so-called logical positivists, and others who marched under the banner of ordinary language philosophy, turned philosophy's attention almost exclusively to language. They examined philosophical talk through analytic techniques and, in the process, hoped to discover something about not just our thoughts, but the world as we understand it through language. We'll only consider some of these strands here, but it should be enough to give you a feel for contemporary philosophy's analytic roots.

Logic and language

The idea of a logical language goes back at least as far as Leibniz. In a natural language, like English, words are structured into sentences according to grammatical rules. Leibniz imagined an artificial language, using pictographs to represent basic concepts, organized according to logical rules. The users of such a language would not need to rely on their own imperfect judgements – they could simply calculate truths, cranking them out like the solutions to algebraic equations. All scientific and mathematical operations – deductions and inductions of every kind – would be expressed perfectly clearly and held together by logic. When Frege attempted to reduce arithmetic to logic, he was partly inspired by Leibniz's rationalist dream, but what really bothered him was our weak grip on mathematics.

In particular, he worried that mathematicians had no understanding of the basic objects of mathematics, numbers. What are numbers? Do we discover them? Do we just construct them in our imagination? What makes the axioms of mathematics true? His mission was nothing less than establishing a firm foundation for arithmetic in pure logic alone. In this, he adopts what is called 'logicism' – the view that mathematics is really a part of logic. It means that all the terms of arithmetic can be defined purely logically, and all the truths expressible in arithmetic can be derived from logical axioms. If you think of logic as something psychological, a formalization of fallible human inferences, then you might think that this is a fairly shaky foundation. But logic, for Frege, is objective. Logic is not how we in fact reason, but how we should.

In preparing the way for this enormous project, Frege wrote *Begriffsschrift* – there's no comparable word in English for it, but it's translated variously as *Concept Script* or *Conceptual Notation*. It introduces a system of logical operations that has become the foundation of modern logic. Among his achievements, Frege formalized the part of logic dealing with the quantification over variables. When we say that every rose has its thorn, most aliens come at night, some of you are in serious trouble, and no man is an island, we're using quantifiers to limit the range of the things under discussion – words such as 'every', 'most', 'some', and 'no'. For the first time, Frege made it possible to symbolize and examine in detail inferences that depend on limiting the domain of discourse in such ways.

Again almost as an aside, Frege wrote a number of papers dealing with the relationship between logic, language, objects and thought. Perhaps the most famous is 'On Sense and Reference'. He devotes pages to meticulous treatments of such things as subordinate clauses beginning with 'that', adverbial final clauses, dependent clauses beginning with 'who', linguistic designations of definite places, and subsidiary clauses beginning with 'although'. Dull stuff, you might think, but Frege was working out the hidden logical structure of language, connections in thought that lie behind our grammar, a move that would influence Russell and Wittgenstein deeply. He also insisted that the meaning of a word is given in the way it is used in a sentence – as opposed to how one might define a word in isolation – a point that would find its way to the centre of Wittgenstein's later thinking, as we'll see.

Frege's main concern in 'On Sense and Reference', however, is the analysis of identity statements – such things as $2 + 3 = 5$, water is H2O, a bachelor is an unmarried man, and so on. When we make identity claims, we say that something is identical to itself, but just how do such expressions work? How can an identity statement ever be informative, if all we're saying is that some object is the same as itself? Before Frege, philosophers had focused on the meaning of words, but he distinguished between a word's sense and its reference. The sense of a word is the 'mode of presentation', what we grasp about the object through the word. The reference is that to which the word refers. This distinction explains why identity claims can sometimes be very informative, not tautological at all. Two words can refer to the same object, but if different senses attach to those words, an identity claim can be quite important. It's why 'Superman is Clark Kent' is a more interesting thing to know than 'Superman is Superman', even though both say that the same thing is identical to itself.

Frege's large project, the attempt to ground arithmetic in logic, depends partly on this understanding of identity, but much more on the notion of sets, logical collections or classes of things. He found a way to define mathematical objects, like zero, in terms of logical objects, like the empty set. As the second volume of his magnum opus went to press, he received a short letter from a young Russell, then working on a similar project at Cambridge with the mathematician and philosopher Alfred North Whitehead. Russell was one of a small number of people who recognized Frege for the genius he was, but in his letter he identified a contradiction at the heart of Frege's conception of sets. Frege tried to patch things up, but it was clear that what came to be known as 'Russell's paradox' ended his hopes of grounding arithmetic in logic.

Frege's attempt to ground the truths of arithmetic in logic depends on the notion of a set or a class – a logical object picked out or determined by some sort of specification. Frege argues that every concept determines a set. For example, the concept 'dog' determines the set of all dogs, which is made up of all dogs; the set of all cities beginning with the letter L includes London, Lisbon, Lynchburg, and on and on. Some sets are empty, of course, like the set of round squares and the set of married bachelors, but as Frege formulates it, any condition should give rise to a set.

But Russell noticed a contradiction showing that not every condition has a corresponding set or class – bad news indeed for Frege, whose project depends on a connection between concepts and sets. Russell begins by noticing that some sets are members of themselves, and some aren't. The set of all things is itself a thing and therefore a member of itself; the set of all sets is a set and therefore a member of itself. The set of all hamsters is not a hamster and therefore not a member of itself. But what about the set of all sets that are not members of themselves? That's a concept that should determine a set, but it leads instead to a paradox. Is that set a member of itself? It is if it isn't, and it isn't if it is – a contradiction. So instead of that concept picking out a set, it picks out nothing determinant.

You can get a feel for the paradox without weird talk of sets that are members of themselves by thinking about a barber in a small town. Suppose you hear that he shaves everyone in town who does not shave himself. Sounds like a good recommendation. But does the barber shave himself? If he does, then he doesn't, and if he doesn't, then he does.

Frege died misunderstood and uncelebrated, never knowing his place at the start of analytic philosophy. He left his papers to his adopted son, with this note:

Dear Alfred,
Do not scorn my handwritten material. Even if all is not gold, there is gold in it nevertheless. I believe that some of it will one day be held in much greater esteem than now. See to it that nothing gets lost.
With love, your father

It is a large part of myself that I here bequeath to you.

Logical analysis

Russell's logicist programme culminated in the monumental three-volume *Principia Mathematica*, in which he and Whitehead use a new theory (of types) to get around the paradox he spotted in Frege's work. A fourth volume of work on the foundations of geometry was planned, but both Russell and Whitehead confessed to exhaustion and couldn't face it. It was never written.

In addition to his early work in the philosophy of mathematics, Russell is remembered for bringing the techniques of logical analysis to the central problems of philosophy. Outside the academic world, he is known for his popular philosophical writings, which are still widely read, especially his *History of Western Philosophy* and *The Problems of Philosophy*. Russell could write as well as think – he won the Nobel Prize for Literature in 1950. He was infamous for his scandalous views on religion and free love (and a string of marriages and affairs), which got in the way of his academic career. A lifelong anti-war campaigner and advocate of civil rights and nuclear disarmament, he took part in protests even into his nineties. His only concession to old age was a cushion for sit-ins.

When Russell, and his younger colleague Moore, studied at Cambridge, British idealism was the dominant philosophical view – in fact, Russell and Moore themselves flirted with neo-Hegelianism in their early philosophical lives. According to this sort of view, reality is not at all as it appears to us, nor is it anything like the world as described by science. The British idealists were a mixed bag, but most thought that there is a deep distinction between appearance and reality, and reason shows us that the apparent world is full of contradictions. Reality must therefore be something else entirely, something akin to Hegel's absolute, a cosmic, spiritual, conscious unity working itself out through history and through us. The world as common sense (and for that matter, science) would have it – a world of different objects existing independently of our minds – is an illusion. Tables and chairs are not inert matter in a mechanistic universe, but mental items governed at some level by purpose. To understand anything, we must understand everything in its interconnected entirety. Russell and Moore turned this part of the view upside down, insisting instead that philosophical progress could only come by breaking things apart, by analysing words and the structure of our language. 'With a sense of escaping from prison,' Russell wrote, 'we allowed ourselves to think that grass is green, that the sun and stars would exist if no one was aware of them.'

Moore's 'Refutation of Idealism' is a careful analysis of the idealist claim, owed to Berkeley, that *esse est percipi*, to be is to be perceived. Although punctuated by repeated claims that his subject is 'quite uninteresting', Moore's paper is actually a fascinating, meticulous study. What does '*esse*' mean here? What does '*percipi*' mean? What is the 'is' doing in this sentence? Is it the 'is' of identity? Is the claim that existence is identical with being perceived? That can't be right. Is it the 'is' of predication – is the claim that being perceived is a property of existence? And how are we to understand the whole sentence? He works through the possibilities, rejecting those that make no sense or don't fit in with what idealism says, arriving at an analysis of what idealists must mean, and then arguing that if their claim means anything important, it must lead to a contradiction.

He very nearly saunters over to yet another question ('I pass, then, from the uninteresting question "Is *esse percipi*?" to the still more uninteresting and apparently irrelevant question "What is a sensation or idea?"') and turns up yet more ambiguity in idealist doctrine. Reading his paper is like standing back as a master craftsman playfully disassembles an intricate old watch at great speed, showing you in the process exactly why it's broken. He concludes that the view of reality as entirely mental rests on a failure to distinguish between the act of awareness and the object of awareness. 'If my arguments are sound,' he concludes, 'they will have refuted Idealism.' Analytic philosophy hit the ground running.

Russell clashed head on with idealist doctrine too, but his response to idealism proceeds mostly indirectly, by just showing how progress could be made on philosophical problems by using what he called 'the logical-analytic method', rather than picking apart the claims of idealists line by line.

Hegelians argue that the ordinary conception of two different things standing in a relation to one another is incoherent – the mysterious idealist doctrine of internal relations had it that ordinary claims like 'the cat is on the mat' were not, strictly speaking, true. If ordinary relations are incoherent, then nothing stands in a relation to anything – nothing is hotter or colder, or bigger or smaller, or to the left or the right, of anything else. Back, then, to Parmenides and the view that all is one. But by recasting talk of relations in a clarified logical form, Russell showed that talk of the relations holding between two different things really could be rendered entirely respectable, and that the idealist leap back to Parmenides rested on a syntactical confusion. 'It gradually became clear,' he reports in the last chapter of his *History of Western Philosophy* (which culminates, incidentally, with him):

> that a great part of philosophy can be reduced to something that may be called 'syntax' . . . some men, notably Carnap, have advanced the theory that all philosophical problems are really syntactical, and that, when errors in syntax are avoided, a philosophical problem is thereby either solved or shown to be insoluble. I think, and Carnap now agrees, that this is an overstatement, but there can be no doubt that the utility of philosophical syntax in relation to traditional problems is very great.

How does this sort of thing work? Consider the philosophical trouble we get into by talking about things that plainly do not exist. When we say, to use Russell's example, 'The present king of France is bald', we seem to be asserting something

362

about a thing that does not exist. But in doing this we're attributing *some* sort of existence to the present king of France. We are talking about something, aren't we? How could this be if the thing we're talking about doesn't exist? Some philosophers supposed that meaningful expressions like this one really do have to refer to something, so the non-existent king has a kind of conceptual existence in a weird, Platonic world. Others thought that the sentence must be meaningless – but that doesn't feel right either, because it seems intelligible enough. In fact, we seem to say all sorts of meaningful things about non-existent people – some of it even looks true. There's no doubt, for example, that Sherlock Holmes smokes a pipe.

Russell begins by identifying certain phrases, like 'a man, some man, any man, every man, all men, the present King of England, the present King of France, the centre of mass of the solar system at the first instant of the twentieth century, the revolution of the earth round the sun, the revolution of the sun round the earth'. What he does is reduce sentences with these sorts of phrases to logically clear sentences without them – so there's no longer a commitment to the existence of possibly non-existent things. Existence, in other words, is only asserted of complete descriptions, which either describe something or not. Offending phrases like 'the so and so', 'the present king of France', 'the golden mountain', and so on, drop out entirely.

For example, the phrase 'Scott was the author of Waverly'

is translated into 'One and only one man wrote Waverly, and that man was Scott.' Similarly, as Russell puts it:

'The Golden Mountain does not exist' means: There is no entity c such that 'x is golden and mountainous' is true when x is c, but not otherwise.

With this definition the puzzle as to what is meant when we say 'The golden mountain does not exist' disappears.

A neat move, but so what? For one thing, Russell argues that saying 'x exists' is simply bad grammar. With logical analysis one can recast badly formed expressions into logically clear ones, and see where truth and falsity lie. But more interestingly, we can now sidestep what look like profound philosophical questions by dissolving them, seeing them as nothing more than logical confusions. Parmenides might have wondered how 'nothing' could be the object of thought. Russell has an answer for him. Shifting our language into logically clear constructions, he says, 'clears up two millennia of muddle-headedness about "existence".' The grammar of a natural language can get us into philosophical trouble, and logic can get us out of it.

For Russell, the point goes deeper still. His view came to be called 'logical atomism', and it was rooted in ideas he says he 'learnt from his friend and former pupil Ludwig Wittgenstein'. He begins with what he considers two truisms: 'the world contains facts, which are what they are whatever we may choose to think about them, and . . . there are also beliefs, which have reference to facts, and by reference to facts are either true or false'. But from those two simple claims, the way Russell spins it, a lot follows. A logical analysis of language not only reveals hidden meaning and the real location of truth and falsity, but much more – logic reveals the structure of the facts, that is to say, the nature of the world.

The logical positivists

A group of philosophers and scientists who took this idea seriously were known as the Vienna Circle. They met throughout the 1920s and early 30s to discuss such things as logic, language, science and meaning. The members changed – Rudolph Carnap, Herbert Feigl, Otto Neurath and Morris Schlick are thought of as the circle's core, with A. J. Ayer remembered as the one who brought their views to the English-speaking world. But their commitment to logical positivism held them together no matter who they were. Logical positivism admits of different interpretations, but it is generally tied to a single principle, the verification principle. What the principle itself amounts to is also a matter of controversy. Its implications, though, were obvious to many: if the logical positivists are right, talk about ethics, religion, metaphysics and aesthetics is literally meaningless.

As Ayer puts it:

The criterion which we use to test the genuineness of apparent statements of fact is the criterion of veri-fiability. We say that a sentence is factually significant to any given person, if, and only if, he knows how to verify the proposition which it purports to express – that is, if he knows what observations would lead him, under certain conditions, to accept the proposition as being true, or reject it as being false.

Put another way, the meaning of a proposition purporting to express a fact (as opposed to an analytic definition or tautology) is given by the method one might use to verify the truth or falsity of the fact in question. You know what 'it's raining' means, because you know how to find out whether or not it's true or false; you know what experience would prove or disprove it. But what possible experience could you have that would enable you to verify 'abortion is wrong', 'God loves you', '*The Waste Land* is beautiful', 'the soul is non-physical', and 'the Absolute evolves'? It seems that no experience could lead one to conclude that such sentences are either true or false, therefore the sentences are meaningless. The logical positivists hit upon a criterion of meaning, and used it to argue that vast regions of philosophy were nothing but nonsense.

You might wish to ask yourself about the status of the verification principle itself. What experience would enable you to verify it? If you can't think of one, you might be led, as many were, to the conclusion that the principle is rendered meaningless on its own terms.

In the hands of the twentieth century's most influential analytic philosopher, Ludwig Wittgenstein, the notion of meaning, or anyway the lack of meaning, was at the heart of all philosophy's problems.

Language-games

Ludwig Wittgenstein was born into a large, well-to-do Viennese family. His early life sounds complicated, difficult in the shadow of a domineering father. Three of his brothers killed themselves – Wittgenstein himself was regularly distraught, sometimes deeply troubled, and thought about suicide too.

He studied mechanical engineering, and from there found his way into the philosophy of mathematics, which led him to read Russell and Frege, and finally to visit Frege in Jena. Frege, he later reported, 'wiped the floor with me', but nevertheless encouraged him to study under Russell at Cambridge. He inherited a fortune but gave it away, served with distinction in the Austrian army during the First World War, and while in an Italian prisoner-of-war camp produced one of philosophy's most idiosyncratic but fascinating books, the *Tractatus Logico-Philosophicus*. (It's said that Moore came up with the title, with Spinoza's *Tractatus Theologico-Politicus* in mind.)

The book is organized into just seven terse statements, with supporting propositions numbered according to their logical place. So the first sentence, '1 The world is all that is the case' is followed by '1.1 The world is the totality of facts, not of things.' 1.1 is a comment on the first sentence. The next item, '1.11 The world is determined by the facts, and by their being *all* the facts' makes a point about 1.1, and so on until we reach the next sentence, '2 What is the case – a fact – is the existence of states of affairs.' On Wittgenstein marches, through 75 finely honed pages.

The book is built around the picture theory of meaning. Take the first sentence, 'The world is all that is the case.' By this Wittgenstein means that the world is made up of facts, states of affairs. His central claim is that propositions are logical pictures of those facts – they stand for or depict the facts. In other words, propositions picture states of affairs.

There are three points to note here. First, when a proposition pictures the facts, the simple elements of both the proposition and the world stand in the same logical relation. So when one says, 'The lunatic is on the grass', the atomic bits of that proposition and the atomic bits of the world stand in the same logical relation to one another – by teasing out the logical structure of our language, we get a grip on the structure of the world. Second, propositions picture the facts by showing them, not by stating them. Just as a picture of Napoleon shows you something about Napoleon (it doesn't tell you anything), so too a proposition shows something about the fact it pictures. Third, logical analysis can unveil the logical structure of propositions, disguised by our untidy natural languages. When we bring analysis to bear on the claims of philosophy, however, we discover something worrying: philosophical propositions are pseudo-propositions. They're attempts to say something where nothing can be said.

Near the end of the book, Wittgenstein makes a number of fairly spooky assertions. Consider this cluster of claims about morality: 'The sense of the world must lie outside the world . . . *in* it no value exists . . . it is impossible for there to be propositions in ethics . . . It is clear that ethics cannot be put into words . . . Ethics is transcendental.' All we can do with language is picture the facts, state the propositions of natural science. When we try to do the impossible – wander outside the world with our language and ask about all the facts, or the scaffolding we use to talk about the world, or whatever it is we're doing when we do philosophy – we're asking badly formed questions. Strictly speaking, we're not even asking questions. No wonder we have trouble finding answers.

So what is the role of philosophy? As Wittgenstein puts it:

The correct method of philosophy would really be the following: to say nothing except what can be said, i.e. propositions of natural science – i.e. something that has nothing to do with philosophy – and then, whenever someone else wanted to say something metaphysical, to demonstrate to him that he had failed to give a meaning to certain signs in his propositions.

In fact, he claims that the *Tractatus*, a book of philosophy, must itself be meaningless. 'My propositions serve as elucidations in the following way: anyone who understands me eventually recognizes them as nonsensical, when he has used them – as steps – to climb up beyond them. (He must, so to speak, throw away the ladder after he has climbed up it.)' The final sentence of the *Tractatus* is the only one without supporting commentary: '7 What we cannot speak about we must pass over in silence.'

In the *Tractatus*, Wittgenstein believed that he solved, or anyway dissolved, all philosophical problems, and with nothing more to accomplish in philosophy, he left Cambridge to become a schoolteacher in little Austrian villages. When the slower pupils didn't keep up with him, it is said he roughed them up, in one or two cases severely, and it might well be that he returned to Cambridge to teach partly to escape a small-town scandal. His views had by then already started to change, and it's useful to distinguish between the early Wittgenstein of the *Tractatus* and the later Wittgenstein, whose views we have primarily in his posthumously published *Philosophical Investigations*.

The later Wittgenstein came to reject the idea that words have a meaning by standing for or naming something in the world. Language is not as fixed, as determinate as this. Instead, 'For a large class of cases – though not for all – in which we employ the word "meaning" it can be defined thus: the meaning of a word is its use in the language.' Words can be used in a huge variety of ways, in a variety of 'language-games': to cajole, to convince, to convey a subtle point, and on and on. And while this insight opened up all sorts of fruitful avenues of investigation, one thing remained the same in Wittgenstein's outlook: philosophical problems are linguistic confusions to be dissolved, not deep questions in need of profound answers.

Whereas in the *Tractatus* philosophical propositions are pseudo-propositions, now Wittgenstein argues that philosophical perplexity arises when 'language goes on holiday'. When we take words out of their familiar language-games, where we know how to use them, and put them in unfamiliar contexts, we end up confused. We can talk ourselves into thinking that there's something deeply profound about the question 'What is an object?', but once we see that we are using a perfectly decent set of words in an unfamiliar way, we'll see that we have been merely 'bewitched by language'.

Those in a state of philosophical perplexity are in need of something like a talking cure, a therapeutic conversation, and *Philosophical Investigations* sometimes reads like a person calmly talking the reader out of a delusion. The confused need to be reminded of the grip that they have on words when used in familiar language-games, and shown that there's just nothing else to say when words are used in funny ways. As Wittgenstein puts it, 'a philosophical problem has the form: "I don't know my way about"'. It's the job of the philosopher to help the perplexed find their way back to more familiar territory and realize in the process that there's nothing to be gained by getting lost in language, by doing philosophy, in the first place.

Mind and Matter

Look inwards, for a moment, and consider the contents of your mind. In the course of an ordinary day, you'll think a huge number of different thoughts. You might believe it's Thursday morning, deny that it's too late to catch the train, expect the coffee shop to be open, want the queue to be shorter, wish the guy in front of you would hurry up, hope it's not now too late to catch the train, suspect that the guy in front of you is an idiot, wonder why you thought you had time for coffee when clearly only a fool would risk missing the train and now you'll never make it, what people are going to think about you showing up late, and so on, for the many hurried moments of your conscious life.

Maybe what makes you think about coffee in the first place is another thing in your head, a feeling of tiredness that gets your attention over and above the other bodily sensations you have, all the pains, tickles, twinges and itches and whatever else you might feel. Colouring all this are other things, not quite thoughts or bodily feelings, but emotions like love, anger, regret and happiness. Of course, there's also the passing show, the perceptual experiences you have when your sense organs bump into the world – all the sights, sounds, tastes, touches and smells that come together to immerse you in a three-dimensional picture of everything around you. All the while you remember some things, imagine others, daydream, wonder, plan, and generally get on with your inner life. In doing all this you might notice another something at the centre of it all: you, or at least the sense that you're doing all the thinking and feeling and seeing and everything else.

But what is all this mental reality? It's not just you, but a lot of world – every person and every creature with a point of view. Is a thought another thing like a book or a boat, or is it an entirely different sort of something? How do thoughts fit in to the physical world? Is it right to think of mental things as really real, or is it all somehow reducible to the physical world of particles and forces? Philosophers zero in on all this with two questions. What is a mind? And what is the relationship between mind and body?

Thinkers as far back as the ancient Greeks have had something to say about our mental life, but contemporary reflection on the mind has its roots in Descartes. In fact, as we'll see, it's hard to think of the philosophy of mind in the last half-century or so as anything other than an attempt to think ourselves free of Descartes' dualism. So we'll start with

Descartes, and work our way through various theories of mind, ending up, more or less, with where we are now.

The mind–body problem

Recall that Descartes' aim in the *Meditations* is to find an indubitable belief to serve as the foundation of knowledge. As he works his way through his beliefs, jettisoning anything that's in even the slightest doubt, he ends up with just one certain proposition: 'I exist'. Maybe there's an evil demon using all of his considerable power to confuse him, maybe there's no world of objects, maybe he doesn't have a body, maybe he makes a mistake every time he counts the sides of a triangle, but even so, he cannot doubt that there's an I, because even if he goes wrong in all these ways, there still has to be an ego, a self, going wrong.

That line of thought, almost as an aside, results in Cartesian or substance dualism, the view that there are two fundamentally different kinds of thing in the universe: physical objects and immaterial minds. In thinking about what he is, Descartes discovers that he can doubt that he has a body, but not doubt that he exists. The two things have come apart for him – so body and mind must be different kinds of things.

What is his conception of a physical body? 'By body I understand all that can be terminated by some figure; that can be contained in some place and fill a space in such a way that any other body is excluded from it.' Does he, Descartes, the 'I' that he can't doubt, have any of these properties? 'I cannot find one of which I can say that it is in me.' None of these bodily properties, in other words, are properties of the indubitable self that he's discovered. There is only one attribute 'which really does belong to me; this alone cannot be detached from me', and that is thinking. As he concludes, 'I am therefore, precisely speaking, only a thing which thinks.'

This is now called the 'conceivability argument' for dualism. It's conceivable that mind and body exist separately, and whatever is conceivable is possible. If it's possible that mind and body can exist apart, then they can't be identical. Mind and body, therefore, must be two different things. Think of other identical 'things'. Wherever Samuel Clemens is, you'll necessarily also find Mark Twain. It's not possible to conceive of them coming apart, because they're exactly the same thing, but it's easy to think of mind and body existing separately. In fact, Descartes does just this in his book.

But if mind and body are two different things, the question of how they are related to one another quickly arises – and this is the very core of the so-called mind–body problem. Descartes is a little cagey here. He says that mind and body are intimately intermingled or that they form a union, but he explicitly denies the picture of a soul somehow within the body, like a captain steering a ship. Souls or minds are not, strictly speaking, anywhere, because in Descartes' view they're non-physical, and that means they're not located in space. But then how can minds and bodies interact? How can a mind, which is not anywhere, stand in a causal relationship with a body, which is most definitely somewhere? If one thing is out of space and the other is in it, how can causality flow between them? Mind and body nevertheless seem to interact all the time – think about raising your arm, and your arm raises; bang your knee on a table, and you experience pain – but how can this be, if Descartes is right, and mind and body are such different things?

In the last century, philosophers came to the conclusion that Descartes must be wrong, and the flight from dualism has been very nearly a panicked stampede. Although things are now a bit mellower, as we'll see, for decades and decades calling someone a 'dualist' was fighting talk, and in many places, it still is. Philosophy has turned to physicalism, which holds that there's just one kind of thing in the universe, physical stuff. Whatever minds are, we'll have to find a way to understand them in terms of the physical furniture of the world.

Objections having to do with interaction were raised in Descartes' day, but with the rise of analytic philosophy, new discoveries in neuroscience, advances in computing and the appearance of cognitive science, the worries have really piled up. Some appeal to Ockham's Razor, and argue that mental life can be explained without positing immaterial minds – and anyway, what explanatory work could something that's not in space actually do? Talk of immaterial minds or souls also just doesn't mesh with the contemporary understanding of human beings as evolved organisms like any other, or with the world as consisting in just matter in motion in space. Souls look like epicycles, bolted on to a conception of the human animal that could get along perfectly fine without them.

And as we get a better picture of how the brain works, we seem to fill in more blanks about our mental lives. Certainly a neuroscientist has more interesting things to say about the mind than a substance dualist. The appearance of computers did not help Descartes much either. Here are physical objects, built by us, which seem entirely capable of doing all sorts of things that used to be the preserve of the mental, like calculating, storing information, even playing a good game of chess. Why not think minds are physical things too, like sophisticated computers? These and other thoughts led to a number of physicalist theories of mind, to which we now turn.

Physicalist theories of mind

In the years just after the Second World War, the reaction against dualism had a lot to do with changing philosophical fashions. The logical positivists, as we saw in the last chapter, argued that the meaning of a proposition was given in its method of verification – to understand what a sentence means, one has to know how to find out whether or not it's true. This view of meaning makes the Cartesian notion of a private, inner, hidden, non-spatial, mental realm seriously suspicious, and talk about it almost certainly meaningless.

But then how are we to understand our mental talk of pains, pleasures, beliefs, desires, and all the rest of it?

Gilbert Ryle, under the influence of Wittgenstein, saw the dualist picture – the 'ghost in the machine', as he put it – as resting on a logical error. To think of mind and body as though they were on a par, just two different kinds of stuff, is to make a 'category mistake'. These mistakes are confusions that depend on putting things in inappropriate logical categories – green ideas, true questions, tired rocks and so on. To borrow Ryle's example, suppose someone walks around campus and visits the library, the student union and all the other university buildings and then says, 'This is all very nice, but may I see the university now?' The mistake is putting the university in the same category as the university buildings – the university is not just one more building to see. Similarly, but Ryle argues, it's a mistake to think of mind as just another thing, like a body only somehow ghostly.

Both logical-positivist reflection on meaning and Ryle's criticisms inclined some to philosophical or logical behaviourism, the view that dubious references to some hidden, unobservable mental realm could be translated into respectable talk of observable behaviour and dispositions to behave. So when someone says that they're in pain, we need not understand them as going on about something ghostly, some state of a non-physical entity. Talk of pain can be rendered meaningful by understanding it in terms of observable behaviour (like shouting 'Ouch!') and dispositions to behave in certain ways (like being inclined to say yes to the offer of painkillers).

Among the problems for this sort of behaviourism is trying to work out exactly what an adequate translation from mental talk to talk of observable behaviour might look like. Suppose Phil wants a bit more salad dressing. There's a very long, perhaps infinite list of further specifications to do with Phil's dispositions to behave that are required to pin his want down. For example, Phil would be inclined to accept more salad dressing, but only if he doesn't think it's poisoned, or that it might deprive Phyllis of some should she also want a bit more, or if he's not already halfway through his salad and can no longer be bothered, etc. Notice also that to translate Phil's mental life into expressions about behaviour, we needed to make use of terms that are mental too, like 'inclined', 'think', as well as making mention of the mental life of Phyllis. Behaviourism looks like a non-starter.

So by the 1950s and 60s, many philosophers considered the possibility of a full-blooded metaphysical alternative to dualism, a view that does not simply look away from mental talk, but reduces the mental to the physical. The identity theory is the view that mental states are identical to physical states. Just as we learned that light is electromagnetic radiation, and water is H_2O, so as we discover more about the brain we'll come to identify mental states and processes with states and processes in the central nervous system, in particular the brain. Minds, in other words, are brains.

The view has a lot going for it. For one thing, there's no longer a problem of interaction, no question of how it is that mental states can stand in causal relation with physical states – because mental states are just physical states of the brain, which itself is conveniently causally hooked up to the rest of the body. The identity theory also makes a kind of sense of the many correlations we discover between brain events and mental events. With an MRI scanner, for example, we have found detailed correlations between activity in particular parts of the brain and our mental lives. Why not think the active part *just is* a pain, or a memory, or a feeling of fear? However, by putting the identification of mind and brain so starkly, you can begin to see a problem. Suppose a part of your insular cortex is stimulated every time you feel a toothache. According to identity theory, that stimulated bit is your toothache, and the 'two things' are really just one thing. But recall Leibniz's talk of the identity of indiscernibles – if two things have all the same properties, they're really one thing. In the case of your brain and your pain, however, there appear to be different properties galore. Does your toothache have the property of being grey and squishy and weighing a few grams, as does, say, the stimulated part of your brain? Conversely, does that part of your brain have the property of being excruciating, sharp, throbbing and, well, painful? The answer has to be yes to both questions, if the identity theory is true, but that seems wrong. How could a pain be grey? How could a pain weigh a few grams? It just sounds all wrong.

Another difficulty for identity theory is the charge of chauvinism – the objection that the view automatically restricts the class of things with mental lives to human beings, and that can't be right. If pain is the stimulation of some bit of the insular cortex, for example, that means that creatures without that structure can't possibly feel pain. Kick an octopus in the tentacles, and no matter how much it writhes around in apparent agony, if it doesn't have an insular cortex, it's not in pain, according to identity theory. The possibility of aliens having mental life is ruled out too, if they happen to have different brains from ours. And no matter how good we get at designing computers, if they're made out of something other than brain tissue, they can't possibly think.

So some philosophers argue for functionalism, the view that it's not what a mental state is made of that matters, but the functional role it plays in the mental life of the creature that has it. Just as the function of the president of the United States is occupied by many different people over time – what matters is what he does, not who he is – the functional role of a kind of mental state like belief or desire might be occupied by different physical structures too.

In humans, mental states are physically realized by parts of our brains, but it might be different for octopi brains, the green goo of alien brains, even an android's silicon chips. Mental states are understood in terms of function – what the state actually does in the mental life of the creature that has it. And function is spelled out in terms of sensory input, changes to other mental states that result, and behavioural output. Itchiness, for example, is that state caused by a light brushing of the skin, which sets in motion other mental states like the belief that your forearm itches, and outputs like scratching your forearm.

But while functionalism gets around the charge of chauvinism, it brings to the surface a problem that arises for every physicalist theory we've considered so far – these views seem to leave out the qualitative aspect of mental states. Philosophers use the term 'qualia' to pick out the raw feelings associated with our mental lives: such things as the stabbing cramp of hunger, the bittersweet taste of black coffee with sugar, the hurtfulness of pain, the redness of red, the pangs of jealousy and so on. Physicalist accounts of mind seem to ignore something crucial to the nature of mental states, namely, how they feel and seem to the person who has them.

In the case of functionalism, the problem is particularly glaring. You can see it with a slightly far-fetched thought experiment. Imagine two identical worlds. There's Boris on one world, and his identical twin Norris on the other. They're exactly the same except for one thing. For peculiar reasons that had something to do with a research grant, a neurosurgeon covertly crossed Norris's retinal wires at birth. As a result the twins have completely inverted colour qualia relative to one another.

If they look at grass, Boris sees green while Norris sees red. But they've been brought up just the same on their identical worlds, so they both call the grass 'green' and react to green things in just the same way. When they walk in their identical parks – lined up in identical causal networks, breaking out identical picnic baskets – their mental lives are functionally identical. They say the same things, do the same things, and their minds have just the same functional descriptions, but from the inside their worlds look completely different. Their colour experiences are inverted relative to one another. One sees red grass and an orange sky, and the other sees green grass and a blue sky. If two people could have identical functional descriptions but radically different visual experiences, that means mental states have to be more than just functional states. Functionalism seems to leave out the qualitative aspect of experience; it leaves out how the world seems to the people who experience it. It leaves out a big chunk of the mind.

It's a problem for the other views we considered too. In behaviourist translations of mental talk into bodily talk, the whole of one's inner life is left behind. But talk about pain is clearly about much more than merely bodily movements. We know behaviourism isn't right precisely because we know that pains hurt, and that crucial aspect of pain is left out of descriptions of behaviour. Even if we grant the identity theorist's claim that brains are correlated with minds, we're left wondering how a bit of a brain could actually be identical to something that has, from the inside, none of the characteristics of soggy grey matter and all of the characteristics of sweetness or agony or the feeling of hunger. Functionalism brings this problem to the fore, because the functional descriptions of two mental states might be identical, but the way the states seem from the inside could be qualitatively different. These troubles for physicalism have, in recent years, made talk of inner lives finally respectable again. In an effort to flee Descartes, philosophy seems to have headed too far away from him. But recent philosophers have begun to take consciousness seriously once more.

Consciousness

In 1974, Thomas Nagel published a paper with an intriguing title, 'What is it like to be a bat?' In it, he famously argues that physicalist attempts to solve the mind–body problem by reducing the mental to the physical are doomed to fail, because of a fundamental feature of mental life: its subjective character. Why? Nagel argues that 'every subjective phenomenon is essentially connected with a single point of view, and it seems inevitable that an objective, physical theory will abandon that point of view'.

Science works by moving closer and closer to objectivity, further and further from mere appearance and facts that are tied to a particular point of view. An alien scientist without taste buds won't understand a subjective account of the taste of beer, but such a creature could perhaps understand a more objective, scientific, chemical or physical account of beer itself. Science proceeds by moving from appearance to reality, from subjectivity to objectivity, but if what we're trying to do is understand subjectivity itself, this is a move in the wrong direction.

Nagel defines consciousness like this: 'an organism has conscious mental states if and only if there is something that it is to be that organism – something it is like for the organism'. He illustrates the point by considering bats, creatures that use echolocation to build up a complex image of their surroundings. What's it like to experience the world in this way? What's it like to be a bat? Nagel's point is that there must be something it's like to be a bat – bats are conscious, they have subjectivity – but it's not clear that any amount of physical information can give us the slightest grip on this aspect of a bat's life. Acquire as much objective information as you can about the physical facts of bat brains, observe bats for as long as you like, and this gets you nowhere near an understanding of what it's like to be a bat. Stacking up a lot of third-person, objective facts is no help if what you want to understand are the first-person facts of experience.

This does not mean that physicalism is false, Nagel says, only that we don't really understand what it means. He concludes, 'At the present time the status of physicalism is similar to that which the hypothesis that matter is energy would have had if uttered by a pre-Socratic philosopher. We do not have the beginnings of a conception of how it might be true.'

The worry that consciousness might be a kind of mystery struck a chord in certain corners of contemporary philosophy of mind. The mystery deepened some years later, when David Chalmers distinguished between easy problems and the hard problem of consciousness. We might be able to explain, in cognitive or functionalist terms, how vision works, how the brain processes visual information and what role vision plays in the behaviour of a creature. That kind of thing is comparatively easy. What is hard is explaining why there's a subjective, qualitative aspect attached to visual experience in the first place. Reflection on the hard problem led Chalmers back to a kind of dualism.

A nearby possibility is epiphenomenalism, the view that the physical world chugs along as it does, perhaps sometimes making mental events happen, but that mentality has no effects back down in the physical world. Physicalism leaves out mentality, but that's because the mental world is partly disconnected, floating free above the causal fray. In a sense, conscious experience is just along for the ride, a by-product of the physical brain, which does all the real causal work. Although he's abandoned epiphenomenalism now, Frank Jackson argued for a version of it with an interesting thought experiment, which seems to tell against physicalism.

Suppose we understand physicalism as the view that all facts are facts about physical things – there's nothing else but physical stuff, and a complete description of the universe would consist in nothing but physical facts. Now imagine

Mary, a brilliant neuroscientist, raised in an entirely black-and-white room. It's far in the future, neuroscience is complete, and she learns all the physical facts there are to know about how brains process visual images. According to physicalism, if she knows all the physical facts, there's nothing else to know – so she ought to know everything about vision.

Now imagine that she's released from her black-and-white room and presented with a red rose. It's the first time she's ever seen the colour red. The question is, how do you think she'd react? Would she be surprised? Would she say 'Ah! *That's* what it's like to see red!' Or would she take it in her stride, having learned everything there is to know about red from her black-and-white studies? If you think she'd be surprised, then maybe you think that physicalism is false, because although she knew all the physical facts about vision, you believe she still learned something when she saw red for the first time. There's nothing physical left for her to learn, so it looks like the physical facts leave something out, namely the qualitative aspect of experience, in this case, what it's like to see red. The alternative, that she'd yawn and somehow already know what it's like to see red just by studying texts about the brain, seems unlikely.

While there is this feeling of mystery in parts of contemporary philosophy of mind, other philosophers are trying to get on with the job – explaining the mystery away, dissolving the hard problem as a confusion in language, identifying various kinds of consciousness and proposing analyses of them, even formulating entirely new theories of consciousness. The philosophy of mind is wide open. There's not much consensus about consciousness, the mind, or the mind–body problem. At the moment, we're stuck with the view that dualism and physicalism are the only games in town, and somehow both look deeply problematic. It's been said before that the philosophy of mind awaits a Newton, a new philosopher with a big idea that might get us beyond the present impasse. And this brings us, conveniently, to the future of philosophy.

Postscript: The Future

Can anything serious be said about philosophy's future? To get a feel for how ridiculous this kind of soothsaying actually is, crowbar yourself into the head of a Presocratic philosopher. Maybe you think that magnets are alive or that 'the way up and the way down are the same'. Would you have seen Stoicism coming? What about transcendental idealism? Anomalous monism? Imagine that you're a Scholastic trudging through Peter Lombard's *Sentences*. Would Nietzsche's Superman make even a small amount of sense to you? Would it be something you might confidently predict as a possibility on your intellectual horizon? In these final paragraphs, we'll have an admittedly unwise think about philosophy's future. Don't take this as anything more than a shot in the dark. It couldn't be anything else.

There certainly are trends that are under way now, but it's hard to say where they are headed. It's easy to spot some patterns in philosophy's demographics, for example. After nearly a whole history of white male domination, more and more women philosophers are appearing, but numbers are still not representative among academics in departments of philosophy. People from ethnic minorities in the West are finding their way into philosophy too, but again it doesn't mirror the numbers in the wider world or even in many other academic disciplines. There are all sorts of guesses as to why this might be, but whatever the reason, the mix of people who do philosophy seems to be changing.

What of the main subdivisions of philosophy: value theory, metaphysics, epistemology and logic? We can say a little something about each. As disparities between rich and poor continue to increase, philosophers have turned their attention to justice, thinking new thoughts about what might now be demanded in our crowded world. It's said that the moral sphere has been expanding for centuries, and maybe that shift will continue to shape moral philosophy. Where once only male citizens were considered worthy of moral concern, gradually men from other groups, women, children, people with disabilities, and animals have found a place in the moral world. As we learn more about anthropogenic climate change, philosophers are starting to place a new kind of value on the environment, and the moral sphere might expand to include even forests, ecosystems and the biosphere as a whole. Metaphysics has been nudged around a little by advances in quantum mechanics, but don't expect the problem of universals to succumb to a particle collider. The philosophy of mind was recently refreshed by advances in computing and neuroscience. Epistemology was lately jolted into thinking again about the definition of knowledge, and work on that problem is likely to continue. And as we saw in the chapter on analytic philosophy, logic has enjoyed a relatively recent renewal, thanks to Frege, and maybe that will carry on for a while. Beyond even this tentative bit of speculation, things get hazy quickly.

If looking straight ahead isn't all that easy, we can at least peer backwards and draw some conclusions. Philosophical shifts have all sorts of different causes, but four things stand out: social and political influences, scientific discoveries, the recent philosophical past, and the intervention of a very few geniuses.

Think about the interplay between politics and early philosophy. Greek philosophy went along for the ride with Alexander the Great. When his empire collapsed, and while the Roman one coalesced, philosophy became a kind of consolation in difficult times. You can spot all sorts of shifts in philosophy that mirror the times, from Scholastic philosophy reflecting the consolidation of Christianity, through Locke's thoughts echoing the political shifts of the Glorious Revolution, to the Frankfurt School responding to the realities of a world that survived the Second World War. Philosophy keeps pace with the ages, and sometimes the influence flows back and forth. Stoicism had effects on the Roman state. Maybe

Marx really did change the world. So if you want a feel for where philosophy is headed, think a bit about the times that we're in. Think more about the likely future of politics and the social shifts ahead. What changes do you foresee, and what might philosophy do in response?

Philosophy has always had a connection to the science of its day. Again, this goes both ways, and much of what we now recognize as science started out as a part of philosophy. But philosophers tend to find inspiration in scientific discoveries. Plato used the cutting-edge mathematics of his day – an understanding of ratios – to make a point about epistemology and metaphysics by dividing up a line. There are instances of this across the whole history of philosophy – perhaps the loudest examples are the modern philosophers who deliberately applied the 'experimental method' and 'the mathematical method' to philosophical enquiry. We're now quite taken with computers, neuroscience and evolutionary theory. If you have a feel for where science and technology are headed, you might also have an idea of where at least a part of philosophy is going too.

But sometimes philosophy does what it does just because of itself. Philosophical movements rise and fall, the pendulum swings, and often the reason can be found in philosophy's recent past. Aristotle reacts to the Presocratics and to Plato; the Church fathers rebound off Plato and Aristotle; the moderns flee the Scholastics; and on it goes. It's important not to make too much of this – part of what we do when we think of philosophy in this way is apply a little artificial order as an aid to understanding. But, for example, it's hard not to think of contemporary philosophy of mind as a reaction to Descartes. It's hard not to think of analytic philosophy as a response to idealism. If you want to know where philosophy might be headed, start thinking about pendulums. Is anything poised for a swing away from where it is now?

The last of philosophy's catalysts is the most difficult to understand, much less predict. Sometimes a new mind appears on the scene and changes everything. There have been maybe ten or fifteen of these creatures – someone did something in Miletus, there were another three in ancient Athens, a few toiled away in the Middle Ages, a fair number emerged in the modern period, and we got lucky in the 18th century. Why, how, when and where they show up is anyone's guess, but they do keep appearing. Maybe we're due for another one soon. These people are the closest thing to certainty we can have about the future of philosophy.

Unless the world ends, we'll always read Plato, Aristotle, Descartes, Hume, Kant and the other giants of philosophy. We're reading Plato 2,000 years after his death – can you imagine an author alive today who will be read in 2,000 years' time? If there are people and something like books in the year 4000, and if we've still got Plato, you can be reasonably sure that we'll read him. Philosophy, we saw from the start, begins in curiosity and wonder. It's tempting to think that curiosity is not going to go away any time soon. Philosophy, whatever it is, will stick around too.

Further Reading

It's said that Wittgenstein called the act of reading philosophy 'a kind of agony'. You can find that comment dispiriting; or perhaps you'll take heart that even geniuses find philosophy rough going at times.

Probably the best way to avoid the more agonizing philosophy is to start with what interests you and branch out from there. Having found your way through this book, you might now be curious about metaphysics, want to know a bit more about epistemology, or perhaps ethical and political questions caught your eye. Maybe you're still uncertain?

Here are some idiosyncratic suggestions, arranged in such a way that they might help you to follow your interests.

All-rounders

If you're not really sure what interests you most, or want to have a closer look at philosophy's various sub-divisions, consider these introductory books, which aim to cover a lot of the philosophical territory.

A.J. Ayer, *The Central Problems of Philosophy*

Simon Blackburn, *Think: A Compelling Introduction to Philosophy*

A.C. Grayling, *Philosophy 1: A Guide Through the Subject*

Thomas Nagel, *What Does It All Mean: A Very Short Introduction to Philosophy*

Bertrand Russell, *The Problems of Philosophy*

Nigel Warburton, *Philosophy: The Basics*

There are also books that take up different aspects of philosophy through a number of puzzles, questions, and bite-sized problems, some with an emphasis on informal logic, and one of these might help you work out what really grabs you. Among them are:

Julian Baggini, *The Pig That Wants to Be Eaten* and *The Duck That Won the Lottery*

Peter Cave, *Can a Robot Be Human?* and *Do Llamas Fall in Love?*

Stephen Law, *The Philosophy Gym*

Alain de Botton's *The Consolations of Philosophy* brings the insights of major philosophers to bear on aspects of everyday life.

And there are a few popular introductions to philosophy aimed at younger readers, such as Jostein Gaarder's *Sophie's World* and Stephen Law's *The Philosophy Files*.

398

On values

Some good books on ethics and politics include:

Simon Blackburn, *Being Good: A Short Introduction to Ethics*
Jonathan Glover, *Causing Death and Saving Lives*
Peter Singer, *The Life You Can Save* and *Practical Ethics*
Michael Sandel, *Justice: What's the Right Thing to Do?*
Bernard Williams, *Morality: An Introduction to Ethics*
Jonathan Wolff, *An Introduction to Political Philosophy*

Some of the above are more introductory than others.

On the history of philosophy

If you want to go into the history of philosophy in detail, Bertrand Russell's *History of Western Philosophy* has been the standard work for many years. If you'd rather dip into a particular era, have a look at Frederick Copleston's eleven-volume history of philosophy, and choose what's of interest. Recently, Anthony Kenny's authoritative and entirely readable *A New History of Western Philosophy* has made a splash. A good treatment of modern philosophy is Roger Scruton's *Short History of Modern Philosophy*. Anthony Gottlieb's *The Dream of Reason: A History of Philosophy from the Greeks to the Renaissance* makes the list too, not only because it's genuinely funny in places.

Very short introductions

Oxford University Press has an ongoing series of 'Very Short Introductions', and a large number of these books are philosophical in nature, often written by excellent philosophers. You'll find Very Short Introductions to parts of philosophy's history, particular philosophers, sub-divisions of philosophy, theories, concepts and more besides.

Original sources

There's nothing better than going right to the source and reading what a philosopher actually wrote. The trouble is that even old hands can find some philosophers very difficult. But some of the big names could write well, among them Plato, Hume, Berkeley, Descartes and Nietzsche. If a philosopher strikes you as particularly worth pursuing, you can probably find a very cheap 'classic' version of his or her main works. Many books are now freely available online. Here are pointers to some readable original texts.

Plato's masterpiece is *Republic* (though admittedly you might find some of it heavy going). *Meno*, *Euthyphro*, *Apology*, *Crito*, and *Phaedo* deal with the trial and death of Socrates, and are often read together. *Symposium* is wonderful too.

Lucretus' *On the Nature of Things* is an ancient Roman poem about the philosophy of Epicurus, which is rather good. While you're back there, you might have a look at Marcus Aurelius' *Meditations*, an emperor's reflection on stoic philosophy.

Machiavelli's *The Prince* is certainly worth your time, even if he's not in the top philosophical tier. If political philosophy interests you, you might also read *The Communist Manifesto* by Karl Marx and Friedrich Engels.

Meditations on First Philosophy by René Descartes is a page-turner, and possibly the most readable and philosophically interesting thing ever written. George Berkeley's *A Treatise Concerning the Principles of Human Knowledge* makes a case for the astonishing view that only minds and the ideas in them exist. It's comprehensible, remarkable and occasionally infuriating philosophy.

David Hume is another readable great, but getting a handle on him can require serious effort. His *Dialogues Concerning Natural Religion*, however, is fascinating, accessible and entirely devastating. Nietzsche is another philosopher with a gift for language. His aphorisms are endlessly diverting, but have a look at *Thus Spake Zarathustra* and *Beyond Good and Evil* too.

Some people new to philosophy find Ludwig Wittgenstein's *Philosophical Investigations* particularly interesting, and much of it is surprisingly accessible.

Any one of the books mentioned here will certainly help you get on with your own study of philosophy.

Index

Acknowledgements

Many thanks to Judy Garvey, Kerrie Grain, Viola Metzger, and Cheryl O'Donoghue.